AI
and
Assembly

Advance praise for *AI and Assembly*

"Much more than expanded calculative power, AI puts culture together in new ways, driven by corporate imperatives rather than social values. This highly imaginative collection approaches this crucial development by asking how AI transforms how we assemble and appear to each other, both on the streets and online: a model example of how to expand public debate about AI beyond mere technology."

—Nick Couldry, London School of Economics and Political Science

"*AI and Assembly* pierces through the AI hype and delivers a thoughtful exploration of AI's place in the history of technology development and its relationship to people and power. The featured community of scholars challenges us to rethink perceived boundaries between physical and digital space and sets the reader on an important path to recognize why assembly and association are critical rights in the modern AI era. It is a must-have volume for anyone writing, teaching, and working on AI issues across disciplines."

—Nicole Ozer, Technology and Civil Liberties Director, ACLU of Northern California, and 2024–2025 Technology and Human Rights Fellow, Harvard Kennedy School Carr Center

"What would human life be like without the ability to choose your relationships and gather with others? This book takes us on a journey to understand the power of collective rights in a digital world that increasingly treats us as individuals. I recommend it to anyone seeking to escape the stranglehold of individualism in conversations about technology."

—J. Nathan Matias, Citizens and Technology Lab, Cornell University

"*AI and Assembly* shifts the speech-dominant perspective to another critical other freedom: that of assembly. Ultimately, AI is about agency—who has it and who does not; what we are able to know and how we can hold the technology companies to account. AI will impact the way we organize and assemble at its core and this critical book helps us understand how."

—Marietje Schaake, author of *The Tech Coup: How to Save Democracy from Silicon Valley*

"New technologies such as artificial intelligence (AI) have profound impacts on all aspects of human interaction, yet predominant scholarly and civil society discourse has focused on privacy rights, access to information, and free expression. This book is a road sign, a forewarning on the broader impact of AI on assembly and association rights. In exploring the intersection of AI and assembly and association rights, the book paves the pathways for the reorientation of frontline civic actions in the face of AI."

—Nicholas Opiyo, Executive Director, Chapter Four Uganda

"*AI and Assembly* reorients readers to threats that AI systems pose to human rights. Nothias and Bernholz brilliantly and convincingly argue that AI jeopardizes our freedom to assemble beyond just freedom of expression. Essential reading for those who want to understand and democratically shape AI's role in civil society and AI's impact on our freedoms."

—Mary L. Gray, MacArthur Fellow and coauthor of *Ghost Work: How to Stop Silicon Valley from Building a New Global Underclass*

AI
and
Assembly

*Coming Together
and Apart in a
Datafied World*

EDITED BY

Toussaint Nothias AND **Lucy Bernholz**

STANFORD UNIVERSITY PRESS
Stanford, California

Stanford University Press
Stanford, California

The Digital Civil Society Lab and the Institute for Human-Centered AI at Stanford University generously helped financially support the editorial process and provided funds for open-access publication

Library of Congress Cataloging-in-Publication Data
Names: Nothias, Toussaint, editor. | Bernholz, Lucy, editor.
Title: AI and assembly : coming together and apart in a datafied world / edited by Toussaint Nothias and Lucy Bernholz.
Other titles: Artificial intelligence and assembly
Description: Stanford, California : Stanford University Press, 2025. | Includes bibliographical references and index.
Identifiers: LCCN 2024054231 (print) | LCCN 2024054232 (ebook) | ISBN 9781503638556 (paperback) | ISBN 9781503642768 (ebook)
Subjects: LCSH: Assembly, Right of. | Artificial intelligence—Law and legislation. | Artificial intelligence—Political aspects. | Artificial intelligence—Social aspects. | Freedom of association.
Classification: LCC K3256 .A93 2025 (print) | LCC K3256 (ebook) | DDC 323.4/7028563—dc23/eng/20241118
LC record available at https://lccn.loc.gov/2024054231
LC ebook record available at https://lccn.loc.gov/2024054232

Cover design: Bob Aufuldish, Aufuldish & Warinner
Cover image: Eric May
Typeset by Newgen in 10.25/15.5 Guyot Text

The authorized representative in the EU for product safety and compliance is: Mare Nostrum Group B.V. | Mauritskade 21D | 1091 GC Amsterdam | The Netherlands | Email address: gpsr@mare-nostrum.co.uk | KVK chamber of commerce number: 96249943

Contents

Tables and Figures

Prologue

In Our Defense

Tawana Petty

Tech giants foster reckless belief in digital intelligence,
Coerce our faith in their omnipotence,
Drive society into gamified surveillance,
Dodge accountability by blaming model hallucinations.

To be watched is never to be seen.
It is to journey through destinations imagined by ChatGPT.
It is to believe in the truths espoused by bots.
It is to surround our communities with panopticons.

But to be seen is to organize for our dignity.
It is to value the intellect of human beings.
It is to resource neighborhoods and families.
It is to regulate toward algorithmic justice and racial equity.

When we protest, we challenge the AGI distraction,
Leverage research and technology for humanity's benefit.
We unite in equitable algorithmic assemblance.
Call out governments when they cower behind technological
ignorance.

It is our duty to gather in pursuit of peace.
A future free of harm, our responsibility.
So, when the scholars, the ethicists, the researchers
and activists speak,
We listen and respond, in defense of our democracy.

February 2024

Introduction

Toussaint Nothias
Lucy Bernholz

What happens in the virtual world happens in the real world. That thing where people think they're different, disabuse your mind of that. There is only one world because we live in both worlds.

Maria Ressa (2022)

Artificial intelligence, predictive software, and automated decision-making tools have moved from the lab into everyday life in ways similar to how Hemingway described bankruptcy: "gradually, and then suddenly." Driven by massive stores of digital data and storage, increasingly powerful computing systems, and competition between both firms and nation-states, artificial intelligence is seemingly everywhere. It is built into our physical systems for energy and transportation management; it powers social media platforms and search engines; it undergirds ever more administrative work and can be found deeply embedded in medical research; educational services; health care; insurance; criminology and judicial systems; social welfare administration; public and organizational policy enforcement; customer service; and home or office lighting, security, and heating controls.

The metastization of AI has galvanized harm prevention scholars and advocates; arguably, there are as many foci of concern about AI as there are implementations of it. Concerns about the existential risks of AI, for example, have led some technologists to insist that the research process be open so that there can be some form of public governance. Others emphasize the geopolitical battles to control the development and use of AI, framing it as an issue of national security and competition. Still others work to de-bias existing systems or advocate for the prohibition of some systems altogether. All of these concerns have a bearing on the focal issue of this book: our ability and freedom to assemble in a world taken over by AI.

Freedom of assembly is a core human right. We assemble when we attend a protest, join a march or rally, organize a community event, or attend a public meeting. Whether you are part of a religious organization, a union, a parent-teacher association, a volunteer community, or a neighborhood group, your involvement in these activities implies some form of assembly. Much like freedom of thought and expression, freedom of assembly is a foundation that ensures and encourages civil society and democratic participation. In this book, we use the term "assembly" as broadly as possible. We neither confine ourselves to the human rights definition and purpose nor abandon it. While some authors make references to the computer science use of the term, we are focused on the human act of gathering. We use "assembly"—and its legal cousin "association"—with a vernacular familiarity, not as professional jargon. How do AI-powered systems change how we gather and how do our gatherings change these systems? This is perhaps the most inclusive version of the question that this volume asks.

Questions of assembly, gathering, and community building used to be central to our understanding of digital systems and their impact on society. In the earliest days of the public internet, scholars, advocates, and users celebrated the community-building aspects of the technology. From studies of New York City's ECHO to San Francisco's WELL, online *spaces* were celebrated for the networks of people who found and supported each other. Early social media sites, such as MySpace and Friendster, aimed to help people find "their people," whether they defined this by identity, geography, social interests, or political allegiances. However, the earliest steps at American regulation, including the 1996 Communications Decency Act, concentrated attention on the internet's link to expressive behavior, a focus that has moved in lockstep with the rise of corporate megaliths such as Google and Facebook. Today, most public discussion, legal analysis, and even safety concerns are examined through the lens of free expression as evidenced in the emphasis on online speech and mis-/disinformation (e.g., Benkler, Faris, and Roberts 2018; Kaye 2019; Persily and Tucker 2020).

This is an incomplete and, we argue, insufficient focus. Scholarship and industry practice surrounding social media and search engines—two dominant AI-powered technologies of the early twenty-first century—over-index on expression as the area of concern. This is due, at least in part, to communications laws in the United States, which have played a defining role in shaping global social media sites, protecting expressive rights. This emphasis made sense when most of our interactions with digital data and their attendant analytic systems occurred through a screen. But this is no longer the case. Software-driven sensors now collect, analyze, and make data-driven decisions about us when we are using screens *and* when we are not. When we are inside our homes and outside in public. When we are in transit or asleep. When we are alone and when we are together. Software, data, and analyses are found throughout our physical spaces, sometimes obscured but often hiding in plain sight. As we move through space, so do the software and AI we carry in our phones or wearable devices. Even when we do not carry these devices, we are tracked by sensors in cars, buses, buildings, parks, and other public spaces. These phenomena require not simply shifting our research focus from expression to assembly. They require an update to our understanding of where and how assembly takes place, what it is, and who participates by choice and who by coercion.

More than three decades after the excitement of modem-enabled community building, we return questions of assembly and association to the foreground and find that a great deal has changed. The shift from screen-based to physical sensors, for example, makes our movements and gatherings as valuable as data-collecting opportunities as social media made our words, images, and social graphs. Not only is what we "say" captured and analyzed by online sites; where we go, what we do, and who we do it with are now also captured in digital representations. The data we generate flow across any preconceived boundaries between physical and digital space.

This plethora of data—and our ability to save and store it, mix it in endless recombinations, and analyze it through multiple lenses, sometimes simultaneously—powers AI and undermines analogue-era understandings of privacy, expression, assembly, and association. Its mere collection may present privacy violations. The substance or content represented by the data may raise expressive issues. And the ability to see data about multiple people in a single place, or interactions between data from different individuals, or spatial locations and relationships between data points threatens private association and public assembly.

Digital and physical spaces are not only expressive spaces; both are places for assembly and association as well. The prevalence of AI in physical space requires us to do more than consider expression beyond the screen. It requires us to consider the interactions between expression and assembly, the very meaning of assembly, and the ways in which digital sensors on screen and in physical spaces serve as a digital sense-taking infrastructure that duly tracks our every word, movement, and gathering.

Wherever we are, we generate data. As our gatherings become digitized, we urgently need to consider the implications of large-scale, semipermanent, inaccessible data trails for how and where and with whom we can take collective action. Assembly and association, two basic human rights, are different in the digital age from what they were in the analogue era. For one thing, time and distance—key differentiators of the two concepts in predigital times—are more complicated ideas in the digital age. Digital systems allow for remote and asynchronous participation in ways that leak through established legal and human rights jurisprudence. Digital mobilization interacts with physical assembly, and physical assembly can lead to new digital associations. AI systems, trained on massive amounts of data, may suggest connections and relationships in ways that remove or at least alter the degree to which we choose with whom we gather. In this way, the chances that we are being assembled not by our own choice but by machine learning or automated pattern detection only increase. Finally, concerns about AI—from its biases to how it is governed—are bringing scholars and activists together to create old-form associations addressing new technological challenges.

No single book can cover all of the ways our dependencies on AI-enabled digital systems are entangled with our sense of community, our ability to gather and our practices of gathering, and our rights to assembly and association. The chapters that follow examine many of these dynamics through diverse perspectives: human rights, organizational behavior, surveillance, discrimination, language and culture, algorithmic power, and others. Each contributor joined this project, however, because of a shared sense that efforts to regulate new digital tools or artificial intelligence will fail if they continue to be rooted primarily, and at times exclusively, in concerns about expressive rights. We must expand our understanding of how these systems influence, interact with, and shift our individual and collective capacities to gather in physical and digital spaces, and factor that understanding into efforts to protect people and communities, be it through regulation, technology design, or community oversight.

As we were finalizing this volume, generative artificial intelligence was dominating public discussion, professional concerns, and regulatory attention on digital technologies. As it had with previous technologies, the media was abuzz with both the promise and the peril of new tools such as ChatGPT or those being built into products from Google, Microsoft, Facebook, and almost all enterprise-facing software. Regions such as the European Union were moving quickly to regulate artificial intelligence, while US legislators were waffling as they so often have when it comes to regulating technology. Industry insiders released several letters of caution, AI company CEOs rushed to present themselves before Congress and the White House as potential partners in regulation, and security experts sounded dire warnings of AI "hallucinations" (Kessler and Hsu 2023). Moments of regulatory opportunity do not come along as frequently as do new technologies. The rules that do result often tend to rigidify even as the technologies they are meant to control continue to embed themselves deeper and deeper into daily life, expanding their reach and impact with every new application.

Freed from the demands of reelection and profit, it is up to independent scholars and community experts to assess the broadest range of impacts these technologies have. Our contribution with this volume is consideration of their impact beyond the expression or privacy concerns they raise. How will artificial intelligence influence who meets whom, who can gather with whom, and where and how those people might congregate? How might artificial intelligence shift "what" participates in a gathering—will chatbots count? Will questions of timing and proximity, which have distinguished assembly from association to date, still matter in an era when evidence of an individual's online action may be stored forever on corporate servers and repurposed for algorithmic training? Will brief and passing online actions take on permanent importance? Will nations come to require registration of informal, digital-first associations? As patterns of private participation are rendered permanent by digital storage options, what lies ahead for the ideas of anonymity, consent, or even personal reconsideration of prior actions? These are some of the questions that emerge when we consider how our practices of gathering for worship, education, political involvement, or community action evolve alongside the technology that enables them.

AI Is Built on Digital Dependencies

What do we mean by AI in the context of this book? "AI" is what cultural theorists call a floating signifier, a term simultaneously instinctive and nebulous. As Veale, Matus, and Gorma put it, "AI has become a loose, umbrella term increasingly saddled with hype, misdirection, and confusion" (2023, 256). As a field of research, artificial intelligence is usually traced back to the middle of the twentieth century and the work of computer scientists to develop machines performing tasks usually associated with human intelligence. Today, the field of AI research is tremendously vast, rich, and made of many subfields. These notably include NLP (natural language processing), machine learning, neural networks, computer vision, and AI ethics, to name only a few. In the public eye, the most recent wave of AI hype concerned generative AI tools like ChatGPT. Powered by large language models (LLMs), these are algorithms trained on huge quantities of text which can seemingly understand and generate text in human-like fashion. While consumers and citizens are entertaining themselves with these tools, global technology companies are racing each other to implement new ones that just weeks earlier were clearly marked as experimental.

Generative AI is only one example of a much broader range of technologies that involve AI in one form or another. In practice, AI-powered technologies have been part and parcel of our digital economies for the better part of the last decade. Social media news feeds, targeted advertising algorithms, automated content moderation tools, and facial recognition software are but a few examples of widespread deployment of AI that predate the current moment of generative AI. In this book, the technological boundaries that we put around the notion of AI reflect this expansiveness. Each chapter touches on one or more technologies that involve some level of AI, even when they might not immediately evoke imaginaries of the sentient machines that animate the current AI hype cycle.

From our perspective, however, AI is neither just a field of research nor a set of technologies. Let us consider here what we can describe as a bingo card of talking points about AI in recent years. You may have heard that "AI can help us solve the biggest challenges the world is facing" and that we should thus develop "AI for good." As the work of Morgan Ames on the One Laptop Per Child Project (2019) and Daniel Greene on poverty alleviation projects in public libraries and schools show (2021), these tech-solutionist refrains have many historical antecedents. Their resurgence in the context of AI shows the endurance of the idea that technology alone can solve complex social issues, which is an idea fraught with problematic assumptions that often lead to the creation of new problems and to the acceleration of damaging social trends, from the privatization of public goods to reinforcement of social inequalities.

Promises that "AI will revolutionize the way we work" awaken familiar libertarian visions of a frictionless automated economy as well as worries from labor advocates—a phenomenon with, again, many historical precedents. As historian Eric Hobsbawm (1952) wrote about the "machine breakers" of the nineteenth century, what often lurks behind these fears are not just concerns about technology per se but also anxieties about broader social inequalities. In the case of AI and labor, these notably include the decades-long rise of globalized neoliberal economies and their associated attacks on collective bargaining, labor protection, growing inequalities, and increased economic precarity.

Discourses pitting the "US and China in a race over AI" generally demonize China as radically different from the US and as responsible for the rise of a dystopian, techno-surveilled, authoritarian society. There are legitimate reasons for these fears, especially considering the Chinese government's use of digital technologies for social control, repression, and discrimination (Qiang 2019). At the same time, this rhetoric reflects a blatant double standard that fails to reckon with the responsibility of the US in building on a global scale, through its corporations and security agencies, a model of widespread, ever increasing, privacy-infringing surveillance—what Shoshana Zuboff (2019) called "surveillance capitalism."

Last example: warnings that "AI carries existential risk for the future of humanity" not only tap into a long-standing sci-fi cultural registry of sentient machines taking over the world. At the time of writing this introduction, an army of industry personalities—led by Open AI's Sam Altman—have been carrying this message and calling for regulating artificial intelligence. At first glance, this position may seem to depart from an historically dominant antiregulatory cyber-libertarianism (Pace 2020). In reality, it aligns with tech companies' efforts in the last few years to get ahead of regulation by publicly embracing it while shaping its contours in the halls of power (Popiel 2018)—a form of regulatory capture familiar to corporate lobbying in other sectors.

In the process, these expert-led conversations tend to ignore or brush aside existing harms of AI that vocal advocates and prominent researchers and public intellectuals—such as Ruha Benjamin, Joy Buolamwini, Virginia Eubanks, Timnit Gebru, Safiya Noble, Cathy O'Neil, and Tawana Petty—have been calling attention to for years. Consequently, a small group of tech entrepreneurs, mostly men racialized as White, hold an oversized influence in public discourse about AI and portray themselves as the saviors who solve problems they largely contributed to creating. This is again not a new phenomenon. Noble and Roberts (2019) described this as a feature of a long-standing "technocratic post-racial order" in Silicon Valley, and it exemplifies what Katz (2020) described as the profound and troubling links between AI and Whiteness. In the AI industrial complex—to riff on Teju Cole's piercing poem about White saviorism (2012)—the tech savior creates brutal algorithms in the morning, funds charities in the afternoon, and receives awards for pretending to support regulation in the evening.

Each of these bingo card statements reveal the many ways in which AI operates—to use the words of Kate Crawford—as a "registry of power"(2021, 8). AI is not just a technology or a field of research. It is also the discourse that surrounds the technology; the economic, political, and social structures that shape its development; and the people behind it, those who benefit from it, and those harmed by it. Today, a vibrant community of activists and scholars are advancing our understanding of these mythologies of AI, where they come from, what they reveal, and what they hide. In this book, we take our cue from these many voices who call attention to the layers of power shaping, and shaped by, socio-technical systems like AI.

Seen in this light, AI is less a unique technological innovation and more the most hyped manifestation of a broader trend decades in the making. Some call it "datafication" (Hintz, Dencik, and Wahl-Jorgensen 2018; Pellegrino, Söderberg, and Milan 2019) or "platformization" (Dijck, Poell, and Waal 2018). Others call it "data colonialism"(Couldry and Mejias 2019), "surveillance capitalism" (Zuboff 2019), the "internet in everything" (DeNardis 2020), or the "society of algorithms"(Burrell and Fourcade 2021). At the Digital Civil Society Lab (where the editors both worked during the writing of this volume), we called it digital dependencies—the ever increasing collective reliance on digital systems for all matters of public and private life, permeating markets, state institutions, and civil society in their many forms. For nearly a decade, our lab worked to understand how these digital dependencies gradually configure the parameters for participation in associational life, activism, philanthropy, and social movement. Today, digital is no longer the "next frontier"; it is common sense. Our current digital ecosystem—characterized by corporate control and government surveillance—continually raises questions about privacy, ownership, power, and the blurring lines between private and public spheres. As AI rolls over for everyone to see and use, the same questions are relevant: Who (should) own the data? What are the privacy implications? How do we bring people—rather than corporations or technological artifacts—to the center? In this book, we understand the current AI moment as the next step in that broader history of digital dependencies.

One might argue that such a perspective on AI considerably expands the boundaries of what it means in the context of this book. One would be right, for indeed our hope is to broaden how scholars, policymakers, technologists, and everyday people think about AI. To understand AI today, we need to foreground what is too often in the background: history, power, and people. By focusing on the intersection of AI and assembly, however, we aim to bound the volume in ways that make it additive and coherent. Perhaps counterintuitively, then, what is most innovative about this volume is perhaps less our attention on AI and more our emphasis on assembly.

AI and Assembly: A Tripartite Relationship

The relationship between assembly and AI is dynamic and multidirectional. A useful starting point is to take stock of existing scholarship on digital systems writ large and assembly to introduce three broad ways to apprehend the relationship between assembly and AI . These can be schematically summarized as follows: (1) AI matters for assembly in physical spaces; (2) AI shapes assembly in online spaces; and (3) individuals and groups assemble to shape the development and deployment of AI.

First, there is considerable scholarship on how digital technologies affect analogue forms of assembly and collective action, such as street protests or demonstrations, particularly in works that examine democracy and mobilization via social media technologies. Spurred in part by the "liberation technology" debates of the early 2010s and the cellphone-powered popular uprisings against authoritarian regimes, this scholarship spreads across social movement studies, political science, sociology, communication, and international relations (e.g., Diamond and Plattner 2012; Tufekci 2017; Feldstein 2021). Over the years, issues of surveillance and censorship—and their circumvention by activists—have been increasingly salient, from the use of cellphone data to monitor racial justice activists (Heh and Wainwright 2022) to internet shutdowns meant to stifle public gathering (Rydzak, Karanja, and Opiyo 2020). Some have questioned the value and efficacy of so-called clicktivism or slacktivism, while others have shed light on political asymmetries in how digital activism impacts offline protest and organizing, and its relevance for different types of advocacy including racial justice and feminist activism (e.g., Chadwick 2006; Tufekci and Wilson 2012; Karpf 2012; Treré and Mattoni 2016; Kreiss 2016; Mendes, Ringrose, and Keller 2019; Schradie 2019; Deibert 2020; Freelon, Marwick, and Kreiss 2020; Richardson 2020; Jackson, Bailey, and Welles 2020).

Although the dynamics between online organizing and physical gathering have been well studied, the findings are nuanced and universal statements of truth do not yet exist. Whether and how online expression interacts with offline behavior are big questions with no simple answers. In January 2021, the world watched as interactions in these categories played out on screens across the globe and in the streets of the US capital: thousands of people organized themselves using mobile apps, listened to a speech, mobilized for action, and swarmed the US Capitol, livestreaming their actions at every step. In subsequent months, digital forensic evidence would contribute to the conviction of thousands of participants and the indictment of a former president. Almost two years to the day, very similar attacks would play out in Brasilia, after Brazil's presidential election. Discussion of the differences between political assembly and attempted coups, from months of mobilization to subsequent arrests, was shaped by political partisanship, criminal law, and constitutional rights. That online behavior was connected to offline behavior in these cases was indisputable. The two January attacks broadcast the dynamics between physical and digital actions to the world. They raised the stakes for our understanding of how digital technologies—including but not limited to artificial intelligence—shape and are shaped by their use for assembling in real life. The episodes are exceptional, but the questions they raise have broad, generalizable application.

Several chapters in our volume add to these debates by assessing the particular affordances that AI-powered technologies—social media news feeds (chapter 3), facial recognition technology (chapter 4), and targeted advertising (chapter 6)—have for different forms of in-person assembly, including protests in public spaces and community gatherings in private spaces.

A second area of vibrant scholarship has been the work done to understand how people assemble in online spaces. Social media platforms, for instance, have always been more than places of expression. They are also spaces for recruiting and gathering people and establishing community norms and conventions—all of which are hallmark practices of assembly, albeit bound here by different constraints of time, space, and technological affordances. In a way, content moderators are equal parts community organizers and speech custodians. The idea of the online world as a *space*—one as much for expression as for gathering—has a history as long as that of the internet, most famously described in John Perry Barlow's canonical 1996 "Declaration of the Independence of Cyberspace." "You have no sovereignty where we *gather*," he warned the governments of the world in the declaration's opening paragraph (Barlow 1996).

Over the years, scholarship from human-computer interaction and media studies have paved the way for deepening our understanding of how communities of volunteers assemble in online spaces (e.g., Reagle 2010); how group dynamics play out on platforms (e.g., Mohan et al. 2017; Soliman, Hafer, and Lemmerich 2019); and how historical contingencies, sociocultural contexts, and the political economy of digital technologies underpin these spaces (e.g., Zuckerman 2013; Firer-Blaess and Fuchs 2014; Coretti and Pica 2015). Much of this scholarship called for understanding how biases from the offline world were brought into online design. For instance, we see how this plays out with Wikipedia (Wagner et al. 2016; McDowell and Vetter 2021; Langrock and González-Bailón 2022). Our volume invites us to think about how online biases are now being brought back into our physical spaces through AI. Consider websites like Reddit and Wikipedia—two paragons of gathering. Today, they are training models for LLMs, effectively turning into sites of extraction not only the speech of users but also the time and labor put into assembling these communities. These same LLMs then feed into the development of a wide range of tools and products found across our physical and digital spaces, from grammar checkers to car infotainment systems. The expansion of AI technologies from screens to streets, homes, cars, workplaces, and more accelerates the porosity of physical and digital realms. A core contribution of our volume, then, is supporting ongoing calls for a theoretical collapse of rigid boundaries between online and offline worlds (for a recent example in the context of African cyber-feminism, see the edited volume by Clark and Mohammed 2023).

Finally, the label "Assembly for AI" summarizes a third way to apprehend the relationship between AI and assembly. Here, we reverse the evergreen branding of AI as a silver bullet for social problems: "AI for good, AI for health, AI for education," and so forth. In contrast, we refer here to emerging efforts by people and communities to organize and assemble to impact the very development of AI technologies. These efforts occur today at the intersection of academia, digital rights advocacy, tech policy, journalism, tech design, and community engage-ment. Some seek to impact product design and the training of engi-neers, while others aim to reveal the exploitative human labor behind AI systems and their ecological costs. Some intend to advance state regulations, while others hope to promote public engagement with AI technologies. Still others call for bans and refusals of specific forms of AI technologies. Therefore, the notion of "Assembly for AI" should not be misconstrued as a reference to communities evangelizing the value of AI but rather to the range of community activities seeking to influ-ence its development.

One example of this form of community: in 2020, amid global pan-demic lockdowns, the editors of this volume launched a listserv—the Digital Assembly Research Network (DARN). Hundreds of scholars and advocates around the world quickly joined. Coming together (via web video), members discussed, debated, and demonstrated research in progress. Absent a pandemic, we probably would have gathered a much smaller, less diverse group in person in physical space. Either way exemplifies the role of gathering, of assembling, in research and in ef-forts to shape tech design and regulation.

While groups assembling to understand and critique AI consti-tute a particularly active space ripe with insights, ideas, activities, and tensions, scholarly analysis of this specific phenomenon itself is rare. Yet research on various forms of advocacy and community organizing about digital technology has been germinating for years now, in partic-ular in work done by data justice and critical data studies scholars, as well as those interested in digital rights advocacy and free and open-source software community organizing (e.g., boyd and Crawford 2012; Irani and Silberman 2013; MacKinnon 2013; Milan 2013; Dubal 2017; Taylor 2017; Treré 2018; Bernholz 2019; Dencik et al. 2019; Gray and Suri 2019; McIlwain 2019; Roberts 2019; Costanza-Chock 2020; Chun 2021; Geiger, Howard, and Irani 2021; Dencik et al. 2022; Driscoll 2022; D'Ignazio 2024). These have paved the way for the possible institu-tionalization of something like an interdisciplinary field of *technology advocacy*—the targeted study of how individuals and groups come together to shape how we engage with technologies. Such inquiry would notably invite perspectives from social movement studies, critical data studies, law, democracy theory, and organizational studies, with recent examples including Waldman's (2024) analysis of the role of privacy nonprofit organizations in crafting the American Data Privacy and Protection Act and Grover's (2022) study of the RightsCon conference as a site of civil society engagement in internet governance. A core contribution of this volume is advancing this line of inquiry by showcasing a multiplicity of advocacy efforts related to AI-powered technologies, demonstrating how these ways of coming together constitute important, pressing, and complex phenomena deserving of study in their own right.

Chapter Overview

The chapters in this volume look directly at issues of artificial intelligence and at the precedent influences of globally networked, data-driven technologies. Some examine how the development and deployment of AI-powered systems are catalyzing new groups of people, from protestors to software professionals. Others examine AI as one element of a much broader digital landscape, in which both laborers and the companies that employ them are being upended by the power of technology. Rather than trying to provide single-sided overarching answers about the impact of AI on assembly, the book explores the multifaceted relationships between AI and assembly and how these relate to complex political, social, legal, and cultural dynamics around the world.

Michael Hamilton starts the book by situating us in the midst of human rights debates about online assembly and association. He quickly clarifies the many ways in which our analogue distinctions between the two terms—which center on questions of temporality and proximity—no longer hold. Redefining assembly and association to fit the reality of socially pervasive AI is ongoing work for the global human rights community.

Ashley Lee brings to the fore the global inequalities central to our datafied world. Her chapter theorizes "algorithmic violence" by showing how algorithmic experiments conducted in the Global South by companies from the Global North upend assembly and harm global civil society. An interdisciplinary scholar trained in computer science and social movement studies, Lee reminds us that our understanding of the social impact of AI ought to consider how global imbalances interact with complex sociopolitical dynamics in local contexts—and that AI harms are about more than just expression and content moderation. After reading this chapter, we are left to wonder: How can there be peaceful assembly where there is algorithmic violence?

Lisa Garbe, Daniel Mwesigwa, and Toussaint Nothias turn to the rise of a paradigmatic AI-powered surveillance technology: facial recognition. In the spirit of Lee's call to think through the nexus of global/local dynamics inherent to AI's expansion, the chapter turns to African contexts, where the rise of facial recognition systems has led to rapidly shifting associations of transnational proponents and critics. It offers an overview of why facial recognition threatens assembly, assesses the pervasiveness of the technology across borders and domains, and reveals a complex tapestry of public, private, local, foreign, and transnational actors involved. These supposed peripheries of the digital economy, they argue, provide compelling insights into the structural forces shaping the future of AI and assembly globally.

In Lucy Bernholz's chapter, the question of agency comes to the fore. As industrial-scale algorithmic analysis of data reveals patterns of behavior that enrich corporations, rideshare drivers and software programmers are taking back control by building their own "mirror" data sets and algorithms to inform advocacy and policy change. An historian by training, Bernholz looks at these civil society tactical responses to consider the implications of algorithmic assembly for community groups, civil society organizations, and democracy.

The chapter by Deborah Raji and Danaë Metaxa takes us inside the world of algorithmic audits, revealing the new assemblages of industry insiders, external scholars, and advocacy organizations building new tools to hold accountable both public and corporate users of AI. They trace the behind-the-scenes process that led to two major algorithmic audits: one on discriminatory bias on Facebook's advertising platform and the other looking at biased performance on Amazon's facial recognition product. Their chapter shows how these technologies themselves became the concern of new civil society organizations and action, and invites us to consider: Are audits becoming a new form of protest?

The volume concludes with a look to the future. Our collective understandings of AI are as much about analogy and metaphor, language, and cultural construction as they are about software code. In the final chapter, Noopur Raval discusses the *New AI Lexicon* project, which is an example of a collective effort to reimagine AI and inform our imagination of it via the language(s) we use. Turning the lens inward to research communities, the chapter allows us to see what it takes to create alternative assemblages of people and ideas to rethink AI by taking head-on questions of power, authority, and collective action.

Assembling the Volume

This book was conceived prior to, and much of it was written during, a global pandemic. In a matter of weeks and months, gathering with others in person went from normal to life-threatening to forbidden. Digital technologies were critical in enforcing the bans and also facilitating continued economic activity. Those that enabled office work to continue via video conference separated some classes of workers from danger while offering no respite for others. Worship communities, political factions, social clubs, and arts programs shifted and shifted again. Some new connections thrived; some preexisting connections withered. Whether they were strengthened or destroyed, the pandemic revealed—again—our deep need to connect to other people, to be part of groups, to come together, to seek like minds, and to find ways to be with others. This most basic human need—to connect—has been and will continue to be—shaped and reshaped by the tools we use to do it.

In seeking to encourage a new or (re)newed focus on assembly, the contributors to this volume drew on the literature and methods of a diverse set of disciplines. Computer science, with its many subareas such as human-computer interaction and AI ethics, is represented. Sociology, history, communication, law, and political science are also represented.

The book was conceptualized by members of the Digital Civil Society Lab. It is not an edited volume in the sense of a collection of essays on a common topic but rather an example of collaborative research production. Building on previous experiences, we invited potential authors to contribute based on their individual expertise and their willingness to collaborate with others in producing an edited volume of some cohesion. In the end, nine scholars from various disciplines (law, history, communication, computer science, information science, and political science) with diverse geographical expertise (North America, Europe, Asia, and Africa) came together to develop their chapters. The contributors gave two rounds of feedback on developmental abstracts, held several online discussions about their work in progress, and spent two days on the Stanford campus to workshop draft versions of their chapters. This process catalyzed several of the jointly written chapters, each of which represents a strong example of cross-disciplinary scholarship. While workshopping, we were able to identify and highlight arguments that spoke to each other across chapters, themes that were widely discussed, and asked/unanswered questions that form the basis of a proposed research agenda. Our goal was to ultimately create an interdisciplinary and integrated volume that is coherent yet still diverse. While individual chapters can be read on their own merit, taken together they also tell a story that progresses from disruption and harm to advocacy and alternatives.

AI, Assembly and Digital Civil Society: Toward Future Research

By focusing on assembly—and assembly across the globe—this volume posits several new perspectives for considering AI in the context of self-governance, collective action, congregational and community boundaries, and global reach. How, where, when, and with whom we come together, for a host of reasons—political, cultural, educational, artistic, religious, familial, or market-based actions—and who or what monitors or restricts those choices will be key chapters in the story of democracy in the twenty-first century. We hope this volume will encourage new research on AI, on assembly, and on their entwined implications.

Our specific interests center on digital civil society, that amorphous, hard-to-define concept that captures collective action on, with, and about digital systems and which sits in interlocking tension with democratic governments and market-based economies. This view foregrounds the role of independent actors—both individuals and collectives—acting on behalf of a public purpose. This is distinct from, though entwined with, purely profit-seeking enterprises or governmental responsibilities.

The chapters in the volume center civil society to think through AI's transformations. Our understanding of civil society goes beyond tax code categorization and reductive normative assumptions about its democratic benefits. We include individuals and not-for-profit, nongovernmental associations, both formal and informal, that come together to address shared social challenges. These include nonprofit organizations and charities, social enterprises, individuals, and collectives, as well as the individuals and private groups that fund them.

Civil society's relationship to digital technologies is found in histories of open-source hardware and software, in scholarship on surveillance and protest, and in studies of the community aspects of specific technological moments, such as phone phreaks, hackers, and, with this volume, the evolution of algorithmic audits. Often, it can also be found in histories of regulatory battles and policy discussions. Rarely, however, is the role of civil society in shaping our digital systems and history discussed in relation to an understanding of its role in democracies. Democracy theory lags behind technological development and is in need of more robust engagement with the power dynamics, capacities, and boundary-crossing nature of digital systems. Scholarship that interrogates the intersections of digital technologies, public participation, and democratic governance is much needed—both for an understanding of governments and from the perspective of technology management.

When it comes to AI-driven changes in civil society, there are countless examples unfolding in real time. Wikipedia, for example, which has stood for more than twenty years as an example of online, voluntary collective action, faces new sustainability challenges as artificial intelligence shifts a once symbiotic relationship with Google to an extractive one. As the nonprofit behind the encyclopedia searches for new funding mechanisms, other civil society organizations—from nonprofits to unions to professional associations—are navigating AI-generated challenges. Gig workers are creating unions built around data and algorithms; distributed content moderators are unionizing, and professional computer scientists are developing independent auditing bodies and transparent methods for unpacking these systems.

While there have been nonprofit associations focused on artificial intelligence since at least 1979, more than sixty-five have emerged in the past decade. These range from well-funded independent nonprofits or university labs to unincorporated associations of protestors who gather and disburse in real time even as they host websites of information that may live on forever (or disappear at any moment). They provide a range of services, from audits to research, advocacy for and against regulation, and training for different sectors such as education, health care, and even fundraising. Nonprofit organizations are not only focusing on AI as their primary purpose; they are being changed by the powers of AI. Foundations across the US and Europe have developed new programs dedicated to understanding AI, and the philanthropic arm of Google is funding efforts to use it to fight climate change.

Nonprofits and civil society organizations around the globe are considering how the use of AI might change their own operations. Pulling back the lens shows that the questions and answers provided in this book on the relationship between AI, assembly, and association raise more existential questions for civil society. We have seen a decades-long move to apply human rights in digital spaces. Artificial intelligence, which both facilitates and represents an expansion of independent, automated agents, raises new questions about nonhuman actors—be they bots, robots, or obscure and embedded algorithms. This in turn raises questions about not only "who" or "what" might be participating but also "how" to interpret the logic and analysis that underpin their actions. Democratic values of transparent and participatory decision-making are challenged by the ability to interpret and reverse-engineer these tools.

At the time of writing, debate is raging about the harms of AI. The loudest voices in most policy-making rooms have been coming from AI industry creators and funders and have largely focused on existential risks to humanity. These existential threats are endlessly debatable. They lead to discussions that center the power of corporate creators and postpone accountability. They are most often brought to attention by the very people building systems they claim may portend the future extinction of humanity. From a civil society perspective, there is an interesting and potentially important alignment here between the effective altruism movement, which has massive philanthropic resources, and an approach to harms that supports rapid and extreme wealth creation of tools, the harms of which one might mitigate through donations and industry-preserving regulations.

In contrast to the potential long-term harms proposed by industry insiders and effective altruists is a focus on the current, real, practical harms of racist, misogynist, discriminatory algorithmic decision-making systems. These are increasingly well documented by scholars and experienced by individuals and communities on a daily basis. Civil society organizations, many of which focus on rights advocacy and protection or direct human services, regularly interact with those being harmed. Future research on civil society's roles in countering AI harm will require analyses of industry and community power, race and gender, human rights advocacy, and development of alternative regulatory foci and regimes, as well as new organizational forms. Scholarship focused on these intersections will provide critical rebuttals to the path dependency assumptions of industry arguments and serve as case studies for a better understanding of civil society advocacy efforts in the digital age.

We hope this volume inspires more research that draws together humanists and scientists, more research that considers experiences of the global majority, and more research that recognizes and wrestles with the profound physical aspects of our digitized connections. By emphasizing civil society—with its dynamic and diffuse organizations, boundaries, and practices—we shine a light on public participation in the making, using, rejecting, and regulating of AI. The type of public participation one finds in civil society—whether through formal organizations or in moments of protest—is critical to sustaining democracies. Participation in activities meant to benefit others is a starting assumption for the grand aspiration of self-governance. Civil society houses "critical defensive work" (Zuckerman 2020) to protect civil liberties and limit the power of Big Tech. But it is also often the site of alternatives—whether open-source, community-managed software projects that provide options beyond proprietary tools, or cultural creation and political advocacy from groups marginalized by dominant systems. Civil society is both generative and preventive. It houses diverse and conflicting convictions, enables those denied formal political power to build their own, and provides space for protest—whether that be in the form of street gatherings or frameworks alternative to corporate understanding of safety, security, and design. By providing a gateway into digital civil society, this volume invites readers to envision a digital future, built byte by byte, beyond the narrow horizon of corporate extraction and state surveillance.

References

Ames, Morgan G. 2019. *The Charisma Machine: The Life, Death, and Legacy of One Laptop per Child*. Cambridge, MA: MIT Press.

Barlow, John Perry. 1996. "A Declaration of the Independence of Cyberspace." *Electronic Frontier Foundation*, February 8. 1996. https://www.eff.org/cyberspace-independence.

Benkler, Yochai, Rob Faris, and Harold Roberts. 2018. *Network Propaganda: Manipulation, Disinformation, and Radicalization in American Politics*. New York: Oxford University Press.

Bernholz, Lucy. 2019. "The Invention of Digital Civil Society." *Stanford Social Innovation Review (SSIR)*. https://ssir.org/articles/entry/the_invention_of_digital_civil_society.

boyd, danah, and Kate Crawford. 2012. "Critical Questions for Big Data: Provocations for a Cultural, Technological, and Scholarly Phenomenon." *Information, Communication & Society* 15 (5): 662–679. https://doi.org/10.1080/1369118X.2012.678878.

Burrell, Jenna, and Marion Fourcade. 2021. "The Society of Algorithms." *Annual Review of Sociology* 47 (summer). https://doi.org/10.1146/annurev-soc-090820-020800.

Chadwick, Andrew. 2006. *Internet Politics: States, Citizens, and New Communication Technologies*. Oxford, UK: Oxford University Press.

Chun, Wendy Hui Kyong. 2021. *Discriminating Data: Correlation, Neighborhoods, and the New Politics of Recognition*. Cambridge, MA: MIT Press.

Clark, Msia Kibona, and Wunpini Fatimata Mohammed. 2023. *African Women in Digital Spaces: Redefining Social Movements on the Continent and in the Diaspora*. Dar es Salaam, Tanzania: Mkuki Na Nyota.

Cole, Teju. 2012. "The White-Savior Industrial Complex." *The Atlantic* (blog), March 21, 2012. https://www.theatlantic.com/international/archive/2012/03/the-white-savior-industrial-complex/254843/.

Coretti, Lorenzo, and Daniele Pica. 2015. "The Purple Movement: How Facebook's Design Undermined the Anti-Berlusconi Protest in Italy." *Journal of Italian Cinema & Media Studies* 3 (3): 305–318.

Costanza-Chock, Sasha. 2020. *Design Justice: Community-Led Practices to Build the Worlds We Need*. Cambridge, MA: MIT Press.

Couldry, Nick, and Ulises A. Mejias. 2019. *The Costs of Connection: How Data Is Colonizing Human Life and Appropriating It for Capitalism*. Stanford, CA: Stanford University Press.

Crawford, Kate. 2021. *The Atlas of AI: Power, Politics, and the Planetary Costs of Artificial Intelligence*. New Haven, CT: Yale University Press.

Deibert, Ronald. 2020. *Reset: Reclaiming the Internet for Civil Society*. Toronto, ON: House of Anansi Press.

DeNardis, Laura. 2020. *The Internet in Everything: Freedom and Security in a World with No Off Switch*. New Haven, CT: Yale University Press.

Dencik, Lina, Arne Hintz, Joanna Redden, and Emiliano Treré. 2019. "Exploring Data Justice: Conceptions, Applications and Directions." *Information, Communication & Society* 22 (7): 873–881.

———. 2022. *Data Justice*. London: SAGE Publications.

Diamond, Larry, and Marc F. Plattner. 2012. *Liberation Technology: Social Media and the Struggle for Democracy*. Baltimore: John Hopkins University Press.

D'Ignazio, Catherine. 2024. *Counting Feminicide: Data Feminism in Action*. Cambridge, MA: MIT Press.

Dijck, José van, Thomas Poell, and Martijn de Waal. 2018. *The Platform Society: Public Values in a Connective World*. Oxford, UK: Oxford University Press.

Driscoll, Kevin. 2022. *The Modem World: A Prehistory of Social Media*. New Haven, CT: Yale University Press.

Dubal, V. B. 2017. "The Drive to Precarity: A Political History of Work, Regulation, & Labor Advocacy in San Francisco's Taxi & Uber Economies." *Berkeley Journal of Employment and Labor Law* 38 (1): 73–135.

Feldstein, Steven. 2021. *The Rise of Digital Repression: How Technology Is Reshaping Power, Politics, and Resistance*. New York: Oxford University Press.

Firer-Blaess, Sylvain, and Christian Fuchs. 2014. "Wikipedia: An Info-Communist Manifesto." *Television & New Media* 15 (2): 87–103.

Freelon, Deen, Alice Marwick, and Daniel Kreiss. 2020. "False Equivalencies: Online Activism from Left to Right." *Science* 369 (6508): 1197–1201.

Geiger, R. Stuart, Dorothy Howard, and Lilly Irani. 2021. "The Labor of Maintaining and Scaling Free and Open-Source Software Projects." *Proceedings of the ACM on Human-Computer Interaction* 5 (CSCW1): 1–28.

Gray, Mary L., and Siddharth Suri. 2019. *Ghost Work: How to Stop Silicon Valley from Building a New Global Underclass*. New York: HarperCollins.

Greene, Daniel. 2021. *The Promise of Access: Technology, Inequality, and the Political Economy of Hope*. Cambridge, MA: MIT Press.

Grover, Rohan. 2022. "The Geopolitics of Digital Rights Activism: Evaluating Civil Society's Role in the Promises of Multistakeholder Internet Governance." *Telecommunications Policy* 46 (10): 102437.

Heh, Eyako, and Joel Wainwright. 2022. "No Privacy, No Peace: Urban Surveillance and the Movement for Black Lives." *Journal of Race, Ethnicity and the City* 3 (2): 121–141.

Hintz, Arne, Lina Dencik, and Karin Wahl-Jorgensen. 2018. *Digital Citizenship in a Datafied Society*. Hoboken, NJ: John Wiley & Sons.

Hobsbawm, E. J. 1952. "The Machine Breakers." *Past & Present* 1 (1): 57–70.

Irani, Lilly C., and M. Six Silberman. 2013. "Turkopticon: Interrupting Worker Invisibility in Amazon Mechanical Turk." In *CHI '13: Proceedings of the SIGCHI Conference on Human Factors in Computing Systems*, 611–620. New York: Association for Computing Machinery.

Jackson, Sarah J., Moya Bailey, and Brooke Foucault Welles. 2020. *#HashtagActivism: Networks of Race and Gender Justice*. Cambridge, MA: MIT Press.

Karpf, David. 2012. *The MoveOn Effect: The Unexpected Transformation of American Political Advocacy*. New York: Oxford University Press.

Katz, Yarden. 2020. *Artificial Whiteness: Politics and Ideology in Artificial Intelligence.* New York: Columbia University Press.

Kaye, David. 2019. *Speech Police: The Global Struggle to Govern the Internet.* New York: Columbia Global Reports.

Kessler, Sarah, and Tiffany Hsu. 2023. "When Hackers Descended to Test A.I., They Found Flaws Aplenty." *The New York Times*, August 16, 2023. https://www.nytimes.com/2023/08/16/technology/ai-defcon-hackers.html.

Kreiss, Daniel. 2016. *Prototype Politics: Technology-Intensive Campaigning and the Data of Democracy.* Oxford, UK: Oxford University Press.

Langrock, Isabelle, and Sandra González-Bailón. 2022. "The Gender Divide in Wikipedia: Quantifying and Assessing the Impact of Two Feminist Interventions." *Journal of Communication* 72 (3): 297–321.

MacKinnon, Rebecca. 2013. *Consent of the Networked: The Worldwide Struggle for Internet Freedom.* New York: Basic Books.

McDowell, Zachary J., and Matthew A. Vetter. 2021. *Wikipedia and the Representation of Reality.* London: Routledge.

McIlwain, Charlton D. 2019. *Black Software: The Internet & Racial Justice, from the AfroNet to Black Lives Matter.* New York: Oxford University Press.

Mendes, Kaitlynn, Jessica Ringrose, and Jessalynn Keller. 2019. *Digital Feminist Activism: Girls and Women Fight Back Against Rape Culture.* Oxford, UK: Oxford University Press.

Milan, Stefania. 2013. *Social Movements and Their Technologies: Wiring Social Change.* New York: Springer.

Mohan, Shruthi, Apala Guha, Michael Harris, Fred Popowich, Ashley Schuster, and Chris Priebe. 2017. "The Impact of Toxic Language on the Health of Reddit Communities." In *Advances in Artificial Intelligence*, edited by Malek Mouhoub and Philippe Langlais, 51–56. Lecture Notes in Computer Science. New York: Springer International Publishing.

Noble, Safiya Umoja, and Sarah T. Roberts. 2019. "6 Technological Elites, the Meritocracy, and Postracial Myths in Silicon Valley." In *Racism Postrace*, edited by R. Mukherjee, S. Banet-Weiser, and H. Gray, 113–30. Raleigh-Durham, NC: Duke University Press.

Pace, Jonathan. 2020. "Cyberlibertarianism in the Mid-1990s." *AoIR Selected Papers of Internet Research*, October. https://doi.org/10.5210/spir.v2020i0.11299.

Pellegrino, Giuseppina, Johan Söderberg, and Stefania Milan. 2019. "Datafication from Below: Epistemology, Ambivalences, Challenges." *TECNOSCIENZA: Italian Journal of Science & Technology Studies* 10 (1): 89–114.

Persily, Nathaniel, and Joshua A. Tucker, eds. 2020. *Social Media and Democracy: The State of the Field, Prospects for Reform.* SSRC Anxieties of Democracy Series. Cambridge, UK: Cambridge University Press.

Popiel, Pawel. 2018. "The Tech Lobby: Tracing the Contours of New Media Elite Lobbying Power." *Communication, Culture and Critique* 11 (4): 566–585.

Qiang, Xiao. 2019. "The Road to Digital Unfreedom: President Xi's Surveillance State." *Journal of Democracy* 30 (1): 53–67.

Reagle, Joseph Michael. 2010. *Good Faith Collaboration: The Culture of Wikipedia.* Cambridge, MA: MIT Press.

Ressa, Maria. 2022. "We're All Being Manipulated the Same Way." *The Atlantic* (blog), April 7, 2022. https://www.theatlantic.com/ideas/archive/2022/04/maria-ressa-disinformation-manipulation/629483/.

Richardson, Allissa V. 2020. *Bearing Witness While Black: African Americans, Smartphones, and the New Protest #Journalism.* New York: Oxford University Press.

Roberts, Sarah T. 2019. *Behind the Screen.* New Haven, CT: Yale University Press.

Rydzak, Jan, Moses Karanja, and Nicholas Opiyo. 2020. "Internet Shutdowns in Africa| Dissent Does Not Die in Darkness: Network Shutdowns and Collective Action in African Countries." *International Journal of Communication* 14: 24.

Schradie, Jen. 2019. *The Revolution That Wasn't: How Digital Activism Favors Conservatives.* Cambridge, MA: Harvard University Press.

Soliman, Ahmed, Jan Hafer, and Florian Lemmerich. 2019. "A Characterization of Political Communities on Reddit." In *HT '19: Proceedings of the 30th ACM Conference on Hypertext and Social Media*, 259–263. New York: Association for Computing Machinery.

Taylor, Linnet. 2017. "What Is Data Justice? The Case for Connecting Digital Rights and Freedoms Globally." *Big Data & Society* 4 (2): 1–14.

Treré, Emiliano. 2018. *Hybrid Media Activism: Ecologies, Imaginaries, Algorithms.* London: Routledge.

Treré, Emiliano, and Alice Mattoni. 2016. "Media Ecologies and Protest Movements: Main Perspectives and Key Lessons." *Information, Communication & Society* 19 (3): 290–306.

Tufekci, Zeynep. 2017. *Twitter and Tear Gas: The Power and Fragility of Networked Protest.* New Haven, CT: Yale University Press.

Tufekci, Zeynep, and Christopher Wilson. 2012. "Social Media and the Decision to Participate in Political Protest: Observations From Tahrir Square." *Journal of Communication* 62 (2): 363–379.

Veale, Michael, Kira Matus, and Robert Gorwa. 2023. "AI and Global Governance: Modalities, Rationales, Tensions." *Annual Review of Law and Social Science* 19 (1): 255–275.

Wagner, Claudia, Eduardo Graells-Garrido, David Garcia, and Filippo Menczer. 2016. "Women Through the Glass Ceiling: Gender Asymmetries in Wikipedia." *EPJ Data Science* 5 (1): 1–24.

Waldman, Ari. 2024. "Compromised Advocates: Civil Society and the Future of Privacy Law." Paper presented at the Privacy Law Scholars Conference, Georgetown University Law Center, Washington DC, 30 May 2024

Zuboff, Shoshana. 2019. *The Age of Surveillance Capitalism: The Fight for a Human Future at the New Frontier of Power.* New York, NY: PublicAffairs.

Zuckerman, Ethan. 2013. *Rewire: Digital Cosmopolitans in the Age of Connection.* New York: W. W. Norton.

———.2020. "The Case for Digital Public Infrastructure." *Knight First Amendment Institute*, Jan. 17, 2020. https://knightcolumbia.org/content/the-case-for-digital-public-infrastructure [https://perma.cc/3NDZ-CCPK].

Two

Illusions of Agency?

Michael Hamilton

Introduction

The risks presented by artificial intelligence (AI) to the public sphere have primarily focused on deliberative and privacy-related predations. Potential distortions relating to *speech* and *information* (including algorithmic shadow-banning and the amplification of disinformation) or privacy intrusions resulting from AI-assisted surveillance (such as the algorithmic processing of data obtained through facial recognition) pose critical challenges. But other potentially profound implications of AI for the freedom to assemble have been overlooked. At the very least, there has been a failure to consider these implications explicitly through the prism of "assembly" and thus to grapple with the ways in which AI might change (or imperil) how we gather with others.

This chapter considers, first, what it means to "assemble" in online spaces. It then addresses the limitations of analogical reasoning, which has so far characterized attempts to understand these spaces (by digital activists, human rights protagonists, and judges). Discussion turns then to the complexity of distinguishing agency from structure in online spaces (not least since this underlies consideration of whether and when AI might amount to an "interference" with the right of peaceful assembly).

Focusing on the affective consequences of AI, the chapter contemplates AI's impact on the authenticity of participation and the dynamic and reflexive forms of agency that the right of peaceful assembly both relies upon and enables. At one level, the very nature of voluntary participation may become atrophied through algorithmic intervention—though arguably too, voluntariness itself is never quite as pure in practice as in abstraction.

These questions are important not only (or even principally) because AI might impact how assemblies are to be represented to others but also because it changes the nature and extent of the choices that participants make about how and with whom they appear. Ultimately, AI stands to impact both how we disclose who we are and how society becomes visible to itself (Jungherr and Schroeder 2023).

Freedom of Assembly Online

The right of peaceful assembly is typically associated with physical forms of gathering—marches and demonstrations in the street. Even then, our intuitive sense of what constitutes an "assembly" (that we know one when we see one) does not always match the protective carapace of the right. For one, "assembly" is often conflated with "protest," obscuring more anodyne forms of gathering that are also integral to the fabric of social interaction and are protected as assemblies under international human rights law.

Both the UN Special Rapporteur on the Rights to Freedom of Peaceful Assembly and of Association (2019) and the UN Human Rights Committee (General Comment 37, 2020, paragraphs 6, 10, and 13) have recognized that the right of peaceful assembly in Article 21 of the International Covenant on Civil and Political Rights (ICCPR) not only protects gatherings in physical spaces (whether publicly or privately owned) but also affords protection to assemblies that take place in online spaces. These are what Peters (2022) describes as "digitally-based" assemblies—in contrast to "digitally-enabled" assemblies (physical gatherings enabled by digital tools). Indeed, online actions need not themselves *be* an assembly for them to engage the right of peaceful assembly: General Comment 37 (2020, paragraphs 33–34) emphasizes that "[a]ssociated activities conducted by an individual or by a group, outside the immediate context of the gathering but which are integral to making the exercise meaningful, are also covered. . . . Many associated activities happen online or otherwise rely upon digital services. Such activities are also protected under article 21."

Such normative claims prompt threshold questions about what it means to "assemble" online or to "participate" in an online assembly—though such questions are not new (Zick 2007; Comninos 2012; Inazu 2013). Nonetheless, uncertainty about the range of activities encompassed by the right of peaceful assembly are magnified when we begin to conceive of assemblies in cyberspace. In particular, given the predominance of *expressive* and *group* activity online—involving interactions that are often more akin to publishing or broadcasting than to assembling (Müller 2019)—there has been considerable imprecision when it comes to pinpointing examples of online *assembly* as distinct from speech and/or association.

John Inazu's (avowedly tentative) application of what he calls virtual assemblies to online forums, churches, and dating services, and to Facebook communications between teachers and students (2013) arguably blurs the distinction between assembly and association (a distinction that is important to retain for our purposes here). Inazu's purpose is less about defining "virtual assemblies" than it is about reading in constitutional protection, under the assembly clause of the First Amendment, for online groups which he defines broadly as "two or more people intentionally pursuing a shared enterprise" (1094, n.2), given the absence of any express guarantee of the right of association in the US Constitution.

The kind of acquaintances, partnerships, and networks that may be established through dating or professional networking apps do not, without more, meet the threshold for an assembly. Nor is every conversation in an online space (such as a chat room) sufficient to engage the right of assembly—speakers and conversationalists do not become assembly participants simply by virtue of their co-presence or mutual interaction. So as not to lose sight of the unique value of the interactions that properly constitute an assembly, it is important to distinguish assembly from mere communication and from online groups in a general sense. Those activities often fall to be protected under speech or association, respectively.

There is, however, overlap and fluidity, and the notion of an assembly is increasingly difficult to fix once it is conceded that remote and distanced groupings may still qualify. As Nothias and Bernholz note in the introduction to this volume, "time and distance . . . are more complicated ideas in the digital age." This concession compels case-by-case consideration of factors such as the spatial proximity of participants, their temporal synchronicity, their unity of purpose, the degree of logistical coordination, and/or their intention to gather—perhaps with no single factor being dispositive (Hamilton 2020; Hamilton et al. 2022). Implicitly, though, this concession is also premised on a recognition that remote online "presence" is no less embodied than is its physical analogue. As Julie Cohen emphasizes, cyberspace is "both extension and evolution of everyday spatial practice . . . [involving] the embodied situated experience of cyberspace users and the complex interplay between real and digital geographies" (2007, 212; similarly, Kalpokas 2020; Bakardjieva 2015). We must therefore recognize that cyberspace users are generally situated in both spaces at once, and that human participants in online assemblies should not be viewed as disembodied avatars but rather as material bodies whose lives and identities offline and online are profoundly entwined.

In order, then, to interrogate the ways in which AI might impact assembly, it is unnecessary to dwell on examples that lie at the definitional periphery of "online assembly"—whether or not this or that hashtag event or distributed denial of service (DDoS) attack (Peterson 2009; Sauter 2014) or mobilization via an anonymously managed messaging app—might properly be classified as an assembly. It is sufficient to point to examples of online assemblies that straightforwardly clear these definitional hurdles.

While "assembly" extends beyond "protest" (encompassing, for example, entirely recreational and social gatherings), online protests by "residents" or "users" on gaming platforms such as Second Life or Meta's Horizon Worlds (Cole 2017) provide a vivid illustration of the concerted type of co-presence that would constitute an online assembly. We might think of the users of Yandex Navigator, a satnav app in Russia, who staged protests by tagging themselves at symbolic locations, both giving the appearance of congestion and posting political slogans in their comments (Buyse 2021; Edwards 2020). We might also point to sit-in protests by World of Warcraft players (Marshall 2021; *The Gamer* 2021), solidarity events on Minecraft, or Hong Kong pro-democracy protests and Black Lives Matter (BLM) demonstrations on Animal Crossing (Bernhard 2020; Schofield 2020), protests against Russia's invasion of Ukraine in the role-playing game Final Fantasy XIV (Fujiu 2022; Harris 2022) or pro-Palestinian demonstrations in Roblox (Azmi 2023; Silberling 2023).

Online spaces make it possible for gatherings that might not otherwise occur. The Roblox protests, for example, involved many young people from Malaysia, where the law prohibits anyone below the age of fifteen from taking part in physical (offline) demonstrations. However, in order to understand the potential effects of AI on such online gatherings, it is important to first consider the affordances (and pathologies) of these different spaces—and to reflect on how such spaces might best be conceptualized (in part so that the design of legal protections and human rights norms correspond to the harms that are likely to arise). In this regard, it is worth recalling Kasinitz's lucent collection that almost thirty years ago positioned the "Metropolis" as center and symbol of our times (1995). Online platforms may be the present-day equivalent—and the as yet untold effects of AI raise complexities and contradictions parallelling concerns that have long preoccupied urban sociologists: AI heralds the prospect of new patterns of interaction, forms of cultural life, and possibilities of civic bonds all catalyzed through synthetically modeled interactions between human and non-human objects.

Of Platforms and Public Squares: The Limits of the Analogy

The public *sphere* has been described as "the collusion of physical space with the everyday world [that] fosters social interactions of both confrontation with otherness and shared experiences that facilitate a communal sensibility overall" (Lang and Cuff 2005, 116). The public *square* is often regarded as its archetype, in large part because it is a space "that prescribes no high-level purpose" (Fleischacker 1998, 292). Here, there is no bright-line division between political and nonpolitical life. As Tamás Györfi has noted, "even when people come together at racecourses, in theatres and stadiums, at festivals or street demonstrations, they have at least the *potential* to become a political entity, capable of acclaiming" (2009, 12).

In the online context, Jessica Beyer similarly emphasizes that "nonpolitical social websites are central to understanding civic engagement in the information age" (2014, 127). It is vital to consider the ways in which political subjectivities are digitally mediated, recognizing that online spaces today play an increasingly important role in political will formation (Müller 2019, 11). Beissinger, for example, notes that "new forms of networking—not face-to-face associations, but digitally mediated social networks—have in a number of instances become vehicles for organizing large-scale mobilizations that have challenged autocratic rule, providing the basis for a civic activism even in the continued presence of anemic 'conventional' civil society association" (2017, 351).

We are confronted with questions about the equivalence or substitutability of aspects of assembling in the material and virtual worlds (e.g., Zick 2006, 648; Müller 2019, 204). In seeking to bridge the two, analogical reasoning pervades the literature and jurisprudence. The X (formally known as Twitter) accounts of certain public officials have been classed as public forums, given their interactivity, general accessibility, and compatibility with expressive activity (*Knight*

First Amendment Institute v. Trump 2018). Pejorative references to disembodied online mobs also echo the atavistic understandings of "crowds" that permeated early crowd psychology (Citron 2009). Privately owned internet platforms have also been likened to shopping malls (see further, Jaffe 2019), nature reserves, vast libraries, or soapboxes that enable modern-day town criers and pamphleteers (e.g., *Reno v. ACLU* 1997; *Packingham v. North Carolina* 2017)—although, as Justice Alito's dissent in *Packingham* emphasized, "there are important differences between cyberspace and the physical world . . . [and] we should be cautious in applying our free speech precedents to the internet."

It is also noteworthy that these physical-world parallels have been drawn not only by those external to online actions (judges, UN Special Rapporteurs, academics, and the like) but also by assembly participants themselves. Discussing early DDoS "sit-ins" against the World Trade Organization in 1999 by the "electrohippies," Molly Sauter notes the desire of these digitally enabled activists to remain "in functional lockstep with existing forms of on-the-street activism" (2014, 44), highlighting how "physical-world parallels were central to their philosophy of practice in the online space" (2014, 48). As Sauter emphasizes, this "necessitates a physicalized view of the internet itself: the internet itself must be seen as a physical place, albeit one with special attributes" (2014, 45).

Fast-forward twenty years. During the drafting of General Comment 37, some commentators still argued that online assemblies should not be brought within the protective fold of ICCPR Article 21. Gerald Neuman, for example, said, "further thought is needed before the Committee concludes that Article 21 is the proper home for this topic, and much more work is needed before the Committee could articulate rules that govern state behavior in regulating an 'assembly' that takes place entirely online" (2020). Such arguments were ultimately unsuccessful, and the assertion of normative equivalency—that whatever rights we have offline must also, by extension, be recognized and protected online—won out (Dror-Shpoliansky and Shany 2021).

No doubt analogical reasoning serves to anchor the unfamiliar (or futuristic) in recognizable tropes, with corresponding explanatory and rhetorical dividends. However, while analogical parallels may have had their place in the struggle to validate rights online, such arguments no longer hold the same strategic currency and it is time to jettison uncritical analogical reasoning, instead focusing on gaining a more granular and critical understanding of these spaces and their different logics.

Taking Justice Alito's cue, it is vital to contextualize and properly understand the differential role and significance of particular spaces for particular individuals and groups in different sociopolitical settings. Dafna Dror-Shpoliansky and Yuval Shany, for example, describe the online ecosystem "as a *new* [my emphasis] realm of human interaction rather than as just a new type of media" (2021, 23). Ian Bogost similarly argues that "Twitter and Facebook and Google aren't 'better' town halls, neighborhood centers, libraries, or newspapers—they are different ones, run by computers, for better and for worse" (2017).

There is also a need for greater nuance when invoking descriptive categories (such as game, chat room, or platform). Harald Trapp and Robert Thum note that "the spatial term 'platform' is used to camouflage a virtual, hybrid market-place organised by algorithms" (2022, 154). Jedd Hakimi, for example, highlights how the concept of video game fails to differentiate "technical conditions that shape a video game's form, content, and reception" (2019, 938). He suggests that in the absence of any unifying characteristic, an exclusive focus on the material platform to the exclusion of the immaterial and experiential qualities of different games results in an overly determinist and unhelpful taxonomy. Tarleton Gillespie makes a similar point about "platforms," arguing that these are "sociotechnical assemblages and complex institutions; they're not even all commercial, and the commercial ones are commercial in different ways" (2018, 18).

Such finespun distinctions suggest that both spaces and events need to be parsed in a highly particularized manner to determine the parameters of online assembly and make sense of what participant agency entails. Stefania Milan, for example, coins the term "cloud protesting" to describe the mobilization that social media platforms enable, observing that "with one-to-one and multidirectional one-to-many exchanges becoming the norm, more and more people potentially communicate directly with each other with the sole mediation of the platform and of its invisible algorithms—as opposed to the mediation of a movement organization or leader" (2018, 120). As such, "social networking platforms and applications, and the algorithms animating them, alter and structure activist agency" (2018, 116).

The underlying logics of some online spaces (ideological, for-profit, or both) can steer users to join or create certain zones or nested enclosures over others, each with their own norms and gatekeepers [cf. Timothy Zick's "tactical spaces" (2006, 584)]. Critically, many of these online spaces in which people assemble function not as the public square but as private or quasi-private rooms—perhaps requiring a digital key, payment, or other form of authentication to obtain access (Anti-Defamation League 2019). Recalling that the UN Human Rights Committee's General Comment 37 on Article 21 of the ICCPR expressly extends protection to assemblies in private spaces, a focus only on the public square overlooks the many significant spaces in which political subjectivities are formed and nurtured. Within and between these myriad spaces, artificial intelligence may have profound implications for the admission and exclusion of users and the "privileges" that they enjoy.

In addition, there must be a careful accounting for the different forms and interventions of AI. Definitions of AI are themselves both contested and somewhat elusive (e.g., Bogost 2017 ("It's just software"); Martinez 2019). Many have highlighted the foundational role that algorithms can play—they "not only reorganize, but define and produce space and new forms of boundaries" (Trapp and Thum 2022, 149). Artificial intelligence potentially performs a range of quite different tasks—from perception and deep learning; classification, aggregation, ranking, and curating; to moderating and communicating. Indeed, industry players may seek to style AI as predominantly enabling: the integration of smart technology in everyday products and the collection and processing of vast amounts of data is claimed to be in the interests of efficiency, prosperity,

well-being, and enhanced quality of life. In an assembly context, benef-
icent claims might be made in relation to, for example, the use of artificial intelligence to verify numbers of protest participants or to fight
harassment and misogyny, discourage trolls, and limit the proliferation
of spam accounts. The dual use of artificial intelligence tools may ultimately make their excesses more difficult to rein in.

The following section focuses on a particular form of action in
which AI operates—the proliferation of chatbots and the scope for these
nonhuman actors to convene or participate in gatherings held in online
spaces.

Participant Chatbots and Astroturfing

In this "dawning age of robo-sociality" (Bakardjieva 2015, 244) and with
the advent of large-language-model (LLM) chatbots, one pressing line
of inquiry, no longer in the realm of dystopian fantasy (listen to Evan
Ratliff's 'Shell Game' podcast) concerns the potential for AI-powered
bots to mimic human behavior and not only interact with assembly participants but actually be considered anthropomorphized participants
themselves. Deshpande et al. argue that "anthropomorphization can
make AI systems human-like decision-taking agents, thus strengthening the case for extending personhood to them" (2023, 4). Moreover,
as Ignas Kalpokas illustrates, the only salient difference between a real
horse and an imaginary horse (or unicorn) is their different *forms*: "What
really matters . . . is their affective capacity vis-à-vis other entities" (2020,
437). Thus Bakardjieva notes that in the world of platformed sociality,
"humans have lost their substantive uniqueness—both humans and bots
are built of combinations of zeros and ones" (2015, 247).The environment renders equivalent the salient characteristics of humans and their
bot—it entails a convergence—"a levelled middle ground where human
and robot appear on significantly equalized footing" (Bakardjieva 2015,
248). In this regard, it is significant, as Nick Monaco and Samuel Woolley note, that "bots programmed with machine learning can even learn
from other people, as well as the creations of other people, such as their

bots. This learning means that their functions or 'personalities' change resulting in a recognition that bots are 'automated social actors (ASAs)'" (2022, 128, citing Abokhodair et al. 2015).

Such innovations portend the possibility of generative "astroturfing" in online environments. The term is used to explain how social movements and demonstrations may not be as they appear—participation can, for example, be incentivized or paid for so as to convey an inflated impression of popular support. Jovy Chan defines astroturfing online as "a practice where a centralized source disseminates colluded information on the internet pretending that such information comes from a large number of unconnected individuals" (2022, 4). Essentially, astroturfing is to assembly what disinformation is to speech. It may, for example, be a tactic used to promote state-mobilized movements (SMMs), which Grzegorz and Elizabeth Perry describe as elite-led countermobilizations amounting to a form of "subsidized publics" (2020, 12). Such practices—potentially enacted through the presence in assemblies of AI chatbots with learned personality traits and bearing voice and visual likenesses to human participants—carry significant manipulative potential (Jungherr and Schroeder 2023; Marcellino et al. 2023).

Moreover, the capacity of chatbots to establish emotional connections cannot be in any doubt—one need only think of the unrequited passions resulting from Replika's decision to withdraw (and then only partly restore) its licentious NSFW chatbot (Tong 2023). So the concern here is not merely or even primarily about informational deficits but rather about the affective implications of AI and the ways in which (unembodied) chatbot participants can influence sentiment and the intersubjective dynamics of assemblies (recognizing too the well-documented potential of AI systems to replicate and reinforce gendered, racial, or other forms of bias).

In this light, we must ask how the potential harms and benefits of such chatbot-driven interactions might be calibrated. One important metric has to be the impact of AI on individual "agency"—the ability of assembly organizers and participants to make strategic choices about how they appear with others. As Giddens emphasizes, agency is different from intentionality—"[a]gency refers not to the intentions people have in doing things but to their capability of doing those things in the first place (which is why agency implies power. . . .)" (1984, 9). On this definition, it is perhaps surprising that even in the sociology of social movements "agency as such has received limited attention" (Milan 2018, 7). But in what circumstances might it be said that AI interventions potentially result in a "reversal of agency?" (Trapp and Thum 2022, 152). What follow are the beginnings of an inquiry—questioning the extent to which participants in assemblies in the offline analogue world may be said to possess agency, and then turning to consider the contingency of individual agency in online assemblies—noting, as Ignas Kalpokas argues, that agency may not be so much "possessed" by a single actor, but rather "remains in-between, a potentiality always circulating among the elements" (2020, 437).

Freedom of Assembly Offline and the Illusion of Agency?

Existing human rights standards on the right of peaceful assembly (especially the UN Human Rights Committee's General Comment 37) ostensibly instantiate protection for the agency of organizers and participants in a number of ways. These include emphasizing that the exercise of the right must be "practical and effective"; that there must be individualized protection for those who remain peaceful even if other participants engage in violent conduct; protection for the right of organizers to choose the time, place, and modalities of their assembly; the freedom to hold spontaneous assemblies; the recognition that the anonymity of participants may be important for individual safety and privacy; and the presumption that assembly organizers should be able to exclude participants whose inclusion might taint or undermine the purity of their message. However, these protections arguably succeed merely in establishing some illusion of agency given the many informal ways in which law and its agencies, combined with myriad contextual factors and relationships of power, operate to condition the exercise of the right in practice.

For the purposes of this chapter, it is notable in particular that legal safeguards have never wrestled with the possibility of testing for, or alerting participants to, inauthentic behaviors on the part of other participants (other than providing for the possibility of disassociation from their violent conduct). It is often the case that assembly participants do not *know* many of those with whom they are assembling but rather assume some shared purpose or values. As such, it might be a stretch to argue that the realization of individual agency is dependent on participants being able to screen, or otherwise obtain certainty about, the motivations of those with whom they are co-present.

It might be suggested, however, that agency does require some baseline assurance that other participants are not there with ulterior and manipulative motives (and that some level of assistance, or compelled disclosure, might be needed to help expose any such nefarious ploys). But even then it is difficult to imagine how this could be achieved. Take state-mobilized movements, for example, which often manage to draw on the seemingly voluntary participation of significant sections of the populace and to attract substantial support (Ekiert and Perry 2020). It is an oversimplification to dismissively claim that participants in these actions are mere dupes—that they have either relinquished (as opposed to exercised) individual agency—or that their agency has somehow been reversed or denied. Thus it would be inconceivable to make a case for the paternalistic protection of participants in the pursuit of some abstract value of individual agency.

These are significant dilemmas for any attempt to ground legal safeguards for assembly participants in the protection of individual agency. As the following section demonstrates, additional complications arise in thinking about ways to protect the exercise of individual agency in online assemblies from possible interference enacted by AI.

AI as "Interference"—Between Agency and Structure?

Assemblies are of course distinct from the spaces in which they manifest, but the nature of the space determines the possibilities for both presence (Gumbrecht 2004) and mobilization (Beyer 2014; Zick 2006; Milan 2018). Whatever confrontations, shared experiences and communal sensibilities occur in online gatherings, they are a function of design decisions and structural affordances and limitations—what Poell and van Dijck refer to as "the techno-commercial infrastructure of social media platforms in today's protest configurations" (2015, 529). By way of example, server stability protocols may determine the maximum number of participants (*The Gamer* 2021). Roblox, for example, has a 200-user limit per session (Azmi 2023). In like manner, weak anonymity protections (or pseudo-forms of anonymity as in Google's Federated Learning of Cohorts, or FLoC) may operate to discourage entry in the first place. More subtly, the digitized personas that we "create"—while holding out the promise of realizing our most authentic selves—are premised on offered choices that are already predetermined and structured by standardized rules and frames, selected by software engineers, such that these personae unfold "based on a predetermined technical script" (Bakardjieva 2015, 246; Bucher 2017).

We are confronted with the question of whether such features should be seen as preexisting conditions, legitimate interventions, or unwarranted interferences. To avoid the most harmful forms of deceptive AI manipulation, legal (and other) protections must somehow develop a register of structural influences and be able to hold a line between those that nudge and those that coerce. In online spaces, the fundamental concept of "*voluntary* participation" may appear to be increasingly attenuated where the underpinning architectures are encoded with features that rely on artificial intelligence and machine learning. In relation to Facebook "friendships," for example, Taina Bucher argues that it is not so much a lack of voluntariness but rather that such relationships are inescapably mediated and conditioned by algorithmic systems (2018). As Anthony Giddens's theory of structuration (1984) illuminated, structure is itself constituted and reconstituted through dynamic interactions with human agents. Actors "routinely . . . maintain a continuing 'theoretical understanding' of the grounds of their activity . . . [and] action is a continuous process, a flow, in which the reflexive monitoring which the individual maintains is fundamental to the control of the body that actors ordinarily sustain throughout their day-to-day lives" (Giddens 1984, 9).

When technology outpaces legal regulation, human expectation bends and adapts accordingly (Zuboff 2019). The routine acceptance of platform terms of service signals the normalization of these logics and our habituation to them. This at once suppresses the assertion of rights claims and potentially shapes and informs the interpretation of legal principles. Our political activities acclimatize to the digital environment rather than the other way around, and so technology evades the prospective application of rule-of-law safeguards. For example, as users become more accustomed to data harvesting, application of the test for "reasonable expectation of privacy" may be torqued accordingly. As Beyer notes, "it is difficult to know which comes first: the chicken of Facebook's profit-driven logic or the egg of individual beliefs about what kind of privacy one can expect online" (2014, 130). Legal doctrine is applied to reinforce newly adopted patterns of behavior. In this context, distinguishing agency from structure, norms from distortions, and interference from architectures is no easy task.

Agency itself emerges through a dialectic engagement with social structure. Neff and Nagy thus use the concept of symbiotic agency to convey the idea that agency is conferred based on our imagined, perceived understanding of emerging technologies (2016). "Technology imprints its own logic on social relations and different actors appropriate it in pursuit of their own interests" (García-Orosa 2021, 2, citing Agre 2002, 311). Specifically in relation to chatbots, as Monaco and Woolley note, "the agency . . . of bots is directly tied not only to the people who build them and interact with them but also to the systems in which they operate" (2022, 132).

Studies of online gaming have advanced the way in which agency online is understood. It is worth concluding here by noting Daniel Muriel and Garry Crawford's seminal work, which casts the notion of agency "as the multiple, distributed and dislocated production of differences and transformations that can take a multitude of forms" (2020, 140): "[F]irst . . . agency produces differences and transformations;

second . . . the characteristics of agency are multiple and do not reside in any one prototypical actor; and third . . . agency is distributed and dislocated" (2020, 142). Agency is also potentially heteromorphic—exercised by human and nonhuman actors (142, citing Garcia Selgas 2007, 144). By further puncturing the illusion of an inert and abstract idea of agency, such understandings provoke difficult questions about the goals and methods of any regulatory intervention purporting to preserve or restore the capacity and power of assembly participants.

Conclusion: Radical Reinterpretations?

It has been suggested here that AI can enact forms of affective, social, and relational manipulation that fundamentally alter the ways in which we gather together and appear with others (including whether, when, and with whom). One such example is through AI-powered chatbots that participate in online assemblies and influence the choices and actions of embodied participants.

Of course, not all manipulation (online or offline) is properly subject to legal regulation—a point aptly demonstrated by the cautious approach (or the "cyber-libertarianism" alluded to by Nothias and Bernholz in chapter 1, citing Pace) to legislating against the potential harms arising from disinformation. Arguments in this regard often instead point to the need to reform the business model of platforms (e.g., Khan 2021). Thus calls for legislative responses to protect against AI-powered interferences have been variously circumspect, nonspecific, or downright skeptical. For example, responding to the oft-repeated call to ensure greater transparency in AI, Charles Jennings is unconvinced: "Enact whatever laws you like, throw tons of money at AI transparency regulation—and we still won't have any idea how a specific AI works" (2023).

The UN Human Rights Committee's General Comment 37 merely emphasizes that

> states should ensure that the activities of Internet service providers and intermediaries do not unduly restrict assemblies or the privacy of

assembly participants. Any restrictions on the operation of information dissemination systems must conform with the tests for restrictions on freedom of expression. (2020, paragraphs 33, 34)

In similar terms, Jonathan Peters has suggested that states "might protect certain aspects of . . . assemblies through laws governing ISPs, artificial intelligence, the spread of misinformation and disinformation,
electronic surveillance, etc." (2022). More specifically, Monaco and
Woolley argue that "targeted, well-crafted legislation against specific
malicious uses of bots would be a step in the right direction" (2022,
144). In particular, they highlight the need to draw a legally defined
bright line to identify "what constitutes deceptive and manipulative
behaviour" (145). Consider too the 'clear and conspicuous disclosure'
requirements proposed by the US Federal Communications Commission (FCC) in relation to voice-cloning and robocalls (e.g., FCC 2024).

Despite the clear challenges, it remains crucial to fully grasp the
forms of AI manipulation for which a human rights framework ought
to provide guardrails. This chapter has argued that the reductive nature
of analogical reasoning ultimately fails to deliver a sufficiently fine-
grained understanding of the different online spaces and heteromorphic actors, and of the harms that AI conceivably enacts.

The affordances of new technologies present an opportunity to re-
evaluate the core of particular rights—to "scrutinize and reassess the
fundamental intuitions, assumptions, and principles upon which the
present doctrine has been built" (Han, 105; also Dror-Shpoliansky
and Shany 2021). Rejecting the "normative equivalency paradigm,"
Dror-Shpoliansky and Shany emphasize "the limited fit between traditional human rights, and the reality of digital technology" (2021, 1266).
They urge greater recognition of "the unique needs and interests of
online users and the new threats and challenges they confront as well as
the radically different configuration of power and control in the digital
ecosystem" (2021, 1256). Moreover, they suggest that "failing to adjust
political rights to conditions of cyberspace might result in privileging

traditional offline political activism at the expense of new forms of online activism" (2021, 1260).

AI forces us to reckon with assumptions about the dynamic and reflexive interplay between agency and structure in assemblies. Such fundamental questions in turn compel reflection on what is intrinsically valuable about the right of peaceful assembly, the nature of participation, and the role of a human rights framework in affording suitable protection (including in relation to the requisite level of certainty and trust in terms of with whom we gather). While it is always an unsatisfactory conclusion to reach, it is no less important for being so—further scrutiny and "technographic inquiry" (Bucher, 2018) is needed to begin to capture the unique and differential harms that might arise from interactions in gatherings instigated or propelled by AI. Given the centrality of assembly to the ways in which we appear and become visible to and with others, such research must be refracted through the prism of the right of peaceful assembly.

References

Abokhodair, N., D. Yoo, and D. W. McDonald. 2015. Dissecting a Social Botnet: Growth, Content and Influence in Twitter. *CSCW '15: Proceedings of the 18th ACM Conference on Computer Supported Cooperative Work and Social Computing.* 839–851. https://doi.org/10.1145/2675133.2675208.

Agre, Philip. 2002. "Real-time politics: The Internet and the political process." *The Information Society* 18: 311–331.

Anti-Defamation League (ADL). 2019. "Telegram: The Latest Safe Haven for White Supremacists" (blog), December 2, 2019. https://www.adl.org/resources/blog/telegram-latest-safe-haven-white-supremacists?s=09.

Azmi, Hadi. 2023. "Malaysian Teens' Pro-Palestinian Rally on Roblox Goes Viral amid Censorship Concerns: 'Things Are Changing.'" *South China Morning Post*, October 27, 2023. https://www.scmp.com/week-asia/politics/article/3239324/malaysian-teens-pro-palestinian-rally-roblox-goes-viral-amid-censorship-concerns-things-are-changing.

Bakardjieva, Maria. 2015. "Rationalizing Sociality: An Unfinished Script for Socialbots." *The Information Society* 31: 244–256.

Beissinger, Mark R. 2017. " 'Conventional and 'Virtual' Civil Societies in Autocratic Regimes." *Comparative Politics* 49 (3): 351–371.

Bernhard, Max. 2020. "On Lockdown, Hong Kong Activists Are Protesting in
Animal Crossing." *Wired*, April 7, 2020. https://www.wired.co.uk/article/
animal-crossing-hong-kong-protests-coronavirus

Beyer, Jessica L. 2014. *Expect Us: Online Communities and Political Mobilization.*
London: Oxford University Press.

Bogost, Ian. 2017. "'Artificial Intelligence' has become Meaningless." *The Atlantic* (blog), March 4, 2017. https://www.theatlantic.com/technology/archive/
2017/03/what-is-artificial-intelligence/518547/.

Bucher, Taina. 2017. "The Algorithmic Imaginary: Exploring the Ordinary Affects of Facebook Algorithms." *Information, Communication & Society* 20 (1):
30–44.

———. 2018. *If . . . Then: Algorithmic Power and Politics.* New York: Oxford University Press.

Buyse, Antoine. 2021. "Pandemic Protests: Creatively Using the Freedom of Assembly During COVID-19." *Netherlands Quarterly of Human Rights* 39 (4):
265.

Chan, Jovy. 2022. "Online Astroturfing: A Problem Beyond Disinformation."
Philosophy and Social Criticism. 50 (3): 1–22.

Citron, Danielle Keats. 2009. "Cyber Civil Rights." *Boston University Law
Review* 89 (1): 61–126.

Cohen, Julie E. 2007. "Cyberspace as/and Space." *Columbia Law Review* 107:
210–256.

Cole, Samantha. 2017. "Second Life Users Are Protesting with Their Avatars."
Vice, February 4, 2017. https://www.vice.com/en/article/kbgnwa/second
-life-users-are-protesting-with-their-avatars.

Comninos, Alex. 2012. "Freedom of Peaceful Assembly and Freedom of Association and the Internet." *Association for Progressive Communication (APC)*, June
2012. https://www.apc.org/sites/default/files/cyr_english_alex_comninos
_pdf.pdf.

Deshpande, Ameet, Tammay Rajpurohit, Karthik Narasimhan, and Ashwin
Kalyan. 2023. "Anthropomorphization of AI: Opportunities and Risks."
openreview.net. https://openreview.net/pdf?id=Z2Ig9ky9HI.

Dror-Shpoliansky, Dafna, and Yuval Shany. 2021. "It's the End of the (Offline)
World as We Know It: From Human Rights to Digital Human Rights—A
Proposed Typology." *European Journal of International Law* 32 (4): 1249–1282.

Edwards, Maxim. 2020. "Russians Launch Mass Virtual Protests Using Satnav
Application." *Global Voices*, April 20, 2020. https://globalvoices.org/2020/
04/20/russians-launch-mass-protests-using-satnav-application/.

Ekiert, Grzegorz, and Elizabeth J. Perry. 2020. "State- Mobilized Movements: A Research Agenda." In *Ruling by Other Means: State-Mobilized Movements*, edited by Grzegorz Ekiert, Elizabeth J. Perry, and Yan Xiaojun, 1–23. Cambridge, UK: Cambridge University Press.

Federal Communications Commission (FCC). 2024. "FCC Fact Sheet: Implications of Artificial Intelligence Technologies on Protecting Consumers from Unwanted Robocalls and Robotexts." July 17, 2024. https://docs.fcc.gov/public/attachments/DOC-404036A1.pdf.

Fleischacker, Sam. 1998. "Insignificant Communities." In *Freedom of Association*, edited by Amy Gutman, 273–313. Princeton, NJ: Princeton University Press.

Fujiu, Takako. 2022. "Ukraine War Protests Find Virtual Platforms as Gamers Speak Out." *Nikkei Asia*, March 11, 2022. https://asia.nikkei.com/Business/Media-Entertainment/Ukraine-war-protests-find-virtual-platforms-as-gamers-speak-out.

García-Orosa, Berta. 2021. "Disinformation, Social Media, Bots, and Astroturfing: The Fourth Wave of Digital Democracy." *Profesional de la información* 30 (6): e300603.

García Selgas, F. J. 2007. *Sobre la Fluidez Social. Elementos para una Cartografía*. Madrid: Council of International Schools.

Giddens, Anthony. 1984. *The Constitution of Society: Outline of the Theory of Structuration*. Berkeley, CA: University of California Press.

Gillespie, Tarleton. 2018. *Custodians of the Internet: Platforms, Content Moderation, and the Hidden Decisions That Shape Social Media*. New Haven, CT: Yale University Press.

Gumbrecht, Hans Ulrich. 2004. *Production of Presence: What Meaning Cannot Convey*. Stanford, CA: Stanford University Press.

Györfi, Tamás. 2009. "The Importance of Freedom of Assembly: Three Models of Justification." In *Free to Protest: Constituent Power and Street Demonstration*, edited by András Sajó, 1–16. Utrecht, Netherlands: Eleven International Publishing.

Hakimi, Jedd. 2019. "'Why Are Video Games So Special?': The Supreme Court and the Case Against Medium Specificity." *Games and Culture* 15 (8): 923–942. https://doi.org/10.1177/1555412019857982.

Hamilton, Michael. 2020. "The Meaning and Scope of 'Assembly' in International Human Rights Law." *International & Comparative Law Quarterly* 69 (July): 521–556.

Hamilton, Michael, Ella McPherson, and Sharath Srinivasan. 2022. "'Deal with Me: Here I stand': Presence, Participation and the Equal Protection of Online Assemblies." In *A Life Interrupted: Essays in Honour of the Lives and Legacies of Christof Heyns*, edited by Frans Viljoen, Charles Fombad, Dire Tladi, Ann

Skelton, and Magnus Killander, 327–346. Pretoria, South Africa: Pretoria University Law Press.

Han, David S. 2020. "Constitutional Rights and Technological Change" *UC Davis Law Review* 54 (1): 71–131.

Harris, Iain. 2022. "FFXIV Players Gather to Show Solidarity with Ukraine." *PCGamesN*, February 28, 2022. https://www.pcgamesn.com/final-fantasy -xiv-a-realm-reborn/ffxiv-ukraine.

Inazu, John D. 2013. "Virtual Assembly." *Cornell Law Review* 98 (5): 1093.

Jaffe, Andrei Gribakov. 2019 "Digital Shopping Malls and State Constitutions—A New Font of Free Speech Rights." *Harvard Journal of Law and Technology* 33 (1): 269–291.

Jennings, Charles. 2023. "Opinion: There's Only One Way to Control AI: Nationalization." *Politico*, August 20, 2023. https://www.politico.com/news/ magazine/2023/08/20/its-time-to-nationalize-ai-00111862.

Jungherr, Andreas, and Ralph Schroeder. 2023. "Artificial Intelligence and the Public Arena." *Communication Theory* 33: 164–173. https://doi.org/10.1093/ ct/qtad006.

Kalpokas, Ignas. 2020. "Agglomerations, Relationality and In-Betweenness: Re-learning to Research Agency in Digital Communication." *Central European Journal of Communication* 3 (27): 426–440.

Kasinitz, Philip, ed. 1995. *Metropolis: Centre and Symbol of our Times*. London: MacMillan Press.

Khan, Irene. 2021. "A/HRC/47/25: Disinformation and Freedom of Opinion and Expression—Report of the Special Rapporteur on the Promotion and Protection of the Right to Freedom of Opinion and Expression," April 13, 2021. https://www.ohchr.org/en/documents/thematic-reports/ahrc4725 -disinformation-and-freedom-opinion-and-expression-report.

Knight First Amendment Institute v. Trump, No. 1:17-cv-5205 (S.D.N.Y.), No. 18-1691 (2d Cir.), No. 20-197 (Supreme Court).

Lang, Kang, and Dana Cuff. 2005. "Pervasive Computing: Embedding the Public Sphere." *Washington & Lee Law Review* 62(1): 93–146.

Marcellino, William, Nathan Beauchamp-Mustafaga, Amanda Kerrigan, Lev Navarre Chao, and Jackson Smith. 2023 "The Rise of Generative AI and the Coming Era of Social Media Manipulation 3.0." *Rand Corporation*, September 2023. https://www.rand.org/content/dam/rand/pubs/perspectives/ PEA2600/PEA2679-1/RAND_PEA2679-1.pdf.

Martinez, Rex. 2019. "Artificial Intelligence: Distinguishing Between Types & Definitions." *Nevada Law Journal* 19: 1015–1041.

Marshall, Cass. 2021. "World of Warcraft Players Are Hosting Sit-In Protests After Blizzard Allegations: If You Can't Protest In California, Try Oribos."

Polygon, July 22, 2021. https://www.polygon.com/22589046/world-of -warcraft-players-protest-blizzard-lawsuit-california-discrimination- harassment-allegations.

Milan, Stefania. 2018. "The Materiality of Clouds. Beyond a Platform-Specific Critique of Contemporary Activism." In *Social Media Materialities and Protest: Critical Reflections*, edited by Mette Mortensen, Christina Neumayer, and Thomas Poell, 116–128. London: Routledge.

Monaco, Nick, and Samuel Woolley. 2022. *Bots*. Cambridge, MA: Polity Press.

Müller, Jan-Werner. 2019. "What Spaces Does Democracy Need?" *Soundings* 102 (2–3): 203–216.

Muriel, Daniel, and Garry Crawford. 2020. "Video Games and Agency in Contemporary Society." *Games and Culture* 15 (2): 138–157.

Neff, Gina, and Peter Nagy. 2016. "Talking to Bots: Symbiotic Agency and the Case of Tay." *International Journal of Communication* 10 (20): 4915–4931.

Neuman, Gerald L. 2020. "The Draft General Comment on Freedom of Assembly: Might Less Be More?" *Just Security*, February 4, 2020. https://www.justsecurity.org/68465/thedraft-general-comment-on- freedom-of-assembly-might-less-be-more/.

Packingham v. North Carolina, 582 U.S. 98 (2017).

Peters, Jonathan. 2022. "Guide on Digitally-Mediated Assemblies and How to Monitor them." *ECNL*. https://ecnl.org/handbook/guide- digitally-mediated-assemblies-and-how-monitor-them.

Peterson, Chris (blog). 2009. "In Praise of [Some] DDoSs?" July 21, 2009. http:// www.cpeterson.org/2009/07/21/in-praise-of-some-ddoss/.

Poell, Thomas, and José van Dijck. 2015. "Social Media and Activist Communication." In *Routledge Companion to Alternative and Community Media*, edited by Chris Atton, 527–537. London: Routledge.

Ratliff, Evan. 2024. *Shell Game* (podcast). https://www.shellgame.co/.

Reno v. ACLU, 521 U.S. 844 (1997).

Sauter, Molly. 2014. "Blockades and Blockages: DDOS as Direct Action." In *The Coming Swarm*, chap. 2, London: Bloomsbury.

Schofield, Daisy. 2020. "Black Lives Matter Meets Animal Crossing: How Protesters Take Their Activism into Video Games" *The Guardian*, August 7, 2020. https://www.theguardian.com/games/2020/aug/07/black-lives-matter -meets-animal-crossing-how-protesters-take-their-activism-into-video- games.

Silberling, Amanda. 2023. "Kids on Roblox Are Hosting Protests for Palestine: Virtual Worlds Provide a Way for Kids to Explore Identity and World Events." *TechCrunch*, October 25, 2023. https://techcrunch.com/2023/10/25/ roblox-palestine-protest/.

The Gamer. 2021. "WoW Players Protest Activision Blizzard with In-Game Demonstrations." *YouTube*, 23 July 2021. https://www.youtube.com/watch?v =OBwmXOQH3lA.

Tong, Anna. 2023. "AI Chatbot Company Replika Restores Erotic Roleplay for Some Users." *Reuters*, March 25, 2023. https://www.reuters.com/ technology/ai-chatbot-company-replika-restores-erotic-roleplay-some- users-2023-03-25/.

Trapp, Harald, and Robert Thum. 2022. "The Algorithmic Construction of Space." In *(Dis)Obedience in Digital Societies: Perspectives on the Power of Algorithms and Data*, edited by Sven Quadflieg, Klaus Neuburg, and Simon Nestler, 148–171. Edinburgh: transcript Verlag.

UN Human Rights Committee. 2020. *General Comment No 37 on the Right of Peaceful Assembly (Article 21)*. CCPR/C/GC/37, September 17, 2020. https:// www.ohchr.org/en/documents/general-comments-and-recommendations/ general-comment-no-37-article-21-right-peaceful.

UN Special Rapporteur. 2019. *Report of the Special Rapporteur on the Rights to Freedom of Peaceful Assembly and of Association, Focusing on the Opportunities and Challenges Facing the Rights to Freedom of Peaceful Assembly and of Association in the Digital Age*. A/HRC/41/41, May 17, 2019. https://daccess-ods.un .org/access.nsf/Get?OpenAgent&DS=A/HRC/41/41&Lang=E.

Wijermars, Marielle. 2021. "Russia's Law on New Aggregators—Control the News Feed, Control the News" *Journalism* 22 (12): 2938–2954.

Zick, Timothy. 2007. "Clouds, Cameras and Computers: The First Amendment and Networked Public Places." *Florida Law Review* 59 (1): 1–69.

———.2006. "Speech and Spatial Tactics." *Texas Law Review* 84 (3): 581–651.

Zuboff, Shoshana. 2019. *The Age of Surveillance Capitalism: The Fight for a Human Future at the New Frontier of Power*. London: Profile Books.

Three

Algorithmic Violence

Ashley Lee

AI Advances: Computing and Democracy

Advances in computing have coincided with recent landmark political events, such as the 2016 US election, the Brexit campaigns, the January 6 US Capitol attack, and the rise of the far right. Consequently, intense debates have arisen in our society about whether technology use is, in fact, as likely to undermine as to advance democratic processes (e.g., Bernholz, Landemore, and Reich 2021; Deibert 2020; Marwick and Lewis 2017; Persily and Tucker 2020; Schradie 2019; Tufekci 2017). These concerns in computing have coincided with a range of challenges faced by democracies, such as the erosion of institutional trust, the rise of authoritarianism, widening inequality, and political polarization. Even as advances in emerging technologies such as generative AI, facial recognition systems, and augmented and extended reality may hold promises for democratic experiments, they simultaneously raise concerns about the erosion of privacy, civil liberties, and human rights (e.g., Buolamwini and Gebru 2018; Garvie and Moy 2019; Renieris, 2023).

There are significant efforts under way to build fairness, accountability, and transparency into AI-driven technologies and machine learning algorithms. Studies have shown how algorithms come to encode values and biases that reflect systemic inequities embedded in sociotechnical structures (e.g., Allen, Friedman, and Nissenbaum 1996; Eubanks 2018; Noble 2018; O'Neil 2017). Research has also extensively documented the ways in which AI-driven technologies and algorithms may be trained on incomplete, inaccurate, biased data sets, leading to harmful results (e.g., Bender et al. 2021; Buolamwini and Gebru 2018). In some instances, the designers of algorithms may make unexamined assumptions about end users, resulting in systems that are discriminatory and in violation of human rights (e.g., Costanza-Chock 2020).

Algorithms increasingly structure and govern our everyday lives as they become integrated into existing sociotechnical systems and structures. In AI research and policy, algorithmic harms are often narrowly framed as technical, rather than structural, sociopolitical problems. This way of formulating the problem can lead to highly technocratic, individualist approaches to addressing algorithmic harms. Social structures and institutions can create "structural violence," which prevents human beings from meeting their full potential (Galtung 1969; see also Farmer et al. 2006). Galtung (1969) distinguishes structural violence from direct violence, which involves an actor who directly commits the violence. Physical bullying and war are some examples. Structural violence, on the other hand, may remain latent and invisible as people accept it as "the way things are," even though it may have serious consequences in their lives (Farmer 2013). This type of violence is built into the structure and affects life chances. Some examples include institutionalized racism and discriminatory laws, which can operate jointly to create harm. Here, even as Galtung (1969) makes an analytical distinction between structural and direct violence, it is important to note that structural violence can create conditions for direct violence.

As algorithms integrate into governance infrastructures, they can create new forms of structural violence. In this chapter, I examine new forms of violence associated with algorithmic systems and infrastructure, which I refer to as "algorithmic violence." Although algorithmic violence may be seen as a structural form of violence, its impact extends beyond abstract realms and can mediate and materialize in more direct,

physical forms. This chapter aims to demonstrate how algorithmic violence arises from both sociotechnical *processes* and *products*, resulting
in *intended* or *unintended* consequences. In the political context, it has
the potential to inflict extensive social harm, affecting the well-being of
both *individuals* and *society at large*. While it is beyond the scope of this
chapter to provide an exhaustive catalogue of all forms of algorithmic
violence, it is important to recognize that it manifests in myriad forms
beyond the examples discussed in this chapter.

In order to understand the nature and manifestations of algorithmic violence, it is critical to look beyond the code. Algorithmic violence
stems from inequities created by an assemblage of algorithms and related practices, norms, and institutions. In efforts to conceptualize the
pragmatic ethics of algorithms, Ananny (2016) makes an important
move to broaden the unit of analysis from computer code to an assemblage of "institutionally situated computational code, human practices,
and normative logic that creates, sustains, and signifies relationships
among people and data through minimally observable, semiauton-
omous action" (2016). Ananny argues for a more expansive model of
ethics of algorithms that goes beyond the code. He observes that the
code may be transparent, its designers may be well-intentioned, and
the institutions involved may follow regulations, but an algorithmic assemblage may still create ethically unsatisfactory relations.

In the global context, algorithmic assemblages shift and flow across
national borders throughout technology life cycles (see Ong and Collier 2008). At the same time, they are co-constitutive of socioeconomic
and political structures (e.g., neocolonial relations between countries,
authoritarianism in some countries). Global algorithmic assemblages
often evade existing governance and accountability frameworks across
national boundaries, introducing gaps and tensions between compet-
ing interests, social practices, and values.

In this chapter, I delve into the development of algorithmic violence and its impact on civil society. With a particular focus on its
implications for assembly and association, I draw on cases of algorithmic experiments in the Global South. While algorithmic violence can

manifest itself in various domains and forms, my primary focus in this chapter is a distinct subclass that directly affects contemporary political infrastructure. I concentrate on this specific subclass because it poses significant challenges to the robust functioning of civil society and democracy.

Digital Political Infrastructure: The Infrastructural Transformation of "Public" Spheres

Today, civil society relies heavily on proprietary algorithmic systems for its essential functioning, including citizen engagement and empowerment, advocacy, and knowledge building (Bernholz 2020, 2021). Privately controlled algorithmic systems—such as Facebook (now Meta)—have become critical components of digital political infrastructures. This development raises concerns about the privatization of digital "public" spheres and underlying political infrastructure and the prioritization of profit over public interest and civic values.

Contemporary digital political infrastructures are data-driven, automated, and algorithmically mediated. While the adoption of AI and algorithmic systems can present new opportunities for civil society actors, these technologies can also expose them to digital surveillance, censorship, propaganda, and other forms of algorithmically mediated repression (e.g., Benjamin 2019; Noble 2018). Today, political content on social media is algorithmically curated in an environment that prioritizes rumors, fear, anger, or other emotional content in order to sell more clicks. As bots and trolls increasingly dominate the political ecosystem online, there may not even be real people behind the production and circulation of content (Zuckerman, 2024). Lines of code mimic human behavior by "liking" and sharing content to drive up engagement and create a false sense of popularity and momentum around a particular individual or idea. Data-driven techniques are leveraged to tailor political messaging to specific users or groups based on their preexisting identity, values, and interests. Behavioral data on social media platforms can be further exploited to mobilize (and demobilize) certain groups and stifle and suppress dissent, effectively influencing assembly and association.

Earlier studies widely examined how malicious actors can deploy social media platforms to spread viral content designed to mobilize certain audiences and suppress others' political participation (e.g., Karell et al. 2023; Marwick and Lewis 2017). To date, analyses of the impact of algorithms on political processes have predominantly focused on the production and circulation of *content* on digital platforms and its impact on individual political behavior, assembly, and association.

Digital political infrastructure spans the material and the virtual, and includes—but is not limited to—the algorithmic systems, platforms, technical protocols and specifications, code, and tools that support and enable civic and political engagement in the digital age. Digital infrastructure includes the deeper physical and virtual layers below the communication and content layer of digital platforms (e.g., Bernholz 2020; DeNardis 2020; Parks and Starosieski 2015). These layers encompass the digital resources and technologies that set norms, mechanisms, and policies not only for facilitating communication and information sharing but also for assembly, association, and other forms of interaction between citizens, civil society, and governments.

Recognizing infrastructure as a form of governing power, Mann (1984, 2008) introduces the notion of infrastructural power, which he defines as the capacity of the state to exert control over civil society and vice versa. Whereas Mann (1984) is most concerned with political power relations between the state and civil society, contemporary digital political infrastructures see a convergence of corporate and state power as private companies become key players in collecting, classifying, and storing data in the civic and political realm.

Although significant focus has been placed on political activities going on at the expressive and discursive *content* layer of digital platforms (e.g., addressing misinformation and disinformation through content moderation policy), less attention has been directed towards algorithmic experiments—including those carried out internally by platforms themselves—that alter digital political *infrastructure* and the functioning of civil society that relies on it.

Algorithmic Violence, Assembly, Dis-Assembly

When it comes to digital political infrastructure, the impact of algorithms on the processes of assembly and association manifests itself at several levels. Ricaurte (2022) aptly calls for a broader, multilayered framing of the ethical AI framework, turning our attention to the entanglement of micro-, meso-, and macro-political relations.

At the micro-political level, behavioral targeting can influence the production of individual and collective political identities. AI-driven technologies can also influence individuals' relationships to others and the world, and alter the perceptions of reality. Further, the entire industries built around personal data extraction (Couldry and Mejias 2019; Zuboff 2019) and algorithmic manipulation (Ricaurte 2022) are sustained by a new global underclass of vulnerable groups, including invisible workers (Gray and Suri 2019; Roberts 2019).

At the institutional level, AI-driven algorithms are increasingly a part of larger systems of governance. They become part of the sociotechnical infrastructure composed of existing actors, relationships, norms, and institutional structures (Ricaurte 2022). An invisible infrastructure operating on "black-box" algorithms, AI-driven systems play a critical role in managing institutions and mediating and shaping people's relationships with institutions and society. Institutional decision-making processes often remain opaque and can lead to unintended consequences, partly because of their reliance on proprietary software. Furthermore, algorithmic systems are often so complex that even their designers cannot anticipate or explain their output.

The production of AI-driven technologies can also contribute to the military-industrial complex (Crawford 2022). There is a concentration of power in a few countries (e.g., the US, China, etc.) where multinational tech corporations are located, and the development of AI technologies can become entangled with state interests in advancing military power and domination, through classifying, sorting, labeling, and surveilling the world's populations (Eubanks 2018; O'Neil 2017).

At the macro-political level, the development of AI technologies relies on the extraction of natural resources for their production and massive consumption of energy and water for data center maintenance and algorithm training—which can lead to environmental degradation and displacement of communities (Crawford 2022). In turn, these actions can exacerbate global inequities and give rise to various forms of violence. Yet the disproportionate harms caused by algorithmic violence in developing countries are often left out of "AI ethics" debates led by tech corporations, advanced industrial nations, and international governance bodies. While generative discussions about algorithmic harms and inequities accumulate at the micro-political and institutional levels, there has been limited discussion of collective harms to civil society that arise from algorithmic violence targeting large swathes of society and communities.

Political AI Experiments with Societies in the Margins

Algorithmic experiments can augment and continue the long legacy of scientific and medical exploitation of marginalized and vulnerable communities. Throughout history, marginalized populations have been exploited for scientific and technological advancements (Corbie-Smith 1999). The British Empire, for instance, used its colonies as a laboratory for new medical and scientific practices (Jasanoff, 2006). African Americans have also been subjected to a long history of scientific experimentation, such as the infamous Tuskegee syphilis study (Brandt 1978). These exploitative practices persist today and may find parallels in the development of algorithmic systems.

Algorithmic experiments involve testing and refining early versions of algorithmic systems to uncover problems in real-world scenarios. However, they often reveal instances of blatant exploitation, where corporations and developers use foreign countries as testing sites. They are often carried out in foreign countries, where data privacy laws are lax or nonexistent, because testing procedures would violate domestic laws. As such, algorithmic experiments can export unethical research and development practices to vulnerable communities, especially those in low-income countries (Mohamed et al. 2020). Even when the harms become known and documented, there is often a failure to take necessary measures to redress them.

In response to various cases of unethical research practices, such as the syphilis study at Tuskegee, the scientific community has established ethical guidelines that strive to reshape the power dynamics between researchers and the communities or individuals affected by their work. The Nuremberg Code (Nuremberg Military Tribunal 1947), the Declaration of Helsinki (World Medical Association 1964), and the Belmont Report (National Commission for the Protection of Human Subjects of Biomedical and Behavioral Research 1978) were among early efforts that led to the establishment of core ethical guidelines. These guidelines outline the minimum standard for human subject research and include respect for persons (research must recognize the autonomy and dignity of individuals), beneficence (research must be designed to maximize societal benefit and minimize potential harm to participants), and justice (research benefits and burdens must be fairly distributed across society). Despite being a landmark for research ethics, these principles continue to be violated. They have been criticized for their limitations in addressing the lived experiences of vulnerable groups. Today, in the context of advances in AI, these guidelines may be inadequate for addressing emergent harms.

The theories of data colonialism (Couldry and Mejias 2019; Ricaurte 2022) and surveillance capitalism (Zuboff 2019) note historical continuity and conceptualize data as both symbolic and material resources that may be leveraged for economic exploitation and accumulation of power. Common to these concepts are concerns about the continuous tracking of digital devices and people's lives, which has created unprecedented opportunities for social discrimination and behavioral influence by corporations. Such concerns go far beyond social media platforms and search engines, as the world becomes increasingly hybrid and the boundaries between the physical and the digital blur. Corporations are able to amass people's data at an unprecedented scale, threatening to colonize everyday life through data and appropriate it for profit (Couldry and Mejias 2019; Ricaurte 2022). Mejias and Couldry (2024) further develop the idea of data colonialism by examining the ways in which digital infrastructure can reproduce extractive social processes and practices with regard to human relations, labor, and the environment. Scholars have variously analyzed digital and data coloniality through the lens of data feminism (D'Ignazio and Klein 2020), postcolonialism (Irani et al. 2010; Mohamed et al. 2020), and critical race theory (Benjamin 2019), among others.

In what follows, I turn to the analyses of algorithmic harms that manifest as mass violence to entire communities and societies, with a focus on the Global South. The first case centers on the impact of algorithmic experiments conducted on the Facebook News Feed on political assembly and association in six developing nations, particularly in volatile political contexts. The second case focuses on the experiments carried out by Cambridge Analytica in developing countries and how they impacted political assembly on the ground. The two cases represent a specific subclass of algorithmic violence that arises from experiments related to digital political infrastructure.

The Case of Facebook News Feed Experiments
AI AND NEW FORMS OF POLITICAL POWER AND VIOLENCE

The Facebook News Feed experiments in this section illustrate how algorithmic experiments can lead to algorithmic violence by rapidly transforming and mutating digital political infrastructure. Algorithmic experiments conducted by private companies internally can lead to significant disruptions in digital political infrastructure, with ramifications for assembly and association in the short and long term. They may have intended or unintended consequences for assembly and association. Control of digital political infrastructure represents a new form of political power.

In October 2017, Facebook (now Meta) rolled out an experiment with its News Feed across six countries: Bolivia, Cambodia, Guatemala,

Serbia, Slovakia, and Sri Lanka (Palatino 2017). Five of them are in the Global South. A new Facebook algorithm one day started filtering out unsponsored content from the regular News Feed. The users had to click on a new button, "Explore Feed," to access posts from news outlets, nongovernmental organizations, and political groups that did not pay to promote their content.

The experiment came at a tense moment in Cambodia, when the country was heading into contentious 2018 general elections. Facebook went ahead with it as the space for free expression was being shut down. Because of the experiment, users stopped receiving critical information from independent news sources that were being buried, essentially cutting off millions of Cambodians from vital sources of information.

According to Facebook, the experiment, which was to last several months, was in service of "our community":

> We always listen to *our community* [emphasis mine] about ways we might improve News Feed. . . . We will hear what people say about the experience to understand if it's an idea worth pursuing any further. (Palatino 2017)

Yet it is not clear who was truly a part of this "community" or who benefited from the experiment. As Burrell and Fourcade (2021, 230) observe, "AI's trajectory in society is not simply a question of whether humanity will benefit or not, but rather of who will benefit."

In Cambodia, an authoritarian country where the prime minister has been in power for nearly four decades, press freedom and freedom of expression and assembly are severely constrained. The population was estimated to be around 15 million at the time, with about 5 million on Facebook—the single most popular social media platform in the country (Palatino 2017). In a survey conducted in 2016, most Cambodians reported Facebook as their main source of news and information (Palatino 2017). The popularity of Facebook as a news source was due in part to the heavily progovernment media, which delivered a constant regimen of state-generated news and propaganda.

The algorithmic experiment had a severe impact on local independent news outlets, nongovernmental organizations, and political groups, all of which already faced significant budget constraints and so could not pay for content promotion. As a result, they reported huge drops in user engagement with their Facebook content, with some losing upwards of 60 percent of traffic to their pages (Palatino 2017).

Under-resourced civil society organizations in Cambodia relied on Facebook to mobilize resources, recruit members, and share news and information. Compared with state-dominated news outlets, they were already at a considerable disadvantage when promoting content to their local and international audiences. Even minor experimental tweaks to Facebook algorithms had the potential to drastically curtail their ability to reach their audience and alter the network structure of civil society. With the disruptions and gaps introduced by algorithmic experiments, opposition and dissident voices in the country, which had been suppressed for generations, were unceremoniously silenced again.

Some people noticed that posts from independent news sources and the opposition party had gone missing. However, locals for the most part would not have perceived any major changes to their News Feed (Palatino 2017). The lack of transparency and the invisibility of the algorithmic experiment deprived Cambodian users of meaningful choice or agency to react proactively to the experiment (e.g., by opting out). Their rights to information, assembly, and association were severely curtailed overnight. Algorithmic violence stemming from such black-box infrastructural experiments can remain invisible to impacted communities and go unobserved and unreported.

When pathways to information sources and networks become obstructed overnight, civil society actors and organizations do not have enough time to forge new ones. Many grassroots organizations and activists in authoritarian regimes are already at the end of their rope in terms of financial and human resources. At the same time, they are constantly persecuted by the government through threats, intimidation, harassment, and abuse. For such groups, even minor disruptions to digital political infrastructure can be the tipping point. The Facebook experiment in Cambodia arguably tipped the scale in favor of the ruling party, as it undermined the social media initiatives of NGOs, independent media, political opposition, activists, and dissidents.

In conflict regions, fragile democracies, and authoritarian contexts, news and information ecosystems are highly volatile and unstable. Facebook's algorithmic experiment highlights the differential risks and impact that such experiments can have on the healthy functioning of digital political infrastructures in diverse contexts. It is vital to attend to the global power inequities that underlie these experiments, from how multinational tech corporations select their "low-risk" experimentation sites to what avenues exist for local communities to intervene. Are there appropriate mechanisms for redress if such experiments lead to large-scale political suffering of certain communities? Communities— especially those lacking material, social, and symbolic resources—may be left without appropriate mechanisms for recourse and redress.

The same algorithmic experiment may exact differential risks and burdens in different contexts precisely because some communities and groups lack social structures, regulatory frameworks, and local institutions and resources that offer "safety nets." In a politically precarious environment, algorithmic experiments have the potential to swiftly introduce disruptions and exacerbate gaps in an already unstable political infrastructure. Algorithmic violence impacts marginalized communities more severely because these communities lack access to resources—material, social, and symbolic—that can mitigate, reverse, or eliminate its adverse impacts.

Further, algorithmic violence can jeopardize individual activists who rely on digital political infrastructures for their livelihood. Digital infrastructures increasingly structure participation across all domains of life (e.g., civic, work). They are dominated by a small group of powerful multinational tech companies, most of them concentrated in tech hubs such as Silicon Valley. Algorithmic experiments with digital political infrastructures can magnify and normalize oppressive social, political, and economic relations between the Global North and the Global South. A women's rights activist in Cambodia, who vlogs about women's issues for living, found herself in a precarious position after her Facebook views saw a sharp decline overnight, as a result of an algorithmic experiment (Pavior 2017):

> I was baffled until I recalled seeing a few posts from people on my Facebook [News Feed] about how the reach on their page had been declining dramatically after Facebook rolled out the new Explore Feed feature. As someone who makes a living through my videos on Facebook (companies pay me for product placement and endorsements), I feel helpless and powerless now. Facebook's sudden change can threaten my way of life. I have talked to other video bloggers and social media personalities; one popular personality told me that she used to get 2,000 to 3,000 watchers when she did a live video. After Explore Feed, the number dropped to 30 people. Still, Facebook will leave me no choice. I need to rethink strategies to adapt and deal with the changes. (Harry 2017)

As online campaigns and content creation increasingly become major sources of income for individual activists and civil society organizations, algorithmic experiments can give rise to precarious labor conditions while simultaneously constraining political participation (for a discussion of the relationship between automation and precarious labor, see Gray and Suri 2019 and Roberts 2019). The disruption they cause may be negligible in the middle- or high-income communities in established democracies under conditions of free press, free expression, and free assembly. Those without safety nets (economic and otherwise)—such as those in developing countries, members of low-income communities, women, and youth—may be more severely impacted, and they may take on disproportionate burdens of such experiments.

Digital political infrastructures exert power transnationally and play a significant role in structuring the global economy and global civil society. The ethnic cleansing of the Rohingya in Myanmar offers another example of how private control of digital political infrastructures can lead to algorithmic violence (Roose and Mozur 2018; Taub and Fisher 2018). Human rights groups have repeatedly pinpointed Facebook as the major platform used to incite the ethnic violence of Muslim minorities in Myanmar (Roose and Mozur 2018). For many years, civil society organizations there had pleaded with Facebook to alter its algorithms (Roose and Mozur 2018). Muslim minority communities and allied NGOs have had little to no power to alter algorithmic systems that are said to have promoted calls to violence. The Rohingya example shows that multiple forms of political violence are co-constitutive and mutually reinforcing—including algorithmic violence, which in this case stems from the platform's lack of response and its inaction. Algorithmic violence intersects with and amplifies existing forms of political violence that arise from oppressive regimes, political repression, human rights abuses, discrimination, social inequality, armed conflict, systemic injustices, and more.

The ways in which algorithmic experiments are deployed by multinational corporations without accountability to the affected communities perpetuate and reproduce power asymmetries between the Global North and the Global South. As one Sri Lankan government official points out, "There needs to be some kind of engagement with countries like Sri Lanka by big companies who look at us only as markets. . . . We're a society, we're not just a market" (Taub and Fisher 2018). In such cases, algorithmic experiments may essentially come down to A/B testing democracy. This is particularly true in fragile political climates against the background of extreme global inequities.

The ability to control digital political infrastructure represents a new form of political power. But when analysis of algorithmic violence remains purely at the level of the individual (e.g., the individual suffering of activists), the social production of society-wide suffering (e.g., social suffering; see Kleinman 1997; Kleinman, Das, and Lock 1997)—political or otherwise—may be overlooked. Algorithmic violence can impact the digital political infrastructures of entire communities, societies, and populations. Therefore, identifying and addressing it requires looking beyond the individual and assessing social determinants of such forms of violence. The notion of algorithmic violence provides a starting point for imagining the means of collective reparation and transformation.

The Case of Cambridge Analytica in Developing Countries

CONTEXTUALIZING ALGORITHMIC VIOLENCE

The emergence of private data brokers and the digital influence industry undergirds the political economy of digital political infrastructure today, creating a political environment that is conducive to algorithmic violence. In the pre-AI era, gaining control of political infrastructure required access to massive state resources and external state support. However, today, as Facebook's News Feed experiments demonstrate, it is possible to gain control over digital political infrastructure with mere tweaks to algorithmic systems. The infrastructural transformation of contemporary "public" spheres (e.g., below the expressive and discursive *content* layer) is further accentuated and accelerated by the emergence of the digital influence industry. In this section, I analyze a series of Cambridge Analytica projects undertaken in developing countries to illustrate how global capitalist arrangements driving the digital influence industry build up transnational infrastructures of algorithmic violence that come to operate at a global scale.

The development of the Cambridge Analytica projects over time shows that algorithmic violence, in fact, begins long before algorithmic systems enter the scene. The accumulation of massive data, the refinement of data processing techniques, and the establishment of data infrastructures laid the foundation for algorithmic violence. Thus in order to understand how algorithmic violence develops, it is crucial to broaden the temporal and spatial horizons of analysis beyond the specific moments when algorithmic systems enter and exit the scene.

In 2018, Cambridge Analytica, a political consulting firm, captured global attention and sparked intense media coverage, igniting furious debates about its interference in the 2016 US elections. The story gained significant traction when *The Guardian* and *The New York Times* published explosive articles exposing the company's data mining and manipulation practices.

Most analyses of Cambridge Analytica have centered on the privacy breach and the responsibility of Facebook in safeguarding user data, along with the ethics of manipulative tactics in political campaigns.

Less attention has been given to the origins of Cambridge Analytica's neocolonialist experiments in Africa, the Caribbean, and other regions. These regions in the Global South, characterized by weak civil societies and lax or nonexistent data privacy laws, provided a fertile ground for testing and refining data collection and analytic techniques (Moore 2018; Nyabola 2018; Rosenberg, Confessore, and Cadwalladr 2018). For over two decades, Cambridge Analytica and its parent company, Strategic Communication Laboratories (SCL), leveraged social scientific research to develop and refine data techniques for manipulating group political behavior.

Founded in 2013, Cambridge Analytica positioned itself as an expert in data-driven political campaigns by amassing big data on voters and employing techniques such as psychological profiling and microtargeting. It acquired personal data from millions of Facebook users without their consent through "This is Your Digital Life," an app created in 2013 by Aleksandr Kogan—a researcher who also collaborated with Facebook—and his company Global Science Research (Hern 2018). By posing a series of questions to users, the app constructed psychological profiles and obtained personal data from their friends through Facebook's Open Graph platform, resulting in the collection of up to 87 million Facebook profiles (Hern 2018). Cambridge Analytica then used this data to provide analytical assistance during the 2016 US presidential campaign. It simultaneously spawned several affiliated companies, including SCL, which acted as the parent company. Cambridge Analytica has been known to strategically shapeshift and operate under different names (Briant 2020).

From its early days, Cambridge Analytica had been involved in political campaigns in developing countries: India, Kenya, Nigeria, Trinidad and Tobago, and Brazil, just to name a few. In India, it worked with the Bharatiya Janata Party during the 2010 state elections in Bihar (Punit 2018). According to a whistleblower named Christopher Wylie, the company used a psychological profiling tool to target specific voters with tailored messaging (Punit 2018). It also worked with the Indian National Congress, although the extent of their involvement is unclear

(Punit 2018). The election was later nullified by the Supreme Court due to irregularities in the electoral process.

In Nigeria, Cambridge Analytica was reportedly hired by a group of wealthy individuals to influence the 2015 presidential election (Kirchgaessner et al. 2023). It allegedly created a video campaign portraying the incumbent president as sympathetic to Boko Haram, the Islamist extremist group responsible for numerous attacks in the country (Kirchgaessner et al. 2023).

In Brazil and Trinidad and Tobago, there is evidence of Cambridge Analytica's involvement in political campaigns. Its precise nature and impact remains unclear, pointing to the challenges in tracing and researching the dark political influence industry in transnational contexts. In Brazil, for example, Cambridge Analytica reportedly worked with several politicians and political groups during the 2014 elections (Coding Rights 2018), allegedly using Facebook data to create psychological profiles of voters which were then used to target them with specific messaging (Coding Rights 2018). The company has also been linked to the Bolsonaro campaign during the 2018 presidential election (Coding Rights 2018).

Further research is necessary to gain a comprehensive understanding of the precise impact of Cambridge Analytica's activities in developing countries. Nonetheless, it is evident that its use of social media data and psychological profiling techniques had a detrimental effect on democratic norms and processes in those nations. It is worth noting that the reach of Cambridge Analytica's projects extended beyond the realms affected by the Facebook data breach (Briant 2020), suggesting a broader scope of influence and potential harm. This list only begins to scratch the surface of the private firm's extensive work (Briant 2020).

FROM DATAFICATION TO ALGORITHMIC VIOLENCE

What is interesting about this long trajectory of development is that well before behavioral targeting through Facebook data came into play, there existed a lengthy "experimental" or incubation phase. During this phase, the data firm extracted, accumulated, and exploited vast amounts of data, refining their techniques on communities and populations in developing countries. Based on journalistic coverage and open-source content, Briant (2020) reconstructs a global map of activities related to Cambridge Analytica, its parent company SCL, and affiliates. My analysis of the data set shows that of the 147 projects that Briant (2020) attributes to them, nearly two-thirds have been carried out in developing countries from as early as 1994 (see Table 1).

Cambridge Analytica and SCL have undertaken a wide range of projects, encompassing not just election and political campaigns but also humanitarian, military, and foreign operations (see Table 1, Column F). These initiatives include youth radicalization, public health and food security, cultural interventions, and more. The majority of the company's projects in the Middle East, for instance, were commissioned by international entities and foreign governments. These projects include intelligence assessments, research on youth radicalization, and assessment of sociocultural attitudes in the region. An illustrative example is a study examining the sociocultural characteristics and attitudes of diverse youth groups in Jordan, Egypt, and Saudi Arabia. In service of anti-radicalization efforts, the project was intended to gain insight into youth recruitment by extremist organizations.

A complex, interconnected global network of influential entities provided financial support for the expansion of the medium-sized Cambridge Analytica and the multi-billion-dollar political influence industry. The company's extensive client base spans governments, political parties and candidates, private firms, international organizations, and NGOs (see Table 1, Column D). It is essential to recognize the inherent power imbalances in these projects, as they are initiated and financed by influential actors and often target the most vulnerable populations, such as children, youth, women, and migrants. By exploiting a profit-driven economic model, data firms like Cambridge Analytica operate on a global scale, wielding an astonishing level of influence over social, cultural, political, and economic domains.

The web of actors also underscores the far-reaching impact of, and economic dynamics underpinning, the operations of such firms. Data

TABLE 1. Cambridge Analytica Projects in Developing Countries

(A) Region	(B) Countries	(C) No. of projects reported in the database	(D) Clients	(E) Targets	(F) Type of sample project
Africa	Gabon, Ghana, Kenya, Mauritius, Nigeria, Rwanda, Somalia, South Africa, Sudan	19	Government agencies (e.g., Ghanaian Ministry of Health), political parties and candidates, international organizations (UN agencies), NGOs	Voters, movements, general public, youth, parents, farmers	Election campaigns, referenda campaigns, youth radicalization, public health projects, cultural interventions (child marriage)
Asia	Afghanistan, India, Indonesia, Macau (SAR), Malaysia, Nepal, Pakistan, Philippines, Singapore, Thailand, Yemen	39	Government agencies, foreign governments, political parties, military contractors, oil and gas companies	Voters, local villagers and communities, political extremist groups (e.g., Al Qaeda, Maoist groups), drug supply networks, youth groups	Election campaigns, voter analysis, public opinion research, census, corporate strategy development, community interventions, foreign influence campaigns
Europe	Albania, Romania, Ukraine	4	Governments, political parties, political coalitions	Voters	Election campaigns, international political campaigns

TABLE 1. (Continued)

(A) Region	(B) Countries	(C) No. of projects reported in the database	(D) Clients	(E) Targets	(F) Type of sample project
Latin America and the Caribbean	Argentina, Colombia, Guyana, Mexico, Antigua and Barbuda, Dominica, Grenada, St. Vincent and the Grenadines, St. Kitts and Nevis, St. Lucia	20	Governments, political parties and candidates	Voters, data mining app users	Election campaigns, foreign influence campaigns, public health campaigns, communication campaigns to counter drug-related crimes, human trafficking
Middle East	Egypt, Iran, Iraq, Jordan, Lebanon, Libya, Saudi Arabia, Syria	14	Government agencies, foreign government agencies, international organizations (e.g., UN agencies), military contractors	Youth groups, general public, political extremist groups (e.g., the Islamic State)	Foreign influence projects, communication strategies, counterterrorism projects, population research

and data analytic techniques, originally developed for military applications or obtained through coercion from vulnerable populations such as migrants and refugees, may be repurposed later to interfere with civil society activities and democratic processes on a global scale (Briant 2020). These experiments can inflict mass political violence on communities and societies.

ALGORITHMIC VIOLENCE AND THE LEGACY OF
DATA EXPLOITATION IN THE GLOBAL SOUTH

Indonesia offers a closer look at how algorithmic violence develops over time, as it was one of the early sites of Cambridge Analytica's experiments. The algorithmic violence targeting Indonesian civil society and electoral processes was not a sudden one-off occurrence but rather a result of decades of exploitative data extraction and experimentation.

As early as 1998, long before Cambridge Analytica harvested the data of 50 million Americans to influence the 2016 US elections, the company's skills were tested and refined during the political upheavals in Southeast Asia. In 1998, Suharto, a military leader, had been in power for more than three decades. The 1998 student protests, sparked by the country's economic crisis, food shortages, and high unemployment rates, ultimately resulted in the downfall of his regime (Goshal 2018).

During this tumultuous period, SCL came into the picture to redirect the anger and dissatisfaction of the Indonesian population (Goshal 2018). The company began its efforts by conducting a country-wide survey of 72,000 Indonesians (Goshal 2018). Based on its findings, SCL provided guidance on political communication strategies to the country's political leaders. However, its operations extended well beyond the conventional scope of a data company. One notable example is SCL's involvement in orchestrating protests on university campuses, aiming to divert students' attention away from actual street protests and demonstrations (Goshal 2018). The company claimed credit for facilitating Abdurrahman Wahid's ascent to the presidency.

Over time, these operations laid the groundwork for data infrastructure and data processing apparatuses underlying algorithmic systems. In 2018, Facebook was again accused of selling the data of over one million Indonesian users to Cambridge Analytica (Goshal 2018). With algorithmic systems in place, the company swiftly employed essentially the same exploitative data extraction practices for political microtargeting, building on its longstanding legacy, infrastructure, and relations of data extraction and exploitation in the Global South.

In today's context of data extraction and algorithmic violence, it is crucial to highlight that the groups targeted by these projects had not been informed about these political "AI" experiments, nor had they given their consent to participate in them. Furthermore, they lacked the ability to simply "turn off" or "opt out of" ongoing algorithmic experiments, which gradually entangled them in a sprawling global network. AI experiments are imposed on target groups by a web of external actors without their consent. In most cases, the communities and societies subjected to such social experiments are unaware of their participation. It is important to note that the powerful users (i.e., clients) who commission and finance the development of algorithmic experiments and systems are distinct from the groups being targeted.

The process of datafication and data privatization frequently involves exploitative and coercive dynamics. Private entities such as third-party data brokers, data analytics firms, and private influence firms have control over the data layers making up digital political infrastructure. Private control of data layers signifies an unprecedented transformation in the global political landscape.

CO-CONSTITUTIVE FORMS OF POLITICAL VIOLENCE

Further, algorithmic violence and the responses to ensuing individual and social suffering are inherently connected to other forms of violence. They are influenced by the institutional, political, and economic structures of a society. For example, algorithmic violence intersects with—and is magnified by—media violence. In the case of numerous

Cambridge Analytica projects conducted in developing countries, there is a lack of media coverage, which presents challenges to transparency and accountability around these emergent forms of violence. Because of the absence of media watchdogs that shed light on algorithmic violence in developing countries, it is difficult to ascertain what measures, if any, have been taken to repair, rectify, and address the algorithmic violence resulting from Cambridge Analytica experiments in politically fragile and vulnerable environments outside of established democracies.

Only a handful of Cambridge Analytica projects associated with US and UK political campaigns have been the subject of substantive media coverage, journalistic investigations, legal actions, and subsequent scrutiny. 2018 saw a sudden, single peak in coverage of Cambridge Analytica in the US (Figure 1) and the West (Figure 2), coinciding with the media frenzy surrounding the Cambridge Analytica scandal. Western media outlets and journalists tend to prioritize stories they deem most relevant to their audience in the West, inadvertently neglecting the experiences of the majority of the world. Figures 1 and 2 show that, even though Cambridge Analytica had been active in the years preceding 2018, English-speaking media outlets did not cover the transnational consequences of algorithmic experiments in developing countries. Consequently, there is a large gap in our understanding of the vast majority of the company's experiments conducted in the majority world. Here, North-South power relations manifest as the absence of data and the silence of media and archives (see D'Ignazio 2024 for a discussion of how power inequities give rise to missing data). Invisibility surrounding projects hinders our understanding of their impact and raises questions about social engineering in these regions. Algorithmic violence disproportionately impacts disadvantaged and marginalized groups (see Crenshaw 1991 for a discussion of intersecting forms of oppression). This disparity stems from global inequities in the distribution of material and symbolic resources necessary to address and alleviate the consequences of algorithmic violence.

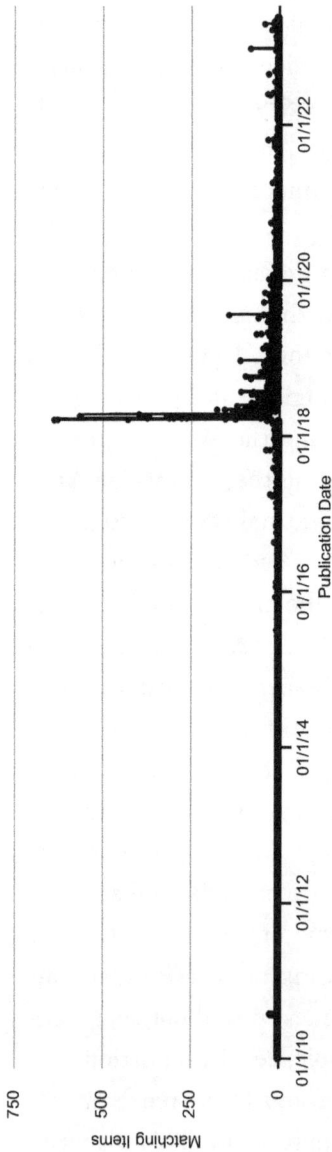

FIGURE 1. Count of news stories containing keywords "Cambridge Analytica" OR "Strategic Communication Laboratories" in the US (via Media Cloud).

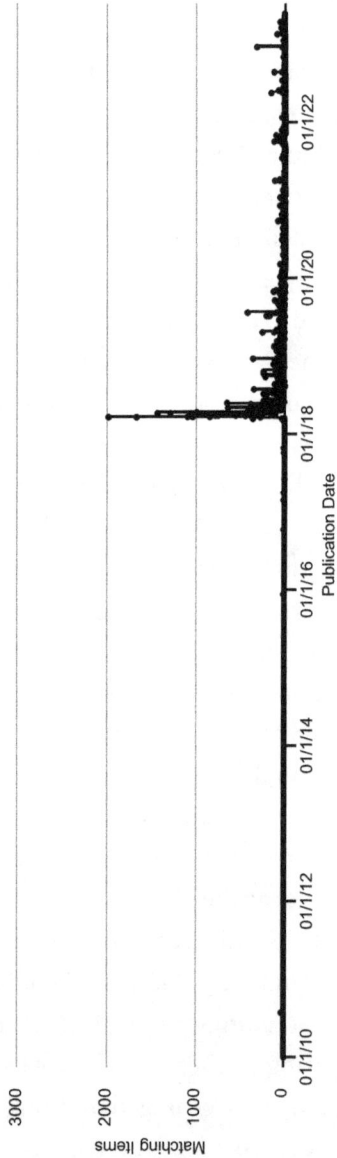

FIGURE 2. Count of news stories containing keywords "Facebook" AND "Cambridge Analytica" OR "Strategic Communication Laboratories" in the US and the West (via Media Cloud).

PROFIT-DRIVEN CAPITALIST LOGICS OF THE
DIGITAL INFLUENCE INDUSTRY

The digital influence industry follows global capitalist logics, ready to offer their services to the highest bidder. On the supply side, it is responsive— and accountable—to profit rather than democratic ideals or civic values. An illustrative example is Kenya's 2013 presidential election, where Cambridge Analytica worked with Uhuru Kenyatta, the incumbent, who faced allegations of crimes against humanity at the International Criminal Court (Nyabola 2018). Collaborating with Kenyatta's Jubilee Party, the company engaged in divisive tactics, conducting smear campaigns against Kenyatta's opponent, Raila Odinga (Moore 2018; Nyabola 2018).[1]

On the demand side, political actors and entities eagerly seek the services of digital influence firms, sometimes solely to prevent their competitors from accessing them. In the lead-up to Mexico's 2018 presidential election, for instance, Cambridge Analytica offered to help the Institutional Revolutionary Party (PRI) by destroying the reputation of its opponent (Ahmed and Hakim 2018). Although PRI believed it could win the presidential race without its assistance, it still paid Cambridge Analytica to prevent it from working with the opposing candidate (Ahmed and Hakim 2018).[2]

Algorithmic violence thrives in the neoliberal social order, where digital influence firms prioritize profit maximization above all other considerations, including democratic values. As the accessibility and affordability of computing and data techniques continue to expand, the digital influence industry is poised to gain further momentum.

Discussion

Algorithmic violence arises from inequitable social arrangements, both old and new. It is a reflection of current social, political, and economic systems. Many instances of algorithmic violence, such as those centered on colonialism, racism, and sexism, have become the very fabric of everyday life to the extent that they are now invisible (Eubanks 2018; Noble 2018; O'Neil 2017). As in the Facebook "Explore Feed" experiment, algorithmic violence may be inflicted without its victims being aware of it. To address algorithmic violence, it is insufficient to mathematically "adjust for" biases in the training data set or "correct for" desired output. Addressing it in its local and translocal dimensions will require transforming the social processes and mechanisms that give rise to these new forms of violence in the first place.

Complex Network Processes Underpinning Algorithmic Violence

From the analytical standpoint, the concept of algorithmic violence surfaces the difficulties and constraints of attributing individual blame and responsibility vis à vis algorithmic assemblage. In AI research, the prevailing approach to tackling algorithmic harms has so far largely centered on individual-level reforms and individual or corporate accountability. However, the concept of algorithmic violence brings to the surface how and why purely individual-level approaches to responsibility and reforms may fall short. Given the vast scale of AI and machine learning code bases, it is a formidable task for individual engineers to acquire a comprehensive understanding of an entire code base, let alone fully grasp its societal impact (Basart and Serra 2013; Debs, Gray et al. 2022). Similarly, political consultants and digital influence professionals may conduct their work in alignment with their professional ethics, with a focus on serving their clients. Arendt's "banality of evil" underscores the disconcerting reality that ordinary people can unknowingly or unintentionally contribute to the perpetration of atrocities in uncritically fulfilling their day-to-day responsibilities (1963). Ethically unsatisfactory relations can emerge from the mundane, bureaucratic, and structural dimensions of institutions and systems—including algorithmic systems. Even in cases where the code is transparent, engineers have good intentions, and the involved institutions adhere to regulations, an algorithmic assemblage can still give rise to ethically unsatisfactory relations (see also Ananny 2016).

The case of Cambridge Analytica in developing countries shows a sprawling global network of states, private firms, clients, funders, and social, economic, and political relations deeply entangled in colonial histories and practices. It demonstrates that algorithmic violence is in part a consequence of complex network processes of global capitalist production and datafication. To achieve transformative social change, it is necessary to go beyond holding individual tech companies or digital influence firms accountable. Discussions need to address society's collective responsibility for structural transformation.

We may draw a parallel with the realm of global health and medical care to better understand how this could happen. In the present day, the prevailing neoliberal, profit-oriented model of medical care treats health care services as commodities, rendering them accessible only to those who can afford them (Farmer et al. 2006). Furthermore, historical, social, economic, and political factors combine to deprive certain individuals of adequate medical care (Farmer et al. 2006). However, it is important to note that medical professionals, much like engineers, are not typically trained to tackle these social forces or the underlying social determinants of a disease. In this context, medical procedures may be transparent, doctors may have good intentions, and medical institutions may operate within regulatory boundaries. Yet the outcome remains ethically unsatisfactory. In the realm of global health, Farmer et al. (2006) introduce the concept of "structural interventions." These interventions encompass a range of actions aimed at preventing the commodification of citizens' health care needs and establishing social safety nets (Farmer 2013). They aim to address inequities in both potential risks and actual outcomes through a broader societal approach rather than focus solely on individual-level reforms.

Reclaiming Global Civil Society

Algorithmic violence provides a starting point for discussing society's responsibility to itself, to its members, and to other societies in addressing the social suffering caused by algorithmic assemblages. It emphasizes the collective rights and responsibilities of all members to seek and pursue transformative changes that contribute to the healthy functioning of civil society.

Today, digital infrastructures have become sites of political contestation. Digital political infrastructures can serve as a site for algorithmically mediated repression and control. Alternatively, they can serve as a site for envisioning and nurturing liberatory politics where people can come together (and apart) freely in peaceful assembly and association.

Future research may examine how the design and deployment of digital political infrastructures might center the agency, dignity, and self-determination of the communities that they are intended to serve. The elimination of algorithmic violence is only a starting point. The healthy functioning of global civil society depends on more equitable and inclusive forms of knowledge production and development, where autonomous communities actively own and govern the design decision-making processes around digital political infrastructures.

Acknowledgments

The author would like to thank Lucy Bernholz, Toussaint Nothias, and all the contributors to this volume for their constructive feedback at various stages of this project. Many thanks also to my research assistants, Victoria Hsieh (Stanford) and Autumn Dorsey (Harvard), for their work on this project. Finally, special thanks to the editor, Marcela Maxfield, and the anonymous reviewers for their insightful comments.

Notes

1. Kenyatta ultimately emerged victorious in the 2013 presidential election (Moore 2018; Nyabola 2018).

2. Despite these efforts though, Cambridge Analytica's client ended up losing to the Morena Party (Ahmed and Semple 2018).

References

Ahmed, Azam, and Danny Hakim. 2018. "Mexico's Hardball Politics Get Even Harder as PRI Fights to Hold On to Power." *The New York Times*, June 24, 2018. https://www.nytimes.com/2018/06/24/world/americas/mexico-election-cambridge-analytica.html.

Ahmed, Azam, and Kirk Semple. 2018. "Mexico Elections: 5 Takeaways from López Obrador's Victory." *The New York Times*, July 2, 2018. https://www.nytimes.com/2018/07/02/world/americas/mexico-election-lopez-obrador.html.

Allen, Robert B., Batya Friedman, and Helen Nissenbaum. 1996. "Bias in Computer Systems." In *ACM Transactions on Information Systems* 14 (3): 330-347.

Ananny, Mike. 2016. "Toward an Ethics of Algorithms: Convening, Observation, Probability, and Timeliness." *Science, Technology, & Human Values* 41 (1): 93-117.

Arendt, Hannah. 1963. *Eichmann in Jerusalem: A Report on the Banality of Evil.* New York: Penguin Books.

Basart, Josep M., and Montse Serra. 2013. "Engineering Ethics Beyond Engineers' Ethics." *Science and Engineering Ethics* 19 (1): 179-187.

Bender, Emily M., Timnit Gebru, Alex McMillan-Major, and Margaret Mitchell. 2021. "On the Dangers of Stochastic Parrots: Can Language Models Be Too Big?" In *FAccT '21: Proceedings of the ACM Conference on Fairness, Accountability, and Transparency*, 610-623. New York: Association for Computing Machinery.

Benjamin, Ruha. 2019. *Race after Technology: Abolitionist Tools for the New Jim Code.* Cambridge, MA: Polity Press.

Bernholz, Lucy. 2020. *Reclaiming Digital Infrastructure for the Public Interest.* Stanford, CA: Stanford Digital Civil Society Lab.

———. 2021. "Purpose-Built Digital Associations." In *Digital Technology and Democratic Theory*, edited by Lucy Bernholz, Hélène Landemore, and Rob Reich, 90-112. Chicago: University of Chicago Press.

Bernholz, Lucy, Hélène Landemore, and Rob Reich, eds. 2021. *Digital Technology and Democratic Theory*. Chicago: University of Chicago Press.

Brandt, Allan M. 1978. "Racism and Research: The Case of the Tuskegee Syphilis Study." *The Hastings Center Report* 8 (6): 21-29.

Briant, Emma L. 2020. "The Interactive Cambridge Analytica Map." *Propaganda Machine*. https://www.propagandamachine.tech/ca-map.

Buolamwini, Joy, and Timnit Gebru. 2018. "Gender Shades: Intersectional Accuracy Disparities in Commercial Gender Classification." In *PMLR Proceedings of the Conference on Fairness, Accountability and Transparency* 81: 77-91.

Burrell, Jenna, and Marion Fourcade. 2021. "The Society of Algorithms." *Annual Review of Sociology* 47: 213-237.

Coding Rights. "Data as a Tool for Political Influence in the Brazilian Elections." *Medium*, November 14, 2018. https://medium.com/codingrights/data-on-the-spot-information-manipulation-and-use-of-personal-data-in-the-internet-election-154e50cf05c8.

Corbie-Smith, Gisells. 1999. "The Continuing Legacy of the Tuskegee Syphilis Study: Considerations for Clinical Investigation." *The American Journal of the Medical Sciences* 317 (1): 5-8.

Costanza-Chock, Sasha. 2020. *Design Justice*. Cambridge, MA: MIT Press.

Couldry, Nick, and Ulises A. Mejias. 2019. *The Costs of Connection*. Stanford, CA: Stanford University Press.

Crawford, Kate. 2022. *Atlas of AI: Power, Politics, and the Planetary Costs of Artificial Intelligence*. New Haven, CT: Yale University Press.

Crenshaw, Kimberlé. 1991. "Mapping the Margins: Intersectionality, Identity Politics, and Violence against Women of Color." *Stanford Law Review* 43 (6): 1241–1299.

Debs, Luciana, Colin M. Gray, and Paul A. Asunda. 2022. "Students' Perceptions and Reasoning Patterns about the Ethics of Emerging Technology." *International Journal of Technology and Design* 33: 143–163.

Deibert, Ronald J. 2020. *Reset: Reclaiming the Internet for Civil Society*. Toronto: House of Anansi Press.

DeNardis, Laura. 2020. *The Internet in Everything*. New Haven, CT: Yale University Press.

D'Ignazio, Catherine. 2024. *Counting Feminicide: Data Feminism in Action*. Cambridge, MA: MIT Press.

D'Ignazio, Catherine, and Lauren F. Klein. 2020. *Data Feminism*. Cambridge, MA: MIT Press.

Eubanks, Virginia. 2018. *Automating Inequality: How High-Tech Tools Profile, Police, and Punish the Poor*. New York: St. Martin's Press.

Farmer, Paul. 2013. *To Repair the World: Paul Farmer Speaks to the Next Generation*. Edited by Jonathan L. Weigel. Berkeley, CA: University of California Press.

Farmer, Paul, Bruce Nizeye, Sara Stulac, and Salmaan Keshavjee. 2006. "Structural Violence and Clinical Medicine." *PLoS Medicine* 3 (10): 1686–1691.

Galtung, Johan. 1969. "Violence, Peace, and Peace Research." *Journal of Peace Research* 6 (3): 167–191.

Garvie, Clare, and Laura M. Moy. 2019. *America under Watch: Face Surveillance in the United States*. Washington, DC: Georgetown Law Center on Privacy & Technology.

Ghoshal, Devjyot. 2018. "From Indonesia to Thailand, Cambridge Analytica's Parent Influenced Southeast Asian Politics." *Quartz*, March 29, 2018. https://qz.com/1240588/cambridge-analytica-how-scl-group-used-indonesia-and-thailand-to-hone-its-ability-to-influence-elections.

Gray, Mary L., and Siddharth Suri. 2019. *Ghost Work: How to Stop Silicon Valley from Building a New Global Underclass*. Boston: Houghton Mifflin Harcourt.

Harry, Catherine V. 2017. "Facebook's Dangerous Experiment in Cambodia." *The Washington Post*, December 12, 2017. https://www.washingtonpost.com/news/global-opinions/wp/2017/12/12/facebook-is-conducting-a-dangerous-experiment-in-cambodia/?utmterm=.58ff53647d55.

Hern, Alex. 2018. "Far More Than 87M Facebook Users Had Data Compromised." *The Guardian*, April 17, 2018. https://www.theguardian.com/uk-news/2018/apr/17/facebook-users-data-compromised-far-more-than-87m-mps-told-cambridge-analytica.

Irani, Lilly, Janet Vertesi, Paul Dourish, Kavita Philip, Rebecca E. Grinter. 2010. "Postcolonial Computing: A Lens on Design and Development." In *Proceedings of the SIGCHI Conference on Human Factors in Computing Systems*. 1311-1320.

Jasanoff, Sheila. 2006. "Biotechnology and Empire: The Global Power of Seeds and Science." *Osiris* 21 (1): 273-292.

Karell, Daniel, Andrew Linke, Edward Holland, and Edward Hendrickson. 2023. "'Born for a Storm': Hard Right Social Media and Civil Unrest." *American Sociological Review* 88 (2): 322-349.

Kirchgaessner, Stephanie, Carole Cadwalladr, Paul Lewis, and Jason Burke. 2023. "Dark Arts of Politics." *The Guardian*, February 16, 2023. https://www.theguardian.com/world/2023/feb/16/team-jorge-and-cambridge-analytica-meddled-in-nigeria-election-emails-reveal.

Kleinman, Arthur. 1997. *Writing at the Margin: Discourse Between Anthropology and Medicine*. Berkeley, CA: University of California Press.

Kleinman, Arthur, Veena Das, and Margaret Lock, eds. 1997. *Social Suffering*. Berkeley, CA: University of California Press.

Mann, Michael. 1984. "The Autonomous Power of the State: Its Origins, Mechanisms and Results." *European Journal of Sociology* 25 (2): 185-213.

———. 2008. "Infrastructural Power Revisited." *Studies in Comparative International Development* 43: 355-365.

Marwick, Alice, and Rebecca Lewis. 2017. *Media Manipulation and Disinformation Online*. New York: Data & Society Research Institute.

Mejias, Ulises A., and Nick Couldry. 2024. *Data Grab: The New Colonialism of Big Tech and How to Fight Back*. Chicago: University of Chicago Press.

Mohamed, Shakir, Marie-Therese Png, and William Isaac. 2020. "Decolonial AI: Decolonial Theory as Sociotechnical Foresight in Artificial Intelligence." *Philosophy & Technology* 33: 659-684.

Moore, Jina. 2018. "Cambridge Analytica Had a Role in Kenya Election, Too." *The New York Times*, March 20, 2018. https://www.nytimes.com/2018/03/20/world/africa/kenya-cambridge-analytica-election.html.

National Commission for the Protection of Human Subjects of Biomedical and Behavioral Research. 1978. "The Belmont Report: Ethical Principles and Guidelines for the Protection of Human Subjects of Research." https://www .hhs.gov/ohrp/sites/default/files/the-belmont-report-508c_FINAL.pdf #page=1.

Noble, Safiya Umoja. 2018. *Algorithms of Oppression: How Search Engines Reinforce Racism*. New York: NYU Press.

Nuremberg Military Tribunal. 1947. "Permissible Medical Experiments." In *Trials of War Criminals Before the Nuremberg Military Tribunals Under Control Council Law No. 10. Nuremberg, October 1946-April 1949*, Vol. 2., 181–182. Washington, DC: U.S. Government Printing Office.

Nyabola, Nanjala. 2018. *Digital Democracy, Analogue Politics*. London: Zed Books.

O'Neil, Cathy. 2017. *Weapons of Math Destruction*. New York: Broadway Books.

Ong, Aihwa, and Stephen J. Collier. 2008. *Global Assemblages: Technology, Politics, and Ethics as Anthropological Problems*. Oxford, UK: Blackwell.

Palatino, Mong. 2017. "Facebook's 'Explore Feed' Experiment Is Hurting Small Businesses, NGOs, and Political Groups in Cambodia." *Global Voices*, November 14, 2017. https://advox.globalvoices.org/2017/11/14/facebooks -explore-feed-experiment-is-hurting-small-businesses-ngos-and-political -groups-in-cambodia/.

Parks, Lisa, and Nicole Starosielski, eds. 2015. *Signal Traffic: Critical Studies of Media Infrastructures*. Champaign, IL: University of Illinois Press.

Paviour, Ben. 2017. "What a Facebook Experiment Did to News in Cambodia." *BBC News*, October 30, 2017. http://www.bbc.com/news/world-asia-4180 1071.

Persily, Nathaniel, and Joshua A. Tucker, eds. 2020. *Social Media and Democracy*. Cambridge, UK: Cambridge University Press.

Punit, Itika Sharma. 2018. "Cambridge Analytica's Parent Firm Proposed a Massive Political Machine For India's 2014 Elections." *Quartz*, March 28, 2018. https://qz.com/1239561/cambridge-analyticas-parent-firm-proposed- a-massive-political-machine-for-indias-2014-elections

Renieris, Elizabeth M. (2023). *Beyond Data: Reclaiming Human Rights at the Dawn of the Metaverse*. Cambridge, MA: MIT Press.

Ricaurte, Paula. 2022. "Ethics for the Majority World." *Media, Culture & Society* 22 (4): 726–745.

Roberts, Sarah T. 2019. *Behind the Screen*. New Haven, CT: Yale University Press.

Roose, Kevin, and Paul Mozur. 2018. "Zuckerberg Was Called Out over Myanmar Violence. Here's His Apology." *The New York Times*, April 9, 2018. https:// www.nytimes.com/2018/04/09/business/facebook-myanmar-zuckerberg .html.

Rosenberg, Matthew, Nicholas Confessore, and Carole Cadwalladr. 2018. "How Trump Consultants Exploited the Facebook Data of Millions." *The New York Times*, March 17, 2018. https://www.nytimes.com/2018/03/17/us/politics/cambridge-analytica-trump-campaign.html.

Schradie, Jen. 2019. *The Revolution That Wasn't*. Cambridge, MA: Harvard University Press.

Taub, Amanda, and Max Fisher. 2018. "Where Countries Are Tinderboxes and Facebook Is a Match." *The New York Times*, April 21, 2018. https://www.nytimes.com/2018/04/21/world/asia/facebook-sri-lanka-riots.html.

Tufekci, Zeynep. 2017. *Twitter and Tear Gas: The Power and Fragility of Networked Protest*. New Haven, CT: Yale University Press.

World Medical Association. 1964. "World Medical Association Declaration of Helsinki." https://www.wma.net/wp-content/uploads/2016/11/DoH-Oct2013-JAMA.pdf

Zuboff, Shoshana. 2019. *The Age of Surveillance Capitalism*. New York: Public Affairs.

Zuckerman, Ethan. 2024. "Are There Any Humans Left on the Internet? *Prospect*, June 24, 2024. https://www.prospectmagazine.co.uk/ideas/technology/internet/66995/are-there-any-humans-left-on-the-internet

Four

From Threat to Advocacy

Lisa Garbe
Daniel Mwesigwa
Toussaint Nothias

In November 2021, Benin Club 1931 in Benin City, Nigeria, celebrated its ninetieth anniversary. It used to be known as the European Club. According to the club's website, "it was established by Europeans for their own private recreation; sport and entertainment away from the prying eyes and alien life of indigenous society, so to speak. The club seldom entertained Nigerians, not indigenous sportsmen or nobility" (Benin Club 2023). The club was a paradigmatic example of what Mamdani called the racialization of civil society during the colonial era. Civil society, Mamdani writes, was, above all, the society of the colonists; for him, the anticolonial struggle was in part "a struggle of the embryonic middle and working classes for entry into civil society" (1996, 148). Shortly after the country's independence in 1960, the European Club changed its name and eventually was no longer exclusive to "Europeans." In a ceremony celebrating its ninetieth anniversary, Edo state governor, Mr. Godwin Obaseki, emphasized the centrality of associational hubs like Benin to the economic growth of the region. He also announced a new investment: "We have done our best to develop the club's infrastructure, and now, the club is working on installing facial recognition to access the club" (*NewsDirect* 2021).

Facial recognition technologies are increasingly expanding to spaces at the core of how people come together and practice their freedom of assembly and association. In postcolonial societies, as the story of Benin Club 1931 reminds us, the spaces where people come together today and where digital technologies expand always carry a broader history of tensions and struggles shaped by racialized global power relations. When students in South Africa protested high tuition fees in 2016, NEC XON—a South African subsidiary of a Japanese company, the world's largest facial recognition provider—tried to identify protesters (Hao and Swart 2022). They gathered images from pictures and videos shared on WhatsApp and various social media platforms, and then compared them with student identification photos stored in university databases. In 2021, when new protests erupted in the country, students reported that riot police filmed them "at close range for so-called 'evidence' collection"; Ntyatyambo Volsak, a nineteen-year-old student, shared with journalists Karen Hao and Heidi Swart their experience of this encounter: "We're trying to make sure that everyone is getting an education," he said, "but the police treat us like animals" (Hao and Swart 2022).

All over the world, public spaces such as city centers, streets, airports, and train stations are increasingly equipped with CCTV cameras, many of which have enhanced functionalities like facial recognition. Facial recognition technologies rely on artificial intelligence (AI) to analyze and identify human faces. Facial recognition technologies work by comparing and mapping a person's facial features to a database of known faces (Purshouse and Campbell 2022). The capability to collect and analyze large amounts of data in real time makes it, in the eyes of civil liberties advocates, a highly intrusive form of surveillance. While governments usually foster the use of facial recognition technologies for security reasons, empirical research raises major questions about their security benefits. Empirical research suggests that governments, especially in authoritarian countries, may systematically abuse surveillance technologies to identify and repress political opposition (e.g., Gohdes 2020; Xu 2021). In addition, studies highlight that citizens are more likely to self-censor and refrain from political participation in light of government surveillance (e.g. Chang and Manion 2021; Eck et al. 2021). As Zalnieriute outlines, anonymity is essential to the right of assembly. It enables people to feel "confident and safe in their ability to gather in public spaces to manifest their disagreement with the status quo" (2021, 2). Since they undermine citizens' anonymity, facial recognition technologies significantly threaten freedoms of assembly and association. In public spaces, they create what Andrejevic and Volcic (2021) call an "operational enclosure"—where biometrics are the operative embodiment of *being* and *access*. Citizens who may not even have direct access to digital devices become subject to vast surveillance. Their mere existence in cities and areas mediated and platformed by facial recognition technologies automatically transforms them into real-time surveillance targets. As a result, the possibility of opting out of this hybrid architecture is reduced and citizens' basic rights might be subsequently curtailed.

Moreover, these technologies revive dangerous ideas core to the pseudo-scientific racism of the nineteenth century. At a basic level, facial recognition implies visually analyzing facial features, classifying them, and using them eventually to inform mechanisms of social order—from policing (Arnett 2023) to immigration (Sumaita 2022) to taxation (Rappeport 2022). In recent years, scholars have dubiously claimed that facial recognition can be used to determine a person's political orientation (Kosinski 2021), sexual orientation (Wang and Kosinski 2018), and criminal tendency (Hashemi and Hall 2020). These claims resemble older, dangerous ideas (Stark and Hutson 2021). Phrenologists, for instance, erroneously claimed that measuring human skulls could determine intelligence, morality, and personality traits. Physiognomists wrongly argued that one could infer criminality by analyzing facial features. The biases of this pseudo-science, now debunked, were instrumental in the establishment of an oppressive racial ordering and justification of violent colonial policies and apartheid regimes (Bowker and Star 2020). Even though facial recognition strikes a chord at the center of this fraught and brutal history, this has not prevented its expansion across the world today.

In recent years, many African governments started employing facial recognition technologies in public spaces, including authoritarian regimes such as Uganda and Zimbabwe (Kafeero 2020; Gwagwa and Garbe 2018) as well as more liberal countries like South Africa and Kenya (Basimanyane and Gandhi 2019; Burt 2019). Facial recognition's recent circulation in Africa has coincided with novel and emerging digital transformations fueled by various actors. For example, partnerships between African governments and transnational entities—that is, multilateral agencies, humanitarian organizations, and international data processing corporations—have often attempted to use technical biometrics to solve intractable and complex problems in health, security, governance, immigration, and development. In many instances, these partnerships are rationalized as win-win situations by the main stakeholders, legitimated as "national security" by state actors, and lauded for their "development" potential by multilateral actors. However, many of these alleged win-win situations have had mixed results for citizens and civil society (Jili 2022b). Some analysts warn that such technologies can "exacerbate existing inequalities if not deployed with proper governance mechanisms and adequate safeguards" (Mudongo 2021, 1).

In this chapter, we focus on the deployment of, and resistance to, facial recognition in various African contexts. We see the technology as one that carries risks for freedom of assembly, and our primary focus is on understanding the extent and nature of its deployment across Africa. At the same time, we are interested in understanding if, when, and how communities come together to advocate for the technology's regulation, oversight, or even banning—in other words, when facial recognition becomes an *object of assembly*.

Far from being entirely new phenomena, we relocate both the deployment of and the resistance to facial recognition technologies in a broader sociopolitical context marked by continuities and changes characteristic of the postcolonial era. Our chapter shows that these supposed peripheries of the digital economy provide a particularly relevant vantage point to apprehend the structural dynamics that shape the future of AI and assembly globally—from the changing cultural norms around biometric capture to the privatization of public goods; and from growing antidemocratic populism to the precarious institutionalization of global digital rights advocacy.

Our chapter proceeds in three sections. The first section offers an overview of the rise of facial recognition technologies across Africa. We provide results from a review of news coverage and gray literature to scope African countries where facial recognition technologies have been deployed, their social domains of application, and the main actors involved. The second section analyzes two case studies to provide a more contextualized account of facial recognition deployment in Kenya and Uganda. We explore the relevant private and public actors involved and analyze various advocacy efforts to oppose them. By shedding light on the emergence and nature of advocacy against facial recognition, the third section addresses pressing questions about the present and future of digital rights advocacy in a globalized world.

Before we start, three clarifications are in order. First, our continental framing does not assume a single story about "Africa." Our analysis aims to highlight and understand heterogeneity: we attempt to map different deployments and actors across different countries, and our two case studies further engage with some of this heterogeneity. At the same time, we recognize that African countries, like most countries in the Global South, have historically been targets of similar foreign forces—states, corporations, NGOs, and international organizations—trying to control, shape, dictate, and exploit their economies, cultures, and political systems. These shared threats have historically shaped the contours of resistance to outside forces, including in the form of pan-African solidarity. We take our cue from this legacy and argue that, while national contexts are often radically different, many of these countries face similar structural influences involving foreign actors; as such, lessons learned from one context can inform resistance in another—for instance by anticipating risks and structural trends and foreseeing pathways for successful advocacy and regulatory interventions at a national, transnational, regional, or continental level.

Second, throughout the chapter we put in dialogue "facial recognition technologies," subsequently abbreviated as FRTs, with other forms of biometric capture. FRTs are forms of biometric capture akin to and often used in conjunction with other biometric data, including but not limited to fingerprints, palm prints, DNA, and iris and retinal scans. Under the FRTs label, we include several phenomena usefully summarized by EFF (Cyphers, Schwartz, and Sheard 2021): "face detection," which consists of identifying faces (as opposed to other objects in an image); extracting features from a face to capture its differentiating features and develop a "faceprint"; "face matching," which consists of comparing two or more face prints for face verification (matching different faceprints to determine if they are from the same person), face identification (matching a faceprint from a new image to a database of faceprints linked to personal identities), face clustering (comparing faceprints so as to group the images including a specific person or group of people), and face tracking (following the movements of a person through a physical space). We use FRTs to refer to the various technologies involved in collecting and processing faceprints. For reasons that should become clear as we move along in the chapter, our normative position aligns with civil liberties and digital rights advocates who see FRTs as worryingly intrusive surveillance.

Lastly, as described in the book's introductory chapter, our understanding of "civil society" is expansive, including formal and informal dimensions. We approach this category more as a set of practices than a rigid type of institutions or organizations. This point is worth emphasizing since the notion of civil society in the context of African politics and history is particularly fraught, as the case of Benin Club 1931 reminds us. Especially used in the 1990s as a policy panacea to bring about democracy and development and fight corruption, the prescription that Africa should build its civil society worryingly assumed, as Willems reminds us, that "Africa did not have a 'civil society'" (2012, 14). In contrast, we see civil society as multifarious and contested. We do not prescribe one of its forms as an obvious solution, and we do not consider it a power-free zone. On the contrary, we show how civil society is at times implicated in the deployment of FRTs and that, as we discuss in our conclusion, even civil society resistance to FRTs is itself fraught with contradictions that should invite us to critically consider the emerging idea of a "global" digital rights community. Notwithstanding a fluid conceptualization of civil society, we believe that a plural, safe, and autonomous associational life remains a marker of, and contributor to, vibrant democratic life. Bound to be impacted by FRTs, this associational life should be involved in the debates and decision-making around the deployment, oversight, and possible curtailing of the technology.

Method

To provide a big-picture overview of the deployment of facial recognition technologies across African countries, we conducted a content analysis of Anglophone and Francophone news coverage published in the last five years (from January 2018 to March 2023). We combined three databases to search for articles: ProQuest, LexisNexis, and Civic Signal Africa. In ProQuest and LexisNexis, we searched for articles that included the words "facial recognition" or "reconnaissance faciale" published in any news source in the world, and then filtered the results using the geographic filter "Africa" (this filter captures any article tagged with a geographic location anywhere on the continent). Civic Signal is a tool designed by Code for Africa, Africa's largest network of civic technology and data journalism, building on the Media Cloud news search tool. It allows searching specifically for articles published by African news sources. We selected all sources available from Civic Signal and searched for the keyword "facial recognition" OR "reconnaissance faciale." With this approach, we sought to cast a wide net that included a dedicated focus on local news.

Across the three databases, our queries initially returned 2,558 news articles. We then looked at the headline of each one to determine its relevance. If the title clarified that the story was about facial recognition in an African context, we kept it (e.g., "Ghana: Facial Recognition Metric

App Saved NSS GH¢112m"). If the title made it clear that the story was irrelevant, we discarded it (e.g., "Wells Fargo and USAA Lead in Offering Mobile Features Consumers Would Switch Banks For"). If the title alone was not enough to make a determination, we read the article to decide whether to include or not (e.g., "Parliament's Failure to Regulate Surveillance Threatens Human Rights in Uganda"). At the end of this process, we had a corpus of 318 articles.

We manually coded every article in an Airtable spreadsheet. For each article, we recorded which country or countries deployed or considered deploying FRTs and for which purposes; what the main actors involved were (companies, governments, nonprofits, etc.); whether the article included concerns about or critiques of the technology; and whether the article included the perspective and voice of community members/civil society.

In addition to our systematic search for news content, we compiled a list of relevant articles, reports, and other publications related to facial recognition technologies in African contexts published by think tanks and digital policy and advocacy groups. Our review of this so-called gray literature also informed our overall assessment of the deployment of FRTs across the continent and in our two case studies.

There were noticeable limitations to this method. Because we focused primarily on news content, we relied on news visibility as a proxy for assessing deployment. In some cases, governments and other actors were keen to publicly advertise their use of facial recognition as a symbol of development, strength, and modernization. In other cases, a culture of secrecy characteristic of the surveillance industry prevailed. We were therefore missing deployments that escaped public scrutiny. Our search was also linguistically limited. English is an official language in twenty-four African countries; French, in twenty. Thus we were missing the many non-English- and non-French-language news stories that might have reported on deployment in non-anglophone African countries. As such, our results were indicative rather than fully exhaustive; they provided a robust baseline assessment of FRTs deployment across the continent.

The Rise of FRTs in Africa

Based on our review, we estimate that FRTs are being deployed in at least forty-one African countries (Figure 3). Far from being a privilege for only a handful of tech-oriented African countries (such as Nigeria and South Africa), we find FRTs to be pervasive and expanding at a rapid pace across most countries.[1]

This expansiveness is reflected in the different domains in which FRTs are deployed. These domains are often interrelated, but we can broadly separate them into six clusters for analytical purposes. A particularly common one relates to identification for election, voter registration, and national identity. These are usually projects led by states looking to integrate biometric identification—including facial recognition—in their voting or national identification system to complement or gradually replace existing systems. For instance, during its 2020 general elections, Ghana procured 75,000 devices to record fingerprints and facial features from voters, at an estimated cost of US$12 million (*GhanaWeb* 2020). The system was to be used to verify the identity of voters only when fingerprints alone were insufficient. This type of bimodal voter accreditation system (BVAS)—combining fingerprint and face biometrics—seems increasingly popular. Countries like Nigeria, Kenya, Zimbabwe, and Liberia are adopting a similar approach, claiming that the technology will prove cost-effective, more reliable, and faster. A similar rhetoric underpins the inclusion of facial recognition in proposed national digital identification systems. In the last decade, Lesotho, Mozambique, Tanzania, Uganda, Zambia, and Zimbabwe introduced digital identification, often in partnership with multilateral or intergovernmental organizations such as the World Bank or the UNHCR. The latter, for instance, has been using biometric identity management systems since 2015 (Haberkorn 2023). In 2022 the UNHCR, in collaboration with the Cameroonian government, issued biometric IDs, including facial photographs, to 6,000 refugees from the Central African Republic (Al Jazeera 2022).

Facial recognition technologies deployed?

yes
n/a

Created with mapchart.net

FIGURE 3. Facial recognition technologies across Africa: A baseline.

A second cluster of applications relates broadly to policing and security. Here, we refer to the inclusion of facial recognition in systems of surveillance of public places. Notably, the Safe Cities program by Chinese firm Huawei has been instrumental in promoting the deployment of facial recognition–enabled CCTV to monitor public spaces in Ethiopia, Madagascar, Uganda, Ivory Coast, Nigeria, Cameroon, Kenya, Angola, Botswana, Mauritius, South Africa, and Ghana (Hillman and Calpin 2019). This is also happening in the context of private security.

In Nigeria, for instance, estate managers are encouraged to consider FRTs to "protect residential estates and offices" (Anaesoronye 2022). In South Africa, private security firms increasingly turn to AI analytics and facial recognition to detect crimes and identify criminals (Hao and Swart 2022). Underpinning all of these efforts is a rhetorical emphasis on facial recognition technologies making people and properties "more secure."

A third area—which intersects with matters of identification and security—relates to the deployment of FRTs at infrastructures of border crossing: airports and ports. In Senegal, for instance, the Blaise Diagne International Airport announced that it would start using facial recognition to "identify people and track suspects"(*Aéronautique.ma* 2021). Similarly, in Morocco the French firm IDEMIA will work with a Moroccan company, Ultranet Multimedia, to implement facial recognition at Rabat-Salé Airport (Ketti 2022); and in Capo Verde's main airport, the Belgian company Zetes installed eleven Panasonic facial recognition eGates (Jarrahi 2020). Meanwhile, in Nigeria, the recently inaugurated Lekki Deep Sea Port uses biometric scanners and facial recognition surveillance systems (*Nigerian News Net* 2023). The result of a collaboration between Nigeria, France, and China, this is now the largest seaport in Nigeria and is slated to become a key hub of import for neighboring countries of Chad, Mali, Niger, and Cameroon.

E-governance and the provision of social services are other domains in which FRTs are being deployed. We see examples of this in education, from proctoring software to prevent and catch "fraudsters" in South Africa (McKenna 2022) to a thousand CCTV cameras being donated to the University of Lagos in Nigeria by the technology company Bionomics Nig. Ltd (*National Daily Newspaper* 2021). We also see examples in the administration of the National Service Scheme (NSS) in Ghana. The NSS provides twelve-month employment postings to recent graduates from Ghanaian tertiary institutions. In this case, a new system of facial recognition identification blocked the enrollment of "14,027 potential fraudsters" in the scheme—an outcome presented by authorities as cost-saving: "Without the use of this technology, we would have paid GH₵94 million, and if they had gone to the private sector, GH₵112 million. All of that money would have gone down the drain to 'ghosts'" (Awal 2022). Similar rhetoric was at play behind the introduction of a biometric system with facial recognition by the Zimbabwean Public Service Commission in collaboration with the World Bank. Following an audit, "they found 3,000 so-called 'ghost workers' and removed them from the payroll hence saving the country some money" (Toesland 2021).

Identification and fraud reduction/prevention is also front and center in commercial applications of FRTs. Several banks and financial technology companies are turning to FRTs for authentication, particularly in Nigeria. The local investment firm Digital Space Capital integrated facial recognition into one of its applications meant to encourage a "savings culture among Nigerians" (Salau 2021). Aella, a Nigerian financial technology startup, was "recognized by Amazon as one of the world's leading financial organizations pioneering the use of facial recognition for customer authentication and credit scoring" (Kimathi 2020). Access Bank, for its part, is set to deploy Facepay, a new payment technology that uses facial recognition and AI (Faith 2020). The telecom sector is also one where FRTs are playing a growing role, specifically for SIM card registration. MTC, Namibia's leading telecom provider, requires citizens to provide biometrics—face and fingerprints—when registering their cards (Macdonald 2023). The trend toward integrating SIM card registration and digital IDs is on the rise; according to Roberts and Oloyede (2022): "Some 30 countries globally require SIM registration linked to digital ID," including Nigeria, Uganda, Zambia, and Kenya. The Tanzanian government even went as far as launching a social media influencer campaign to promote biometric registration by enrolling 150 of Tanzania's top social media personalities (Hersey 2019).

Last, and perhaps surprising, we saw FRTs being used in the domain of conservation. French scientists in Zimbabwe, for instance, used a deep learning system primarily for facial recognition of humans "to re-identify individual giraffes in Hwange with 90 percent accuracy" (Truscott 2021). And in Kenya, the "Lion Guardians" built a database of lions, including photographs of their faces. They argued that the project would help better monitor the animals' movements and reduce the cost of tracking with GPS transmitters (Kerr 2015).

Cumulatively, these domains of application paint a somewhat dystopian picture of our near future: whether you want to vote, prove your identity, cross a border, walk in the street, attend school, use a bank, make phone calls, or access social services, your face will be captured, processed, stored, cross-checked, and most likely used to train new AI systems. Even animals are not exempt from it, making South African activist Ntyatyambo Volsak's remark about being treated like animals even more poignant. At the moment, FRTs are on track to become a core feature of our world, inevitably shaping how people live their lives and how communities come together, leaving people with seemingly a handful of choices: accept FRTs, set limits to them, or challenge them altogether via obfuscation, collective advocacy, and/or regulation.

Invariably, we find a handful of types of institutions involved in deploying FRTs, often in collaborations. Spurred by hyped promises of safety, efficiency, and modernization, states adopt these technologies and generally turn to foreign companies to implement them. These companies aggressively compete to obtain contracts. A handful of few prominent ones kept appearing in our corpus: IDEMIA (formerly known as OT-Morpho), a French multinational particularly prominent in biometric systems for policing, digital ID, and elections; NEC, a Japanese multinational and a major player in digital ID; Travizory, a Swiss company that sells facial biometric gateways to airports; Thales Group, also a French multinational company that sells biometric election systems; and Chinese companies Huawei, Cloudwalk, and Hikvision, which install FRTs in public spaces via Smart Cities programs tied to the country's One Belt, One Road campaign. Experts have been quick to frame China as the sole culprit in exporting digital surveillance and even evangelizing its authoritarian model of digital sovereignty. It is clear, however, that technology providers from Europe, Japan, and the United States are also complicit in exporting and circulating FRTs in Africa. According to Clearview AI's leaked pitch deck, the US facial recognition company with a dataset of 10 billion images scraped off the internet, was planning to roll out its technology in airports in Senegal and Côte d'Ivoire in 2022/2023 (Harwell 2022). The global surveillance technology industry knows neither creed nor geography; it flows where invited. Local private security companies are involved as well, such as the South African Vumacam, which was the focus of an investigation by the *MIT Technology Review* detailing the network of 6,600 AI-powered CCTV cameras installed by the company (Hao and Swart 2022). Meanwhile, intergovernmental organizations play a crucial role in continuously encouraging states to adopt these technological solutions presented as "cost-saving"; for example, the World Bank's ID4D program incentivizes states to establish digital ID systems.

The result is a patchwork of local, foreign, international, and transnational actors contributing to so-called public/private partnerships or, instead, to the privatization of the public sector—a process in the making since the advent of structural adjustment plans in the 1980s. The previously mentioned integration of digital ID with SIM card registration provides a valuable case in point. A state mandates telecom operators to register customers obtaining a new SIM card. Some operators are private companies; others are publicly owned; and many are a mix of both and often multinational. Meanwhile, national digital ID systems—which arguably should be a quintessential object of national sovereignty—are implemented by foreign private companies incentivized by intergovernmental organizations. When Nigeria requires SIM card registration to be linked to a citizen's digital ID (including their biometric data), the result is the increasingly complex intermingling of private and public actors, with hybrid companies involved for digital ID, for SIM card registration, and for integration of the two. These new technological intermediaries not only create new types of vulnerabilities; they also fragment national sovereignty and encourage the influence of foreign actors, a process that led Kenyan writer Nanjala Nyabola to talk about a form of "digital colonialism" (Nyabola 2018).

We found that civil society voices were directly quoted in 84 of our 318 stories and appeared on all sides of this issue. In 54 stories, civil society actors criticized and worried about the deployment of facial recognition. As our case study of Kenya will show, they emerged mainly from human rights and digital rights advocacy organizations, raising concerns about the racial biases of the technologies toward dark-skinned individuals, building on the foundational work of activists in the US. Deploying this technology on the African continent would risk supercharging these biases. Interestingly, some analysts have linked the expansion of Chinese FRTs in Africa to an attempt to "be better able to train racial biases out of its facial recognition systems"(Hawkins 2024). This could give the country a competitive advantage—a strategy that mirrors the successful expansion of Chinese Tecno Mobile phones in Africa, which provided Tecno a competitive edge through its much touted camera optimization for darker tones (Lu and Qiu 2022).

Activists also had worries about technical glitches and possible manipulation of data associated with integrating biometric information into voting systems. Another concern was the nature of the investment and the procurement process. When the Electoral Commission of Ghana decided in 2020 to procure a new biometric system including FRTs, opposition parties and some civil society groups expressed concerns and protested (Anaba 2020). They asked why a new system was needed when the previous one worked well; they argued that the money spent could have been used for more pressing purposes for their constituents, and ultimately they cast a shadow over possible corruption in procurement. Last but not least, we noted concerns about privacy infringement and mass surveillance reinforcing the power of autocratic governments to monitor and target protestors, opponents, and minorities—an issue we discuss in more detail in our case study of Uganda in particular.

Still, we found that thirty-five stories included civil society actors who generally welcomed the deployment of FRTs. This was the case notably for organizations in the humanitarian sectors, like the UNHCR and the WFP, that saw tremendous possibilities in integrating biometrics into their operations. Others welcomed FRTs for their supposed broader benefit to a community, such as more confidence in election results. This was the case in Nigeria, where some members of civil society welcomed the announcement of the inclusion of BVAS during general elections. Samson Itodo, the executive director of a nonprofit organization called Yiaga Africa, which focuses on democracy and human rights, largely praised the technology as one of the "most significant innovations and reforms to Nigeria's electoral process"—one that will enhance transparency and boost public trust (Itodo 2022). Importantly, it should also be noted that civil society was seemingly absent from nearly three-quarters of the articles. Whether this number represented a willful silencing of a broader range of civil society perspectives or a lack of engagement by civil society actors with FRTs in these contexts remains an open question.

Kenya: Surveil and Identify

In the past fifteen years, Kenya has raised its profile as a key technology hub on the continent, with its local scene dubbed the Silicon Savannah. Expectedly, the use of FRTs in the country is on the rise. FRTs are not only used as part of private sector innovations to improve health care and education services (Toesland 2021); rather, the Kenyan government started rolling out projects involving FRTs over the last decades. This case study sheds light on two fields in which FRTs play an important role—the fight against terrorism and the management of identity systems—and briefly summarizes developments in both fields.

Countering Terrorism

Over the past decades, Kenya has seen a massive increase in CCTV cameras in public spaces. The recordings captured by CCTV cameras are used in combination with FRTs by Kenyan police and other security forces. To understand Kenya's rapid deployment of CCTV cameras and FRTs in public spaces, it is necessary to situate these advancements in the historical context of antiterrorism policies in the country. Kenya has been subject to several large-scale Islamist terrorist attacks, such as the attack on the US embassy in Nairobi in 1998, the 2002 bombing of the Paradise Hotel in Mombasa, the 2013 attack on the Westgate shopping mall in Nairobi, and the 2015 attack on Garissa University, along with several comparatively smaller attacks during the same time. In response to these attacks, the Kenyan government introduced a number of counterterrorism (CT) efforts. One of these was the advancement of surveillance, notably in areas with many so-called vulnerable targets. In 2014, the Kenyan government introduced a new bill amending several security laws to provide a legal basis for surveillance (Roberts et al. 2021).

In the early 2000s, the government installed CCTV cameras at airports to protect vulnerable targets supported by the US Safe Skies for Africa program (Mogire and Mkutu Agade 2011). Later, the Japanese firm NEC provided CCTV cameras and the FRT NeoFace for several Kenyan airports, including Jomo Kenyatta International Airport (JKIA) in Nairobi (Burt 2019). Following Al-Shabaab's terrorist attack on Nairobi's Westgate Mall, the government deployed thousands of cameras along with FRTs to enhance security and reduce crime (Jili 2022a). According to Jili, footage from these cameras feeds into "a national police command center that supports more than 9,000 police officers and 195 police stations" (2022a, 446). The infrastructure for this project is provided by the multinational Chinese technology corporation Huawei. Kenya is among at least seventy-three countries that have entered a Safe Cities agreement with Huawei (Hillman and McCalpin 2019). While Huawei claimed that its technology reduced crime rates in the affected cities of Nairobi and Mombasa by more than 40 percent, official Kenyan police statistics contradict Huawei's numbers and the police are, in fact, much less enthusiastic about its success (Hillman and McCalpin 2019).

Ultimately, it remains challenging to assess the technology's actual impact on crime rates and even more on efforts to combat terrorism. Several accounts highlight that, while the benefits of the massive rollout of CCTV cameras to enhance security are unclear, negative ramifications may be severe. Somali Kenyans have been disproportionately policed ever since the terrorist attacks in the early 2000s. Increasingly preventive and indiscriminate forms of policing contribute to a culture in which "many fear . . . the consequences of speaking out" (Al-Bulushi 2021, 3). Especially given the absence of regulation, there are concerns that there are no limits to the scale of surveillance through CCTV, further reducing the space for freedom of expression and assembly (Kapiyo and Githaiga 2014).

International NGOs like Privacy International have criticized the expansion of surveillance in the name of security and emphasized privacy concerns related to sharing data from video surveillance with third parties (Privacy International 2014). Local human rights organizations supporting members of minority communities, such as HAKI Africa and Muslims for Human Rights (MUHURI), have also raised concerns about privacy with particular consequences for their communities. However, resistance by HAKI, MUHURI, and others was impeded in 2015 when the Kenyan government banned eighty Kenya-based NGOs, including HAKI and MUHURI, for alleged support for Al-Shabaab (Hansen, Lid, and Okwany 2019). Kenya's High Court lifted the ban later that year, stating that the government had not provided sufficient evidence to link the organizations to terrorist activity (*Freedom House* 2015). The ban exemplifies resistance to surveillance as particularly challenging for organizations representing minority groups that have a history of conflict with and marginalization by the government.

Managing Identity

More recently, FRTs have been discussed in the context of a new identity management system in Kenya. In 2019, the government proposed a mandatory national integrated identity management system (NIIMS), more commonly known as Huduma Namba ("service number" in Swahili). In this program, Huduma cards would be the only valid proof of identity entailing biometric information stored in a centralized government database. The government allowed NIIMS to collect vast amounts of information about its citizens including "GPS location information and biometric information such as fingerprints, facial images, DNA" (Open Society Justice Initiative n.d.). According to the government, the new system will substantially improve service delivery as it enhances the state's knowledge about individuals and whether they qualify for access to state support (Ministry of Interior & Coordination and for National Government, n.d.).

Already, before the introduction of NIIMS, the US was encouraging the Kenyan government to collect the biometric information of refugees coming to Kenya to further protect the country's borders. In 2013, the UNHCR and the WFP introduced a pilot project using a biometric identity management system (BIMS) for the distribution of aid in the Kakuma refugee camp in Turkana County in 2013 (Iazzolino 2021). It is instructive to quote directly from one of the WFP's materials describing its partnership with UNHCR in Kenya. The system used fingerprints to determine if a person was eligible for food. If the fingerprints or photo did not match the UNHCR refugee registration database, they would be rejected. The WFP estimated that this resulted in savings of US$1.5 million per month and described the program as a success (World Food Programme, n.d.):

> This was at a time when donors were signaling fatigue and we were at risk of not being able to feed our real refugees. The savings are real and impressive and the donors' confidence is higher. Our relationship with UNHCR is also very strong which will mean other opportunities in future. (2)

The inclusion of biometrics becomes a way to make savings and to create sharp boundaries between deserving and undeserving hungry people. Streamlining resource management, appeasing donor anxieties, strengthening partnerships, and opening new opportunities—all of these take precedence over the foundational mission of the WFP—to feed communities in need and end hunger irrespective of their status in a database.

While biometric data are typically collected by international organizations such as the UNCHR, several accounts indicate that data were shared not only with the Kenyan government but also with the US Department of Homeland Security (DHS) (Weitzberg, 2021). As Iazzolino

(2021) highlights, while such technologies are often used under the pretense of improving access to state resources for refugees, they bear the risk of further marginalizing people who already face systemic discrimination.

The government mostly cites efficiency as the reason that NIIMS should be implemented. In contrast, critics suspect that security has been one of the core motivations. After the initial rollout of the program, three Kenyan NGOs—the Nubian Rights Forum, the Kenya Human Rights Commission (KHRC), and the Kenya National Commission on Human Rights (KNCHR)—petitioned the High Court of Nairobi to halt its implementation. These organizations were concerned about the different implications of Huduma Namba. On the one hand, they raised concerns about the privacy implications for the groups they were representing and Kenyans more generally. On the other hand, they highlighted that the proposed scheme would further exclude already marginalized groups. The Nubian Rights Forum, for instance, a civil society organization representing the Nubian ethnic minority, expressed concerns that Huduma Namba would further exclude Nubians from political participation since many of them lacked the birth certificates required to obtain a Huduma Namba card (Gonzalez 2023).

The petition was successful, and the High Court of Nairobi ordered a halt to implementation "until a comprehensive regulatory framework was put in place" (Manby 2021, 6). One of the main arguments brought forward by the petitioning NGOs was the high risk of privacy violations that would enable the government to "conduct mass surveillance through searching aggregated data on individuals across linked databases and easily allow the government to profile individuals and groups" (Open Society Justice Initiative n.d.). In 2021, the court halted the program's rollout again, ordering it to be subject to a data impact assessment. Especially since it is unclear which government agencies would have access to the data under which conditions, the system might eventually disadvantage minority groups like the Somali Kenyans. If an ID card like that issued by Huduma Namba would affect the surveillance of different groups in society unequally, it might exacerbate rather than reduce existing inequalities (Garbe et al. 2023).

The program was technically supported by French information technology firm IDEMIA, formerly OT Morpho, which provided the hardware to collect data for Huduma Namba. IDEMIA had been criticized in the aftermath of Kenya's 2017 elections, for which it provided 45,000 biometric voter registration and identification kits (Statius et al. 2022). The servers to which election results were transmitted had allegedly been hacked, and the election was ultimately nullified by the Supreme Court (Passanti and Pommerolle 2022). Against this background, the KHRC and the Nubian Rights Forum, together with European NGO Data Rights, sued IDEMIA for "failing to adequately identify and address human rights risks linked to its provision of a technology" (*Plan Vigilance* 2022, 1) for Huduma Namba. Their case was an ingenious feat of transnational advocacy and strategic litigation: they appealed under the French Due Vigilance Law, which requires companies to identify adverse human rights that may result from their operations. In July 2023, the two Kenyan NGOs, Data Rights, and IDEMIA reached a settlement under this law, with the company agreeing to substantially revise its vigilance plan "to provide for stronger safeguards to avoid adverse impact of the use of its products by governments" (*Data Rights* 2023)

Uganda: From Walk-to-Work Protest to Safe Cities

The 2011 postelection walk-to-work protests radically impacted the freedoms associated with assembly in Uganda, paving the way for advanced surveillance technology for monitoring and managing restive publics. The 2011 general presidential elections had been marred by numerous cases of vote-buying and electoral violence, and it was alleged that the incumbent's electoral profligacy and vote-buying had directly contributed to consumer inflation and higher costs of living in the election's immediate aftermath. In response, a coalition of leading opposition politicians organized walk-to-work protests. Dr. Kizza Besigye, a political activist and then presidential aspirant, led the most significant and sustained public protests against high living costs. The protests rallied citizens all over the country to rise against the unprecedented levels of inflation marked by commodity price hikes that the country had not experienced since the ascendance of the current president, Yoweri Museveni, in 1986. Faced with contestation, the state responded swiftly: tens were killed and hundreds injured. As Bareebe argues in his work on military-state relations in Uganda, "when confronting anti-regime protests, the orders seem clear: shoot first and ask questions later" (2020, 146). The proliferation of FRTs in Uganda needs to be understood in the context of the government's fear of potential spillovers of citizen activism seen in the Arab Spring in the early 2010s. The deployment of FRTs is part of a long process of legal and technical work-arounds to address national security concerns, perceived or real, and the enduring fight for fundamental freedoms.

While the plans to develop a broad state surveillance apparatus had been publicly shared by president Yoweri Museveni and his cabinet since the 1980s, little was known about FRT-enhanced CCTV cameras prior to their implementation in late 2019 (*Privacy International* 2015; Mwesigwa 2019; *Center for Human Rights* et al. 2021). The relative secrecy of the project meant both a lack of information about the technology's actual impact on security and a lack of consultation related to its impact on privacy and anonymity, and assembly more broadly. In many instances, such security and surveillance plans in Uganda have often coincided and aligned with regional and global efforts, such as the war on terrorism, and ideals, such as strengthening democracy. For example, since the early 2000s various biometrics technologies have been adopted to supposedly curb electoral fraud and malpractice. Since the early 2010s, there have been massive campaigns to implement mandatory SIM card registration of citizens and residents for a range of reasons, among them stamping out crime and integrating citizen data in one central national identification database.

The president has often blamed inadequate surveillance methods and technologies for security lapses—large public protests, terrorism attacks, high-profile murders, and others. Following a shocking spate of assassinations of high-profile Ugandan citizens, including government and security officials, and Muslim clerics from the mid-2010s to the early 2020s, the president revealed that he would personally champion the procurement of CCTV cameras: he did not mention facial recognition. However, the goal, or at least the hope, was for "his" cameras to finally observe crime as it happened in real time. In 2014, Huawei donated twenty CCTV cameras to the Ugandan government (Special Correspondent 2022). In 2019, the government accelerated installation of facial recognition CCTV cameras along major highways around Kampala, the capital, and surrounding urban areas, allegedly undermining public procurement rules and regulations (Kahungu 2019). Close to 2,000 cameras were installed in Kampala in the first phase in 2019, and over 3,000 have been installed in subsequent phases, spanning two years and covering towns and cities beyond Kampala (*The Independent* 2019; Kafeero 2020).

Yet a *Wall Street Journal* (*WSJ*) investigative article published in August 2019—and subsequently republished in the *Daily Monitor*, a leading daily in Uganda—pierced the mystery surrounding the government's surveillance programs. In rich detail, the article revealed that Uganda had signed a US$200-plus million contract with Huawei for the Safe Cities program. The program would include an assortment of facial recognition CCTV cameras and other FRTs, such as face and gait and license plate recognition, centrally controlled at monitoring and command centers. The article further revealed that the Ugandan government had not only entered a contract with Huawei for the Smart Cities program but had also drawn on the expertise of Huawei's technicians for other tasks. These included infiltrating and cracking encrypted communication channels of fast-rising politicians, activists, and bloggers in anticipation of opposition-party rallies and assemblies. Although a government spokesperson confirmed to the *WSJ* that Uganda was working with Huawei technicians to "bolster national security," he denied that the government was targeting opposition politicians and stated that he could not reveal any specifics of the government's national security operations. The Uganda Police Force (UPF) response to the article was extremely lacking (*Uganda Police Force* 2019). In trying to refute claims of spying on the opposition, the police accused the *WSJ* of telling the story through the eyes of Robert Kyagulanyi, popularly known as Bobi Wine, an Afro-ragga star turned Museveni's most serious political contender in recent time. While the police did not mention Bobi Wine by name, their statement was equivocal, suggesting media bias: Why "would [*WSJ* and *The Daily Monitor*] single out one leader, yet there are many other players in the political arena of Uganda including other politicians?" The tone seemed to suggest that there were more fish entrapped in the police net whose stories mattered too, and that the attention on Mr. Wine was "being used to sabotage and smear the UPF." As if that were not enough, they added that the article had malicious intent, arguing that "we believe [it's] pure sabotage and a trade war against Huawei and its clients" (2019).

Uganda is one of the many countries all over the world that have enrolled in Huawei's program to manage national security and social cohesion in public spaces. Although the uptake and efficiency of the company's Safe Cities program across the Global South was already facing public scrutiny, as we previously mentioned in the case of Kenya, little was publicly known about Uganda's engagement with Huawei and other technology vendors in the facial recognition arena. There is also evidence of selective and partisan use of the technology in Uganda. In 2020, images from the CCTV surveillance system were used by the police to identify and arrest 836 persons suspected to have taken part in antigovernment protests (Kafeero 2020). That same year, there were reports that state forces killed at least 45 protestors and bystanders in a clamp-down against rallies sympathetic to Bobi Wine in central and northwestern Uganda (Ntale et al. 2020). While FRT cameras had been installed in the areas of Kampala where the police had shot and killed multiple protestors and bystanders, the police claimed that there was no "documented" evidence because the cameras were dysfunctional that day; yet, for better or worse, citizen journalists had captured important mobile phone footage that the BBC used to reconstruct scenes of state violence (Burke 2021).

Members of civil society and sections of the public have raised concerns about FRTs in Uganda and elsewhere in the region. This culture of alarm bell ringing is not new, as these groups had previously confronted reactive government directives and rollout of technologies meant to combat threats, perceived or real. From civil society's perspective, these technologies are often assembled in an architecture of violence and intimidation and the expedited adoption of "mass data sweep[ing]" technologies as "substitutes for trust"—a combination that Nanjala Nyabola has argued often results in chaos (Pilling 2019). CIPESA, for instance, is a Ugandan ICT policy and advocacy group that works across East and Southern Africa. It plays a role in coordinating efforts across borders and routinely highlights the importance of strong data protection laws and the human rights implications of digital technologies. Unwanted Witness, a Kampala-based NGO, embarked on a project with the Centre for Intellectual Property and Information Technology Law at Strathmore University in Kenya. Together, the two organizations analyzed data policies and practices of a handful of key private technology companies in Kenya and Uganda. They gave all of them a zero on accountability: not one published transparency reports to answer questions about the data they collect (Unwanted Witness and Center for Intellectual Property and Information Technology Law 2022; Special Correspondent 2022). Pollicy, another Kampala-based organization, released a report on surveillance technology expansion in the context of the pandemic. It reported that the government used its cameras' surveillance network to track and identify "individuals who participated in anti-government protests during the first year of the pandemic, resulting in their arrests" (Mwanzia, Kapiyo, and Ayazika 2021, 15).

Despite some civil society engagement, popular understanding of and involvement in digital policy debates remains limited. In 2021, the Africa Freedom of Information Centre, a pan-African organization based in Kampala, published a report on people's knowledge of government procurement of FRTs in Uganda. Thirty-eight percent of the respondents said they were unaware of government procurement of facial recognition, and about 50 percent were unaware of laws and policies regulating digital technologies (*Africa Freedom of Information Centre* 2021). Who should bridge this gap and how? These are vital questions that those committed to democratizing digital policy issues must grapple with urgently.

African Digital Rights Advocacy, Against and Beyond FRTs

In this last section, we focus on emerging efforts to advocate against facial recognition in Africa. We touched on several examples in Kenya and Uganda. However, these should be understood in the broader context of the emerging "global" community of digital rights advocacy. In what follows, we relocate African resistance to FRTs in this broader context and highlight its key challenges and possible futures.

The African digital rights community has joined many global coalition campaigns while leading domestic and regional campaigns related to facial recognition and biometric technologies. By "African digital rights community," we mean the individuals, organizations, coalitions, and campaigns defending digital rights in various African contexts. This is a community in the making. However, it already has some key institutional anchors: CIPESA, Unwanted Witness, and Pollicy in Uganda; Paradigm Initiative in Nigeria; KICTANet in Kenya; the Media Institute of Southern Africa; Research ICT Africa in South Africa; the African Digital Rights Network; the annual Forum on Internet Freedom in Africa; the Africa Digital Rights hub in Accra; and the African Civil Society on the Information Society. These are only a few of the key actors.

These groups are part of what is routinely called the global digital rights community, which is shorthand for a tapestry of organizations, movements, and individuals who advocate for digital rights from global, transnational, cross-national, domestic, and local perspectives. It encompasses strictly digital rights–focused organizations—like Privacy International, Access Now, S.T.O.P., Big Brother Watch, and AlgorithmWatch—as well as more broad-based civil society organizations that increasingly attend to the harms that digital technologies pose to human rights—such as Human

Rights Watch and Amnesty International. A hallmark of this community is its ability to foster coalitions across civil society fields and geographies. With regard to facial recognition, for instance, Access Now, Amnesty International, European Digital Rights, Human Rights Watch, and Internet Freedom Foundation Instituto Brasileiro de Defesa do Consumidor (IDEC) penned an open letter in 2021 opposing rights-abusing biometric surveillance at every level, "from city council to the U.N." ("*Access Now* 2021). Over 200 civil society organizations from across the world, including a few African countries, signed the letter, which was translated into seventeen languages, none of them African.

Like the rest of the global digital rights community, the African community assembles in physical spaces—at conferences, workshops, hackathons, and other events—and digital spaces—from listservs and Telegram groups to X (formerly Twitter) conversations. It is not uncommon to hear these activists describe themselves as born on the Internet or children of the Internet. In that sense, they represent a perfect example of what international relations scholar Nina Hall terms transnational digital advocacy organizations.

> They share common progressive values and operate in a highly connected, globalized world, where issues spill over borders. They can easily communicate across borders and share campaign material, thanks to email and social media. . . . Through this network, digital activists meet frequently in person, and exchange online, to share new technologies, skills, and tactics. They have developed deep relationships through regular summits, staff secondments, and the sharing of campaign failures and successes. (2022, 3)

In the past decade, Internet shutdowns, connectivity costs, and government censorship and surveillance have mainly dominated the agenda of African digital rights (Roberts 2021). However, FRTs and other forms of biometric data collection are gradually becoming part of their national and regional agenda. As previously discussed, the efforts of the African digital rights community have produced some results. In Kenya, they halted the implementation of Huduma Namba. They also held the biometric company IDEMIA accountable by raising its public profile and engaging in transnational strategic litigation to bring the company in front of a French court. In Morocco, civil society was involved in a 2019 moratorium on facial recognition technologies put in place by the government, though eventually lifted. Even when they may not immediately impact regulation, civil society communities play a role in public discourse. Activists like the founder of the African Digital Rights Hub in Ghana, Teki Akuetteh, or Achieng Akena, the executive director of the International Refugee Rights Initiative (IRRI) in Uganda, now routinely call for the development of comprehensive privacy policies related to biometrics (Speed 2020). Similarly, local civil society groups like the Association des utilisateurs des Tics in Senegal raised concerns about biometric driver's licenses and mandatory SIM card registration (Sarr 2019); in Sierra Leone, with regard to the integration of digital ID in election systems (*CIPESA* 2022). By raising concerns and piercing the hype that underpins government and company narratives about FRTs, these groups contribute to developing what scholar Simone Browne calls "critical biometric consciousness" (2010, 131).

On the one hand, the growing presence of FRTs and biometrics on the agenda of African digital rights advocates is a response to governments, including many authoritarian and repressive ones, embracing these technologies. On the other hand, it constitutes a discursive alignment of the African digital rights community with the advocacy agenda of the global digital rights community. In recent years, FRTs have become a central point of global tech advocacy, largely stemming from the US and the groundbreaking research and advocacy of people such as Joy Buolamwini, Timnit Gebru, and Tawana Petty. From protests and coalition campaigns to regulatory hearings, FRTs have become an object of assembly around the globe, with technologists, community members, and civil society organizations coming together to challenge their largely unaccountable and unregulated deployment.

The efforts of the global digital rights community have led to noticeable product changes and regulatory interventions. For example, in 2020 the Court of Appeal in the UK ruled that the use of facial recognition by the police and other forces "breached privacy rights and broke equalities law" (Sabbagh 2020). In the US, about two dozen jurisdictions banned FRTs between 2019 and 2021 (*Fight for the Future*, n.d.), although recent news reports show that some are rolling back the restrictions following "surges in crime" (Dave 2022). In 2022, following advocacy and public pressure, Meta (formerly Facebook) discontinued its decade-old facial recognition tool. That same year, civil society efforts in Brazil led to São Paulo metro to halt its use of FRTs (Article 19 2022, 19). These efforts herald pathways for successful advocacy and regulatory interventions to curb FRT deployment.

Still, the discursive alignment between African and primarily Euro-American advocacy campaigns highlights a key challenge ahead for the African digital rights community: its institutional reliance on Euro-American funders, be they states, corporations, or foundations. Through grants, fellowships, donations, partnerships, or paid travel, North American and European funders play an instrumental role in shaping and institutionalizing the African digital rights community. For instance, the Forum on Internet Freedom in Africa (FIFAfrica)—a flagship yearly event hosted by CIPESA—is sponsored by, among others, the Ford Foundation, ICNL, Internews, and Meta. Much of the African digital rights debates take place in English and, to a lesser extent, French. CIPESA, for its part, was established with funding from the UK's Department for International Development. This applies to most of the organizations previously mentioned, with tech companies Google, Meta, and Microsoft routinely implicated.

This is also true for the "global" digital rights community at large. For all its aspirations to engage with digital rights worldwide, the community remains structured on an institutional scaffolding shaped by Euro-American organizational constraints and funding. Grover, for instance, analyzed the programming of the annual flagship RightsCon conference—arguably the most prominent event for the global digital rights community. Notably, he found that 37% of the organizations hosting sessions at the conference were US-based and that 49% of the organizations claiming a global scope were, in fact, nonprofits registered in the US (2022, 21).

This dependency mirrors older patterns of North–South inequalities that shaped the institutionalization of a certain idea of civil society in the Global South (Wickramasinghe 2005); one that over-determined its agenda, forms of advocacy, and organizational shape. A particular risk is that these organizations, much like companies in a competitive market, become specialized in digital advocacy issues en vogue with Euro-American funders and eventually disconnected from local communities.

Dependency, however, does not necessarily mean path dependency, and it would be reductive to see this as the sole path forward for African digital rights advocacy. For example, while many campaigns against Internet shutdowns were uplifted by the more institutional networks of global digital rights advocacy, they largely emerged from grassroots advocacy and social protests with firmly local roots (Rydzak, Karanja, and Opiyo 2020). Another relevant example is the #datamustfall movement. This grassroots, citizen-led campaign emerged in South Africa to oppose the exorbitant costs of mobile Internet connectivity (Moyo and Munoriyarwa 2021) and then spilled over into neighboring countries. The movement relied not only on transnational digital activism but also on more traditional and local forms of protest, such as demonstrations and sit-ins in front of the offices and stores of telecom operators. As digital technologies become ever more entangled with basic needs for food, work, transportation, health, and public services, so do the chances that digital rights issues will become more palpable and less esoteric to everyday people. Part of the challenge ahead for digital rights advocacy across Africa and elsewhere will be navigating the tensions between inward- and outward-looking activities, and in managing to make digital policy issues much less niche and much more urgently relevant to local communities and their specific sociopolitical contexts and cultures.

Conclusion

This chapter shed light on AI through the spyglass of African politics. Against dominant policy and scholarly discourse that sees African contexts needing to catch up technologically, we see these as testing grounds for the global, unregulated deployment of FRTs which carry important lessons for the future of AI and assembly. The profound risks that FRTs pose for assembly become particularly clear when considering, for instance, their expansion in Uganda for political repression and surveillance of protesters. Look at how bimodal voter accreditation systems are implemented in dozens of African countries, and you will see the ongoing privatization of public goods and new layers of technologies paving the way for private foreign actors to be involved in matters of national and public governance. The complex web of transnational actors involved in projects like digital ID in Kenya means that scholars, activists, and regulators should assume "global" to be a core feature for analysis, regulation, and accountability. Civil society, for its part, is on all sides of these issues, from humanitarians embracing FRTs to global digital rights activists calling for their regulation. The latter may be facing an uphill battle—from the speed and scale of FRT deployment to global digital rights advocacy's own institutionalization and legitimacy challenges. Yet their fight is worth it, for their existing efforts pave the way toward a world where people can come together freely.

Notes

1. In our analysis, we focus on the deployment of FRT in public rather than private spaces. Therefore, we do not include the face unlock features found on smartphones (such as Apple's Face ID)—a globally endemic use of facial recognition that is now taken for granted around the world. Similarly, our mapping does not account for the use of facial recognition technologies by worldwide social media companies. Its added value is to highlight region-specific deployment of FRT.

References

Aéronautique.ma. 2021. "Sénégal: L'Aéroport international Blaise Diagne se met à la reconnaissance faciale." *Portail marocain de l'aéronautique et du Spatial,* June 22, 2021. https://www.aeronautique.ma/Senegal-L-Aeroport-international-Blaise-Diagne-se-met-a-la-reconnaissance-faciale_a4843.html.

Africa Freedom of Information Centre. 2021. "Sunlight in Digital Technology: What Does the Public Know about Transparency and Safeguards in the Procurement and Deployment of Digital Technology Systems in Africa?" November 15, 2021. https://www.africafoicentre.org/what-does-the-public-know-about-transparency-and-safeguards-in-the-procurement-deployment-of-digital-technology-systems-in-africa/.

Al Jazeera. 2022. "In Cameroon, Refugees Get a New Lease of Life with Digital IDs." August 29, 2022. https://www.aljazeera.com/news/2022/8/29/in-cameroon-refugees-get-a-new-lease-of-life-with-digital-ids.

Al-Bulushi, Samar. 2021. "Citizen-Suspect: Navigating Surveillance and Policing in Urban Kenya." *American Anthropologist* 123 (4): 819–832.

Anaba, Daniel. 2020. "18 CSOs Reject Proposals for New Voters' Register." *Citinewsroom—Comprehensive News in Ghana* (blog), January 16, 2020. https://citinewsroom.com/2020/01/18-csos-reject-proposals-for-new-voters-register/.

Anaesoronye, Modestus. 2022. "Expert Proffers Solution to Managing Security Threats to Residential Estates, Offices." *Businessday NG*, November 18, 2022. https://businessday.ng/news/article/expert-proffers-solution-to-managing-security-threats-to-residential-estates-offices/.

Andrejevic, Mark, and Zala Volcic. 2021. "'Smart' Cameras and the Operational Enclosure." *Television & New Media* 22 (4): 343–359. https://doi.org/10.1177/1527476419890456.

Arnett, Chaz. 2023. "Black Lives Monitored." *UCLA Law Review* 69: 1384. https://www.uclalawreview.org/black-lives-monitored/.

Article 19. 2022. "Brazil: Civil Society Blocks Facial Recognition Tech on São Paulo Metro." May 9, 2022. https://www.article19.org/resources/brazil-civil-society-blocks-facial-recognition-tech-on-sao-paulo-metro/.

Awal, Mohammed. 2022. "NSS Uncovers and Blocks GH₵112M Payment to 'Ghosts' Names." *The Business & Financial Times* (blog), February 3, 2022. https://thebftonline.com/2022/02/03/nss-uncovers-and-block-gh₵112m-payment-to-ghosts-names/.

Access Now (blog). 2021. "Ban Biometric Surveillance." December 21, 2021. https://www.accessnow.org/campaign/ban-biometric-surveillance/.

Bareebe, Gerald. 2020. "An Army with a State or a State with an Army? The Military and Post-Conflict Governance in Uganda and Rwanda." Ph.D. thesis. University of Toronto. https://www.proquest.com/docview/2425008987/abstract/734FE050EFC141A7PQ/1.

Basimanyane, Dorcas, and Dumisani Gandhi. 2019. "Striking a Balance Between CCTV Surveillance and the Digital Right to Privacy in South Africa." *APCOF*, December 2019. https://apcof.org/wp-content/uploads/027-cctvsurveillanceanddigital-dorcasbasimanyanedumisanigandhi-1.pdf.

Benin Club 1931. 2023. About Benin Club. https://www.beninclub1931.com/about.

Bowker, Geoffrey, and Susain Leigh Star. 2000. *Sorting Things Out. Classification and its Consequences.* Cambridge, MA: MIT Press.

Browne, Simone. 2010. "Digital Epidermalization: Race, Identity and Biometrics." *Critical Sociology* 36 (1): 131–150.

Burke, Jason. 2021. "Uganda Police Drive-By Killings Revealed Using Mobile Phone Footage." *The Guardian*, May 30, 2021. https://www.theguardian.com/world/2021/may/31/uganda-police-killings-reconstructed-using-mobile-phone-footage.

Burt, Chris. 2019. "NEC Facial Recognition Border Tech for Kenya as Airport Biometrics Rollouts Continue." *Biometric Update*, October 7, 2019. https://www.biometricupdate.com/201910/nec-facial-recognition-border-tech-for-kenya-as-airport-biometrics-rollouts-continue.

Center for Human Rights and Global Justice. 2021. "'Chased Away and Left to Die: How a National Security Approach to Uganda's National Digital ID Has Led to Wholesale Exclusion of Women and Older Persons," June 8, 2021. https://chrgj.org/wp-content/uploads/2021/06/CHRGJ-Report-Chased-Away-and-Left-to-Die.pdf.

Chang, Charles, and Melanie Manion. 2021. "Political Self-Censorship in Authoritarian States: The Spatial-Temporal Dimension of Trouble." *Comparative Political Studies* 54 (8): 1362–1392.

CIPESA. 2022. "State of Internet Freedom in Africa 2022: The Rise of Biometric Surveillance," September 2022. https://cipesa.org/wp-content/files/reports/State_of_Internet_Freedom_in_Africa_2022.pdf.

Cyphers, Bennett, Adam Schwartz, and Nathan Sheard. 2021. "Face Recognition Isn't Just Face Identification and Verification: It's Also Photo Clustering, Race Analysis, Real-Time Tracking, and More." *Electronic Frontier Foundation*, October 7, 2021. https://www.eff.org/deeplinks/2021/10/face-recognition-isnt-just-face-identification-and-verification.

Data Rights. 2023. "NGOs and IDEMIA Agree to Vigilance Plan Improvements in Settlement over Kenyan Digital ID Human Rights Challenge," July 24, 2023. https://datarights.ngo/news/2023-07-24-ngos-and-idemia-agree-to-vigilance-plan-improvements/.

Dave, Paresh. 2022. "Focus: U.S. Cities Are Backing Off Banning Facial Recognition as Crime Rises." *Reuters*, May 12, 2022. https://www.reuters.com/world/us/us-cities-are-backing-off-banning-facial-recognition-crime-rises-2022-05-12/.

Eck, Kristine, Sophia Hatz, Charles Crabtree, and Atsushi Tago. 2021. "Evade and Deceive? Citizen Responses to Surveillance." *The Journal of Politics* 83 (4): 1545–1558.

The Herald (blog). 2020. "Access Bank Set to Launch Face Recognition Payment System in Nigeria," March 4, 2020. https://www.herald.ng/access-bank-set-to-launch-face-recognition-payment-system-in-nigeria/.

Fight for the Future. n.d. "Ban Facial Recognition," accessed October 26, 2023. https://www.banfacialrecognition.com/.

Freedom House. 2015. "Kenya: Court Declares NGOs Did No Wrong," November 11, 2015. https://freedomhouse.org/article/kenya-court-declares-ngos-did-no-wrong.

Gallagher, Ryan. 2019. "Export Laws: China Is Selling on Surveillance Technology to the Rest of the World." *Index on Censorship* 48 (3): 35–37.

Garbe, Lisa, Nina McMurry, Alexandra Scacco, and Kelly Zhang. 2023. "Who Wants to Be Legible? Digitalization and Intergroup Inequality in Kenya." WZB Discussion Paper SP VII 2023-101. Wissenschaftszentrum Berlin für Sozialforschung (WZB). https://www.econstor.eu/handle/10419/274672.

GhanaWeb. 2020. "EC Spends GH¢151m on Biometric Devices," November 9, 2020. https://www.ghanaweb.com/GhanaHomePage/NewsArchive/EC-spends-GH-151m-on-biometric-devices-1103995.

Gohdes, Anita R. 2020. "Repression Technology: Internet Accessibility and State Violence." *American Journal of Political Science* 64 (3): 488–503.

Gonzalez, Bianca. 2023. "Nubian Rights Forum Urges Equitable Rollout to Kenya's UPI System." *Biometric Update*, June 13, 2023. https://www.biometricupdate.com/202306/nubian-rights-forum-urges-equitable-rollout-to-kenyas-upi-system.

Grover, Rohan. 2022. "The Geopolitics of Digital Rights Activism: Evaluating Civil Society's Role in the Promises of Multistakeholder Internet Governance." *Telecommunications Policy* 46 (10): 102437.

Gwagwa, Arthur, and Lisa Garbe. 2018. "Exporting Repression? China's Artificial Intelligence Push into Africa." *Council on Foreign Relations* (blog), December 17, 2018. https://www.cfr.org/blog/exporting-repression-chinas-artificial-intelligence-push-africa.

Haberkorn, Axel. 2023. "Keeping UNHCR's Biometrics System Up To Date." *UNHCR* (blog), August 2, 2023. https://www.unhcr.org/blogs/keeping-unhcrs-biometrics-system-up-to-date/.

Hall, Nina. 2022. *Transnational Advocacy in the Digital Era: Think Global, Act Local*. Oxford, UK: Oxford University Press.

Hansen, Stig Jarle, Stian Lid, and Clifford Collins Omandi Okwany. 2019. "Countering Violent Extremism in Somalia and Kenya: Actors and Approaches." *OsloMet*, April 2019. https://www.cve-kenya.org/media/library/oslomet.pdf.

Hao, Karen, and Heidi Swart. 2022. "South Africa's Private Surveillance Machine Is Fueling a Digital Apartheid." *MIT Technology Review*, April 19, 2022. https://www.technologyreview.com/2022/04/19/1049996/south-africa -ai-surveillance-digital-apartheid/.

Harwell, Drew. 2022. "Scoop: I Got Clearview AI's Big Pitch to Investors." *Twitter.* February 16, 2022. https://twitter.com/drewharwell/status/1494036 439314620419.

Hashemi, Mahdi, and Margeret Hall. 2020. "Retracted Article: Criminal Tendency Detection from Facial Images and the Gender Bias Effect." *Journal of Big Data* 7 (1): 2.

Hawkins, Amy. 2024. "Beijing's Big Brother Tech Needs African Faces." *Foreign Policy* (blog), July 24, 2024. https://foreignpolicy.com/2018/07/24/beijings -big-brother-tech-needs-african-faces/.

Hersey, Frank. 2019. "Biometrics and Digital ID Across Africa This Week: Biometric Influencers in Tanzania, a 'Techno-Political Nightmare' in Nigeria." *Biometric Update*, December 15, 2019. https://www.biometricupdate .com/201912/biometrics-and-digital-id-across-africa-this-week-biometric -influencers-in-tanzania-a-techno-political-nightmare-in-nigeria.

Hillman, Jonathan E, and Maesea McCalpin. 2019. "Watching Huawei's 'Safe Cities.'" *Center for Strategic and International Studies*, November. https://csis-website-prod.s3.amazonaws.com/s3fs-public/publication/ 191030_HillmanMcCalpin_HuaweiSafeCity_layout_v4.pdf.

Iazzolino, Gianluca. 2021. "Infrastructure of Compassionate Repression: Making Sense of Biometrics in Kakuma Refugee Camp." *Information Technology for Development* 27 (1): 111–128.

Itodo, Samson. 2022. "Inspiring Confidence in BVAS and Electronic Transmission of Election Results: Seven Urgent Actions for INEC." *Premium Times NG* (blog), October 20, 2022. https://www.premiumtimesng.com/ opinion/560517-inspiring-confidence-in-bvas-and-electronic-transmission -of-election-results-seven-urgent-actions-for-inec-by-samson-itodo .html?tztc=1.

Jarrahi, Javad. 2020. "Zetes Launches Panasonic Facial Recognition at Cape Verde Airport." *Biometric Update*, December 22, 2020. https://www .biometricupdate.com/202012/zetes-launches-panasonic-facial -recognition-at-cape-verde-airport.

Jili, Bulelani. 2022a. "Africa: Regulate Surveillance Technologies and Personal Data." *Nature* 607 (7919): 445–448.

———. 2022b. "The Rise of Chinese Surveillance Technology in Africa (Part 1 of 6)." *EPIC—Electronic Privacy Information Center* (blog), May 31, 2022. https:// epic.org/the-rise-of-chinese-surveillance-technology-in-africa/.

Kafeero, Stephen. 2020. "Uganda Is Using Huawei's Facial Recognition Tech to Crack Down on Dissent after Protests." *Quartz*, November 27, 2020. https://qz.com/africa/1938976/uganda-uses-chinas-huawei-facial-recognition-to-snare-protesters.

Kahungu, Misairi Thembo. 2019. "Uganda: MPs Okay Shs386b Loan for City Spy Cameras." *The Monitor*, April 26, 2019. https://allafrica.com/stories/201904260210.html.

Kapiyo, Victor, and Grace Githaiga. 2014. "Kenya: Is Surveillance a Panacea to Kenya's Security Threats?" *Global Information Society Watch*. https://www.internetrights.info/sites/default/files/is_surveillance_a_panacea_to_kenyas_security_threats.pdf.

Kerr, Millie. 2015. "Lion Facial Recognition Debuts in Africa." *Scientific American*, July 7, 2021. https://doi.org/10.1038/scientificamerican0715-21.

Ketti, Souleiman. 2022. "Après la CINE, le Français Idemia pour développer la reconnaissance faciale à l'aéroport Rabat-Salé." *Le Desk*, December 28, 2022. http://mobile.ledesk.ma/enoff/apres-la-cine-le-francais-idemia-pour-developper-la-reconnaissance-faciale-a-laeroport-rabat-sale/.

Kimathi, Sharon. 2020. "Nigerian Fintech Start-Up Aella Raises $10m." *Fintech Futures* (blog), February 11, 2020. https://www.fintechfutures.com/2020/02/nigerian-fintech-start-up-aella-raises-10m/.

Kosinski, Michal. 2021. "Facial Recognition Technology Can Expose Political Orientation from Naturalistic Facial Images." *Scientific Reports* 11 (1): 100.

Lu, Miao, and Jack Linchuan Qiu. 2022. "Empowerment or Warfare? Dark Skin, AI Camera, and Transsion's Patent Narratives." *Information, Communication and Society* 25 (6): 768–784.

Macdonald, Ayang. 2023. "Amid Criticism, Namibian Official Explains Why Biometrics Is Required for SIM Registration." *Biometric Update* (blog), February 14, 2023. https://www.biometricupdate.com/202302/amid-criticism-namibian-official-explains-why-biometrics-is-required-for-sim-registration.

Mamdani, Mahmood. 1996. "Indirect Rule, Civil Society, and Ethnicity: The African Dilemma." *Social Justice* 23 (1/2): 145–150.

Manby, Bronwen. 2021. "The Sustainable Development Goals and 'Legal Identity for All': 'First, Do No Harm.'" *World Development* 139 (March): 105343.

McKenna, Sioux. 2022. "Neoliberalism's Conditioning Effects on the University and the Example of Proctoring during COVID-19 and Since." *Journal of Critical Realism* 21 (5): 502–515.

Huduma Namba (blog). n.d. "Huduma Namba." Accessed October 25, 2023. https://www.hudumanamba.go.ke/background/.

Mogire, Edward, and Kennedy Mkutu Agade. 2011. "Counter-Terrorism in Kenya." *Journal of Contemporary African Studies* 29 (4): 473–491.

Moyo, Dumisani, and Allen Munoriyarwa. 2021. "'Data Must Fall': Mobile Data Pricing, Regulatory Paralysis and Citizen Action in South Africa." *Information, Communication & Society* 24 (3): 365–380.

Mudongo, Oarabile. 2021. "Africa's Expansion of AI Surveillance—Regional Gaps and Key Trends." *Research ICT Africa*, January 2021. https://researchictafrica.net/publication/africas-expansion-of-ai-surveillance-regional-gaps-and-key-trends/.

Mwanzia, Sigi Waigumo, Victor Kapiyo, and Phillip Ayazika. 2021. "Unseen Eyes, Unheard Stories: Surveillance, Data Protection, and Freedom of Expression in Kenya and Uganda during COVID-19." *Article 19*, April 2021. https://www.article19.org/wp-content/uploads/2021/04/ADRF-Surveillance-Report-1.pdf.

Mwesigwa, Daniel. 2019. "'Cameras, Mobiles, Radios—Action!': Old Surveillance Tools in New Robes in Uganda." In *Artificial Intelligence: Human Rights, Social Justice and Development*, edited by Alan Finlay, 232–236. Global Information Society Watch. https://giswatch.org/sites/default/files/gisw2019_web_uganda.pdf.

National Daily Newspaper (blog). 2021. "UNILAG Gets 1000 CCTV Cameras." October 14, 2021. https://nationaldailyng.com/unilag-gets-1000-cctv-cameras/.

Isaac Olamikan. 2021. "Obaseki Pledges More Projects to Develop New Areas, Towns in Edo." *Nigerian News Direct* (blog), November 25, 2021. https://nigeriannewsdirect.com/obaseki-pledges-more-projects-to-develop-new-areas-towns-in-edo-by-isaac-olamikan/.

Nigerian News Net. 2023. "Nigeria's First Deep Seaport Opens for Operation." January 24, 2023. https://www.nigeriannews.net/news/273424055/nigerias-first-deep-seaport-opens-for-operation.

Ntale, Samson, David McKenzie, Brent Swails, and Ivana Kottasová. 2020. "At Least 45 People Have Been Killed During Uganda Protests." *CNN*, November 23, 2020. https://www.cnn.com/2020/11/23/africa/ugandan-protest-death-toll-intl/index.html.

Nyabola, Nanjala. 2018. *Digital Democracy, Analogue Politics: How the Internet Era Is Transforming Politics in Kenya*. London: Bloomsbury.

Open Society Justice Initiative. n.d. "Nubian Rights Forum et al. v. the Honourable Attorney General of Kenya et al. ('NIIMS Case')," accessed October 25, 2023. https://www.justiceinitiative.org/litigation/nubian-rights-forum-et-al-v-the-honourable-attorney-general-of-kenya-et-al-niims-case.

Passanti, Cecilia, and Marie-Emmanuelle Pommerolle. 2022. "The (Un)Making of Electoral Transparency Through Technology: The 2017 Kenyan Presidential Election Controversy." *Social Studies of Science* 52 (6): 928–953. https://doi.org/10.1177/03063127221124007.

Pilling, David. 2019. "The Fight to Control Africa's Digital Revolution." *Financial Times*, June 20, 2019. https://www.ft.com/content/24b8b7b2-9272-11e9 -aea1-2b1d33ac3271.

Plan Vigilance. 2022. "IDEMIA in Kenya." Accessed August 27, 2024. https:// plan-vigilance.org/wp-content/uploads/2022/12/PDF-Idemia-EN.pdf.

Privacy International. 2014. "The Right to Privacy in Kenya," accessed September 4, 2024. https://privacyinternational.org/sites/default/files/2017-12/ UPR%20Kenya.pdf.

———. 2015. "For God and My President: State Surveillance In Uganda," October 15, 2015. http://privacyinternational.org/report/1019/god-and-my -president-state-surveillance-uganda.

Purshouse, Joe, and Liz Campbell. 2022. "Automated Facial Recognition and Policing: A Bridge Too Far?" *Legal Studies* 42 (2): 209–227.

Rappeport, Alan. 2022. "I.R.S. Will Allow Taxpayers to Forgo Facial Recognition Amid Blowback." *The New York Times*, February 21, 2022. https://www .nytimes.com/2022/02/21/us/politics/irs-facial-recognition.html.

Roberts, Tony. 2021. "Repressive Governments Play Whack-a-Mole with Africans' Digital Rights." *openDemocracy*, March 30, 2021. https:// www.opendemocracy.net/en/digitaliberties/repressive-governments -play-whack-a-mole-with-africans-digital-rights/.

Roberts, Tony, Abrar Mohamed Ali, Mohamed Farahat, Ridwan Oloyede, and Grace Mutung'u. 2021. "Surveillance Law in Africa: A Review of Six Countries." *Institute of Development Studies*, accessed September 8, 2024. https:// doi.org/10.19088/IDS.2021.059.

Roberts, Tony, and Ridwan Oloyede. 2022. "Why Millions of Africans Are Right to Resist SIM Card Registration." *Thomson Reuters Foundation News* (blog). May 3, 2022. https://news.trust.org/item/20220503084813-z74ni/.

Rydzak, Jan, Moses Karanja, and Nicholas Opiyo. 2020. "Internet Shutdowns in Africa—Dissent Does Not Die in Darkness: Network Shutdowns and Collective Action in African Countries." *International Journal of Communication* 14: 24.

Sabbagh, Dan. 2020. "South Wales Police Lose Landmark Facial Recognition Case." *The Guardian*, August 11, 2020. https://www.theguardian .com/technology/2020/aug/11/south-wales-police-lose-landmark-facial recognition-case.

Salau, Seyi John. 2021. "Digital Space Launches Digikolo to Deepen Financial Inclusion." *Businessday NG* (blog), December 15, 2021. https:// businessday.ng/technology/article/digital-space-launches-digikolo -to-deepen-financial-inclusion/.

Sarr, Antoine. 2019. "Asutic: 'Le permis de conduire biométrique est dangereux et illégal. '" *Senego:* Actualité au Sénégal, December 3, 2019.

https://senego.com/asutic-le-permis-de-conduire-biometrique-est
-dangereux-et-illegal_1010014.html.

Special Correspondent. 2022. "Across East Africa, Big Brother Is Watching Your Every Move." *Nation*, December 8, 2022. https://nation.africa/africa/news/across-east-africa-big-brother-is-watching-your-every-move-4047340.

Speed, Madeleine. 2020. "Activists Sound Alarm over African Biometric ID Projects." *Al Jazeera*, December 10, 2020. https://www.aljazeera.com/economy/2020/12/10/activists-sound-alarm-over-african-biometric-id-projects.

Stark, Luke, and Jevan Hutson. 2023. "Physiognomic Artificial Intelligence." *Fordham Intellectual Property, Media & Entertainment Law Journal* 32 (4). https://doi.org/10.2139/ssrn.3927300.

Statius, Tom, John-Allan Namu, Daniel Howden, and Lionel Faull. 2022. "Biometrics in Africa's Elections." *Lighthouse Reports* (blog), May 2022. https://www.lighthousereports.com/investigation/biometrics-and-the-enslavement-of-african-elections/.

Sumaita, Inma. 2022. "Losing Dignity: Eroding Privacy Rights of Immigrants in Technology-Based Immigration Enforcement." *The University of Cincinnati Intellectual Property and Computer Law Journal* 6 (2).

The Independent (blog). 2019. "More than 1900 CCTV Cameras Installed in Kampala." April 15, 2019. https://www.independent.co.ug/more-than-1900-cctv-cameras-installed-in-kampala/.

Toesland, Finbarr. 2021. "African Countries Embracing Biometrics, Digital IDs." *Africa Renewal*, February 2, 2021. https://www.un.org/africarenewal/magazine/february-2021/african-countries-embracing-biometrics-digital-ids.

Truscott, Ryan. 2021. "French Scientists in Zimbabwe Use Facial Recognition Technology to ID Giraffes." *RFI*, May 12, 2021. https://www.rfi.fr/en/africa/20210512-french-scientists-in-zimbabwe-use-facial-recognition-technology-to-id-giraffes.

Uganda Police Force. 2019. "Statement on Alleged Spying by Huawei Https://T.Co/SUgUApGy9n." *Twitter*, August 20, 2019. https://twitter.com/PoliceUg/status/1163800900160372736.

Unwanted Witness and *Center for Intellectual Property and Information Technology Law*. 2022. "Privacy Scorecard Report: Kenya & Uganda." November 2022.   https://www.unwantedwitness.org/download/Privacy-Scorecard-Report-2022.pdf.

Wang, Yilun, and Michal Kosinski. 2018. "Deep Neural Networks Are More Accurate Than Humans at Detecting Sexual Orientation from Facial Images." *Journal of Personality and Social Psychology* 114 (2): 246–257.

Weitzberg, Keren. 2021. "Biometrics and Counter-Terrorism. Case Study of Somalia." *Privacy International*, May 2021. https://privacyinternational.org/sites/default/files/2021-05/PI%20Counterterrorism%20and%20Biometrics%20Report%20Somalia%20v6.1_0.pdf.

Wickramasinghe, Nira. 2005. "The Idea of Civil Society in the South: Imaginings, Transplants, Designs." *Science & Society* 69 (3): 458–486.

Willems, W. 2012. "Interrogating Public Sphere and Popular Culture as Theoretical Concepts on Their Value in African Studies." *Africa Development* 37 (1): 11–26.

World Food Programme. n.d. "WFP Innovative Food Assistance Instruments—The Biometrics Project, Kenya." Accessed September 9, 2024. https://documents.wfp.org/stellent/groups/public/documents/resources/wfp271054.pdf.

Xu, Xu. 2021. "To Repress or to Co-Opt? Authoritarian Control in the Age of Digital Surveillance." *American Journal of Political Science* 65 (2): 309–325.

Zalnieriute, Monika. 2021. "Protests and Public Space Surveillance: From Metadata Tracking to Facial Recognition Technologies.". Submission to the Thematic Report to the 50th Session of the UN Human Rights Council, July 8, 2021. https://ssrn.com/abstract=3882317.

Five

Machine-Made

Lucy Bernholz

> Technologies actually determine groups, through their clustering and typification.
>
> Linnet Taylor et al. (2017, 216)

Over the last few decades, discussions about "digital rights" and "human rights" have grown ever more interconnected. At the same time, academic and policy debates about the rights of robots or the oversight of algorithmic decision-making tools have increased in importance. This chapter looks at the intersection of these issues in the context of algorithms and data processing systems that are used to cluster, categorize, and sort people, resulting in new, "machine-made" associations and assemblies. These machine-made or data-driven groups are then used as the basis for predicting the future behavior of any individual in or like the group. Without our knowledge or recourse, these data manipulations result in each of us being assigned to invisible associations and assemblies that shape our lives in significant ways. Individuals have long fought against these coerced assemblies, using measures designed to either withdraw or complicate the data that they contribute to this system. More recently, people have been taking collective action with their digital data to counteract the effects of invisible and forced clusters. These collective actions—some of which result in new organizational forms, new technology, and new applications of law—are signals of new forms of digital civil society. In an ongoing cycle, the collection and analysis of data on individuals are leading to new incursions on civil and human rights as well as new forms of organizing and resistance.

Computer Clustering and Human Rights of Association and Assembly

To understand how we are being machine-made or "coercively assembled," we need to examine how our digital data trails are used by those who have control of them. This includes commercial enterprises built on data extraction and governments using algorithmic decision-making tools or predictive algorithms. Civil society organizations that collect data also fit into the supply chain of data driving the digital economy. Actions in all three sectors are challenging long-standing definitions of assembly and association.

In building systems to collect, store, and analyze large, digitized data sets, computer scientists rely on clustering data using an array of algorithms (Xu and Tian 2015). This process is key to all further steps in machine learning. Clustering algorithms have been designed for different purposes and different types of data set, but they all begin by developing mathematical representations of similarity and difference (difference is usually referred to as dissimilarity). In some cases, an algorithm may determine how far certain points are from a mathematically determined center point in a data set; in other cases, the focus is identifying hierarchical relationships between data points. There are many others, including those based on "fuzzy theory" (Xu and Tian 2015). Regardless of algorithmic approach, the underlying process is one of determining clusters of data through mathematical analysis, checking the validity of the clustering using more math, and then using the resulting clusters for any number of purposes. These clusters lay at the root of many of the digital decisions that shape a person's online experience—including the content shown to her, job opportunities she is presented if she is looking for work; potential love interests on dating apps; loan rates; school assignments; or qualification for welfare, insurance, or disability support (Eubanks 2018; O'Neil 2016).

When we replace the word "data point" in the paragraph above with "people," we begin to see this process with new eyes. Our digital tools assign us to different groups of people through ongoing processes of pattern recognition. These processes act at lightning speed, are based on relationships that matter mathematically (but perhaps in no other way), include information on other people about whom we know nothing, and may use or even prioritize characteristics of a data set that have little to do with how we see ourselves. We have no control over how we are clustered, and we may only wonder at the whole system when it serves us something we do not understand or recognize.

A Hidden and Expanding Universe of Data Collection

Public awareness of pervasive data collection has grown over the last few years. Increased media attention, scandals such as the Snowden revelations and Cambridge Analytica, privacy-focused interventions by Apple, the long, hard work done by civil society–based advocates, and implementation of the EU GDPR and the California Community Privacy Act all contribute to this increased awareness. However, these efforts lag far behind simultaneous accelerations in data collection. Companies such as Google and Meta are constantly adjusting their data collection practices under the cover of proprietary trade secrets, and so external constituents—including advocates, researchers, and policy makers—can only ever play catch-up.

Google's 2021 proposal to replace individual cookies with federated learning of cohorts (FLoC) garnered negative attention from both advertisers and privacy advocates and led the company to postpone release. As is often the case, privacy was the primary issue as described by both the company and its critics. Buried in this now familiar dynamic, however, is the question of whose privacy—individuals' or communities'? FLoC involves categorizing people, grouping them—seeing each of us in the cohorts that machine learning algorithms derive from our behaviors. Looked at another way, this approach to data collection assembles individuals into groups not of our own choosing but as determined by proprietary advertising systems. Google has since shifted to an alternative approach, called Topics (Lardinois 2022). Like FLoC, Topics is based on the company's ability to match users to their interests via web browsing history and then deliver advertising based on groups of those interests.

But an even greater shift is occurring in data collection as it moves beyond the screen and infiltrates physical spaces. This is often referred to as the Internet of Things. We have surrounded ourselves with connected devices of every sort, from toys to transit systems (Scheier 2018; deNardis 2020). We have allowed companies and governments to embed a growing number of sensors in our cars, appliances, buildings, streets, and public infrastructure. From the black boxes in our cars to customer loyalty cards, from building swipe card systems to internet-connected lightbulbs and fitness trackers, these devices capture a steady stream of data. Unlike search engines or social media, these devices and the data they collect are directly linked to physical spaces. The data are easily compiled into detailed dossiers of where we are, where we go, whom we are with, and how long we are together. In addition to these devices, many of which people actively select for themselves, is an ever expanding suite of surveillance systems used by law enforcement, including license plate readers, CCTVs, and facial recognition systems. The companies behind these technologies are not the usual suspects of data privacy concerns (e.g., Google, Meta, Amazon, Apple).

In addition to the role that internet-connected sensors play in our physical spaces (both public and private), data collection has become a fundamental part of many work and educational contexts. Students and teachers are subject to pervasive data collection via the technology used for everything from attendance to grading, testing, and proctoring. Office workers, especially those who work remotely, are often monitored by screen and keyboard software. Rideshare drivers and other gig workers are dependent on surveillant apps for work assignments; these apps also collect copious amounts of data on their users. To paraphrase Laura Denardis, the world of digital data collection has become an "on/off switch, with no off," for areas of life as disparate as worship, education, associational life, and political mobilization (2020).

We have increased the number of data collection points in our offline and online environments. As the number of companies and places where our data can be captured increases, the role of data brokers also grows. These companies purchase data from other companies and public records, categorize it, and make it (and the insights derived) available for purchase. They create data sets that draw from social media, physical location, work activities, and personal health. Composite profiles of individuals, as well as composite archetypal profiles, are at the core of what is bought and sold. Individual data points are aggregated, categorized, and clustered in ways that enable purchasers of the data sets or insights to identify likely political allies, potential product purchasers, people in the earliest stages of pregnancy or last stages of their lives, adherents of certain religions, and endless other affiliations. Assembling these composite profiles and associating individuals with them for ever more precise advertisement targeting is the core purpose of pervasive data extraction.

Situating Association and Assembly in the Digital World

In the physical world, we have some degree of choice over how we characterize ourselves and with whom we assemble or associate. Choice and individual agency are so important to these concepts that Article 20 of the Universal Declaration of Human Rights (UN General Assembly 1948), which names the right of peaceful assembly and association, has two clauses. The second clause addresses the importance of individual agency by declaring, "No one may be compelled to belong to an association." In the physical-world incarnation of this right—the incarnation in which the UDHR was written—this freedom from compulsion was intended to protect people from being forced to join certain political parties or religious groups.

The legal literature on assembly and association has struggled with developing clear distinctions between the two activities. What is the difference between assembly and association? In the past, one distinction was temporal—assemblies, it was argued, are often time-limited. A protest, a march, a petition for rights before a governing body may last hours, days, or weeks. However, assemblies are rarely understood as long term. Association, on the other hand, can be understood as an extension of the right of assembly, involving the structures and rules that guide ongoing collective gathering (or associating). In the broadest sense, assembly protects groups coming together to promote or defend collective ideas or identities, particularly in public places. Association is understood as the right to join groups, with a particular focus on labor unions (outside the US) and for those groups to exist without formal legal status (Rutzen and Zenn 2014).

Our use of digital tools for organizing groups, petitioning for change, or protesting complicates this temporal distinction. Digital protest or assembly can be both synchronous (e.g., changing your avatar on this day or taking down all websites at a moment in time) and asynchronous (e.g., petition signing, sharing digital photos from physical events). The digital trails of an assembly may live on long after a specific moment, stored on the devices of participants and servers of telecommunication companies (and others).

Similarly, the use of digital tools changes whether participation in an association or assembly requires in-person participation. It is now easy to follow, share, donate to, or otherwise support time-limited protests and ongoing associations from a great distance. As Michael Hamilton discusses in more detail in this volume, digital systems require us to redefine what it means to be present at an assembly or participate in an association, and the distinction between the two in our hybrid digital/physical world (Hamilton 2025).

Acknowledging the extent to which digital systems change the lived experience of assembly and association, we need to reconsider what it means to be compelled or coerced into participation. The clustering of people (data points) into relationships by characteristics that they do not choose is a form of compelled association. You may have nothing more in common with a serial killer than the time of day at which you check social media, but that alone may be significant enough to cluster you together.

Because pattern recognition and clustering happen behind the scenes and is repeated, with different results, by companies and governments for many reasons, it is tempting to argue that clusters are not meaningful associations. However, the very range of purposes and the extent of the opacity are precisely why we should seek to understand them better. Once individuals are part of a certain cluster, the characteristics of that cluster are applied to them. Because you and the serial killer check social media at the same time, other attributes you share may be surfaced by future algorithmic analysis. If this information is never used for any purpose, then it may simply be interesting, or perhaps upsetting, to know what you have in common. However, when the characteristics of the cluster are broken down and arrest records or parole violations or unregistered gun purchases are projected onto everyone in it, the potential for harm becomes evident.

The dynamics of algorithmic clustering shift how we must think about assembly and association. As shown in the oversimplified discussion above, commercial and government systems are constantly assigning us to groups even though we are unaware of the process and the attributes being prioritized. These clusters are used to inform decisions both big and small, from showing us certain advertisements or videos to bounding our labor choices, eligibility for services, access to financial products, and potential interactions with systems of criminal justice. Our personal ability to choose with whom we associate, when and how, for what purpose, and according to which interests are, at best, mediated by these algorithmic systems. It is also possible that our choices are overcome by clustering systems—as they simply become more fuel for the ever extractive data collection that feeds them.

How Civil Society Fits In

Governments situate their uses of digital data in terms of their obligations to protect and serve their citizens. Commercial enterprises promise consumers better service and more useful advertising while also investing in data extraction and collection as part of their strategy to dominate markets. Nonprofits and other civil society organizations must navigate a more muddled set of principles to inform their data collection practices. Given the weight the sector places on trust, some civil society organizations have been at the leading edge of developing transparent and easy-to-use consent practices, clear statements of data use that include efforts to rename "privacy policies" to "data usage policies," and as advocates for greater integrity in how organizations in the sector collect and use data. Efforts to change both public policy and organizational behavior regarding data use often involve campaigns organized in civil society.

However, just because the leaders of these calls are based in civil society, this does not mean the sector abides by them. There are still many civil society organizations that do not have in place the most basic data protections or governance rules. In addition, many are robust and highly prized sources of the data necessary to train, test, and use commercial and governmental algorithms. Grassroots community organizers, for example, are a key link in the chain of voter data. Their door-knocking efforts produce high-quality data, often on hard-to-reach households. For the community group to gain access to voter data already cleaned and collected by the national parties, it must not only pay a fee but also contribute its data to the larger set. Once the community-level data points are integrated into a data broker's data sets, they become part of the broker's product lines, which it sells to the next group of organizers (Griffin 2022). Similarly, nonprofits that rent or sell their donor lists do so via data brokers, either contributing data to these lists or buying the lists or both. Even as civil society activists decry the work of data brokers and the purchasing and use of data for clustering and other algorithmic products, they are both buyers and sellers of the resultant pooled data.

Data-Driven Associations

All data extraction mechanisms feed another system, that of data brokers, who take the next step in generating machine-assembled associations or assemblies. The technologists at a social media, search, or closed-circuit television company determine the first set of data parameters, the brokers further divide and classify, creating data sets of people's preferences or characteristics and assembling and reassembling them for sale according to their customers' preferences. These data sets of individuals, clustered by religion, age, shopping preferences, travel patterns, or entertainment habits, are off limits to the people whose information they contain. They, the "members" of the data set, have little if any modes of recourse to see the information held on them, how it is used, to whom it is sold, or what downstream purchasers do with it. Unlike members of a physical association, members of digital associations are the objects of the association, not its subjects. While we may be aware of these data practices, we have few options to avoid them. At best, we will be aware of the primary actors with access to our data such as the social media or car companies we use directly. It is unlikely that we will know anything about the downstream users of the data streams—the data brokers with whom they work or the brokers' customers. In this stream of machine assembly, we have none of the protections against coerced assembly that exist in human rights law.

Civil Society's Reactions

The result of such data practices is an obscure, intangible web of associations in which everyone who uses the internet or transits certain sensor-dense areas or shops with a reward card is captured and constantly reanalyzed. This reality requires us to expand our understanding of assembly and association in ways that build on the insights of Michael Hamilton (in chapter 2 of this volume) to account for the impact of digital technologies. As he once noted, our digital dependencies change the way we think about time and space (2020). The clustering processes of machine assembly further challenge our assumptions about agency, choice, and consent.

The depth of these changes might best be understood through the scale of reactions to them, which broadly divide into two categories: individual and collective. Individual reactions extend from concerns about privacy and include efforts to "fool" algorithmic systems by either flooding them with noisy data, confusing them with false data, or withholding as much information as possible. These are largely practices of obfuscation, studied and promoted by Finn Brunton, Helen Nissenbaum, and others (Brunton and Nissenbaum 2016).

In 2018, regulatory changes in the United States allowed internet service providers (ISPs) to aggregate and sell data from their customers, including information on websites they visit. One response to this has been the creation and free distribution of a small piece of software called Noisy, designed to mix your real data with false information, creating a data stream in which truth cannot be separated from fiction— or signal from noise (Hoid 2018). Other approaches to controlling your data stream involve limiting the data trail you leave online by using ad blockers, cookie blockers, do-not-sell lists, and do-not-track add-ons. These individual actions do not aggregate to a great deal of damage or confusion for the data collectors and sellers, but they do provide individuals with small acts of agency.

Not surprisingly, individual acts often aggregate into collective actions. One way we see this is in the growth of data hygiene or protest hygiene information and training now available. Activists and protestors have long been aware of two things: their digital trails are valuable to law enforcement and the safety of the group depends on the actions of individuals. Teaching new participants how to minimize their trail of data to keep everyone safe is a regular part of organizing protests today.

Another place we see individual actions aggregate into collective actions is in the development of algorithmic auditing. As the harms generated by algorithmic clustering and sorting became more and more apparent, the critical voices drawing attention to these harms began to organize themselves. Some of this involved the creation of civil society and/or academic watchdog groups such as AlgorithmWatch (Germany) and the Algorithmic Justice League (US). Some of it is less organization-based and more a matter of practice and identity, as can be seen in chapter 6 of this volume. A 2022 field scan found 438 individuals and 189 organizations who engage in, or whose work directly relates to, algorithmic audits (Costanza-Chock, Raj, and Buolamwini 2022). Auditing is done by both companies and external groups, and its parameters are still emerging. According to Meredith Whitaker, now CEO of Signal but previously with the AI Now Institute when the scan was done, "AI auditing isn't really a thing at this point. . . . By and large that's sort of an aspirational category." Aspirations are fine, as the purpose of these examples is to show that the world of big data and algorithms has sparked two changes: first, new forms of association and, second, familiar associational models intended to monitor the new mechanisms.

The creation of new civil society organizations to explicate and monitor the implications of big data and algorithms is a predictable response to new corporate and government practices. Civil society is often home to the first responders to harms created or amplified by the private and public sectors. But we cannot see civil society as only part of the solution; it is also very much a part of the problem. Intentionally or not, nonprofit organizations are big contributors to the data sets that serve as raw material for machine assembly. Community organizations, for example, are often frontline data collectors for politicians or political campaigns. The information they collect on individual voters or nonvoters is often fed into larger data sets maintained by political data companies, and then sold, repackaged, and resold over time and across campaigns. Providing community-generated data is often a contractual requirement for an organization gaining access to these data products (Griffin 2022). Nonprofits and other civil society organizations also participate directly in the sale of their data, selling membership information to other nonprofits or to data brokers. Thus, they both contribute to the problem of coerced-assembly and are major actors in combatting it. What civil society has not done, at any scale, is tackle conceptual, normative, and regulatory challenges in a world where the concepts of assembly and association include physical activities, physical activities with digital components, and machine-assembled, opaque, intermediated associations.

Mirror Databases and Data-Dependent Reactions

Existing organizations are trying new tactics to address the associational challenges created by big data and algorithms. Among these are legal tactics, such as strategic litigation, which includes fights over group privacy—a legal concept emerging from the bowels of big data technologies. For example, because machine assemblies are built *of* individuals, not *by* them, the individuals involved have no say in what is done with their information or how decisions about them are made. Those are issues decided by external forces—the holders of the data. Interrogatories or lawsuits about these groups must assert that the privacy of the whole group has been violated, which is a difficult task in legal systems built around individual rights. One example is *Privacy International and Others v. UK*, filed in the wake of the 2013 revelations of US government spying by Edward Snowden. The case pit five human rights organizations against British intelligence services, claiming that the government's collection of data on these groups was a privacy violation. The case has continued for more than a decade, going first to the British Investigatory Powers Tribunal, which found in the government's favor. This decision was appealed to the European Court of Human Rights, where it was dismissed for technical reasons in 2020 (Privacy International v. UK 2020). So far, Privacy International's arguments have failed, but they represent a new line of legal action. They also have succeeded in generating public awareness of mass surveillance (Eijkman 2017).

In addition to legal actions, civil society organizations are pioneering digitally specific tactics to address issues of algorithmic bias and harm. These include advocacy for individual data rights, advocacy for tools to aggregate individual rights, and the creation of their own databases and algorithms. The aggregation of individual data rights and the creation of their own databases or digital tools are new, purpose-built tactics, developed for the age of machine assembly.

Mechanisms to aggregate individual data rights are built into new data protection regimes. Most significantly in terms of reach, the European Union's General Data Protection Regulation includes requirements for both individual data access and the ability to aggregate both the right to the data and the data. This works through a mechanism called data subject access rights (DSARs), which allow individuals in a covered jurisdiction to request copies of the data held on them by a commercial enterprise. The law requires that companies respond within a certain time frame. By making companies provide the data and enabling individuals to see the data, it is attempting to pierce some of the obscurity and information asymmetry that currently define our data relationships with companies. Building from these individual rights, several civil society innovators have taken the next step—creating mirror databases of their constituents in ways that allow independent analysis and monitoring.

It is easiest to understand this with an example. The Workers Information Exchange (WIX) in London is the brainchild of James Farrar, a technology worker turned workers' rights activist. WIX focuses on gig workers, specifically Uber and Deliveroo drivers, who may have nothing in common other than their driver status. They are all subject to the data collection and algorithmic allocation of work opportunities of the apps deployed by these companies. The apps collect data on all drivers which company analysts use to update the job assignment or pay-per-ride algorithms in line with corporate incentives and objectives. As Fred Turner notes,

> Ride-share companies track everything from real-time supply and demand to the work habits of their drivers. Because they don't let ride-share drivers know how they use that data to set prices, drivers have no way to know if the "upfront price" that Uber or Lyft offers to pay them for a ride is in fact the same price they are offering other drivers. (Turner 2023)

While analysts in the company can see all the data, individual drivers can only see their own phones and paychecks.

To address this imbalance, WIX developed a process by which individual drivers can assign their data subject access rights to WIX, making the organization a proxy for the drivers. If WIX can convince its members to do this, it can build and analyze a small, representative database—one that mirrors the full data set owned by a company. The result is a subset of the company's databases. WIX aims to reverse-engineer the algorithms used by rideshare companies to identify whether they are prioritizing certain groups, discriminating against others, or manipulating prices in ways that harm riders or drivers. WIX can also create algorithms that show possible alternatives to corporate priorities.

Of course, rideshare companies have little interest in enabling this kind of analysis, nor are they big fans of the data subject access requirements. A 2019 review of DSARs in Europe found that corporations were deliberately slow to respond to requests, often provided the data in printed, not digital (e.g., analyzable), format, and without the contextual information and labeling that would enable sensemaking (Ausloos, Mahieu, and Veale 2019). From a corporate perspective, DSARs are costly, requiring database systems that extract (and in some cases remove) individual records. Complying with DSAR requests is burdensome enough that a new line of intermediary businesses and software has emerged to facilitate their processing.

DSAR processing is ground for a new tug of war between civil society and corporations. In seeking DSARs, researchers have noted that the raw data are insufficient; useful analysis requires additional information about the data sets from which an individual's records are plucked. These early years have generated numerous ideas for improving the legal requirements around DSARs, including calls for more information about entire data sets, proximity between data points used in recommender systems, and other analytic factors that enable people to see how they are being profiled. For their part, corporations are uninterested in increasing the costs of complying with DSARs, nor are they interested in sharing more information about their algorithmic analysis or the insights they gather. Understanding how well corporations are complying with DSAR requests is another issue. Where researchers have attempted to crowdsource insights about these procedures, they have inadvertently fed the corporate argument against making the process easier. In one case, where scholars helped people send multiple DSARs to compare responses, the corporations being studied referred to the resulting requests as comparable to a distributed denial-of-service attack, equating the pursuit of legally established rights to acts of malfeasance or protest (Mahieu, Asghari, and van Eeten 2018).

The response from corporations about data access was like the response from government agencies when the Freedom of Information Act (FOIA) first came into being. Both DSARs and FOIA requests are regulatory avenues intended to assist transparency and accountability efforts. Because DSARs have the potential to be aggregated into a mirror database, which in turn generates its own insights, they can also facilitate collective action.

Working conditions are a good fit for this kind of advocacy. While many people have adjusted to having their data extracted and often feel there is little recourse, "when data games hit their paychecks, people care," as Dan Calacci of MIT observes. Calacci is a computer scientist and "accidental" labor activist. He has developed software called Gigbox that allows individual gig workers to track their time, rides, distances, fares, and other useful information on their own phones, in a system that runs parallel to the companies' software. This allows individuals to do two things: (1) check their own data against a company's claims and (2) share their data with their peers so they can see a collective picture. Gigbox, a technological contribution to data advocacy, rides alongside WIX and its use of DSARs, which are organizational and regulatory tactics to help individuals build the advocacy capacity of their peer groups.

Such tactics—technical, organizational, regulatory, advocacy—are of great interest to labor unions. Christina Colclough has spent much of her career working with unions, and the last several years helping them understand and address data access concerns as part of their negotiations. Getting to the point of building new software or establishing a program to aggregate DSAR requests requires much education, training, and capacity building for most unions and their leaders. The starting advantage for them, however, is that they have identified their shared interest (their labor) and they feel the implications of massive online data collection where it hurts—in their paychecks. Colclough now runs a training and research organization for unions, betting that questions about data collection, use, and analysis will be part of most labor negotiations moving forward.

Workers are not the only ones who recognize that they can benefit from building mirror databases to inform their analysis. In the US, where data subject access is not guaranteed or protected, consumer rights groups have turned to so-called data-raising to get what they need. Consumer Reports (CR), a national consumer rights group, led an effort over many months to solicit copies of people's home cable bills. They removed or redacted information they did not need and built a mirror database from the information they could use to determine disparities in cable costs and speeds by location and in comparison with company promises. They were able to study 22,000 cable bills and determine average fees charged, speeds available, and areas with no access. Doing so required several new functions or skills for CR, a nonprofit. It needed to bring on data science skills, information technology security expertise, and new ways of reaching out to ask people for their data. This was possible because CR was already moving in the direction of more consumer advocacy around digital systems; moreover, it was still a significant investment by the organization to work in this new way.

Having invested in organizational capacities, CR has been able to roll out other new services to help people with their personal data. One example is an online service it calls Permission Slip. This online service makes it easier for people (in California, where the privacy law allows this) to request their data from companies and choose a data protection option for each one. Permission Slip makes it easier for Californians to access the protections of the California Consumer Protection Act. People who sign up "sign over" some of their data to CR, which then reaches out to every company that collects their data and initiates a streamlined process for reviewing, requesting, or deleting the information. While both WIX and CR have members, the two organizations have very different meanings for this term. WIX members are all gig drivers, and their relationship to WIX is based on that shared identity. CR members are subscribers to the full spectrum of CR's product testing and advocacy work; they may have no specific interest in digital data. Permission Slip is open to anyone, and CR is depending on its near-century-old reputation to attract nonmembers to the software.

Digital data-raising—asking people to donate their data instead of their time or money—is new but not without precedent. Medical research has long depended on people contributing tissue and data. Citizen science projects, whether focused on the stars or the seas, depend on data collected and contributed by volunteers. Apps focused on the natural world, whether iNaturalist or eBird, are the human interface to massive data sets built from donated data that include photos, audio files, location information, and participant observations.

Databases of contributed data have the potential to advance both advocacy and research. Consumer Reports' efforts to build mirror databases and provide people with tools like Permission Slip, which allow them better control of their data, may be the tip of a trend. Other nonprofits, including Mozilla, a nonprofit foundation that makes opensource software, have tried to help society reap the benefits of data donations without ceding the rules of these donations to corporations.

Mozilla built a web-based tool called Rally that makes it easy for a person to donate data directly to a study. The Rally system has been used in partnership with universities and by Mozilla and has produced information on privacy violations that then inform advocacy efforts.

Digital data-raising has enabled the building of massive datasets for a wide range of purposes—from cataloging biodiversity to generating increased profits via variable pricing to digitally mediated gig work in just about every corner of the economy. In response, civil society activists and organizations are adapting their tactics to make better use of it. People and communities are finding new ways to organize with and around data, just as companies are using our data to assemble us.

Conclusion

Digital systems and norms are changing the definition of assembly and association. Computers, big data sets, algorithmic analysis, and machine learning are used to cluster people into groups that are invisible but powerful. These groups inform decisions and opportunities of all kinds, from superficial to life changing. But the existence of these clusters and the extent of their effects on our lives are largely invisible. We do not make the choices to align with, participate in, or leave these groups—machines make these decisions. Whether our association with a particular set of characteristics or groups is long- or short-lived is not up to us. We may or may not prioritize the same characteristics that algorithms do.

Framed as a human right, assembly and association are guaranteed to all, and defined by consent, participation, and choice. Viewed through our real experiences in a digitally dependent world, our options for assembly and association now include those that we control and those that may be controlling us. While we are just beginning to understand the extent of machine-made assembly and association, it would be wise to assume that it is as pervasive and knotty an issue as online expression, and that the two are more entangled than distinct. How machine-made clusters interact with assemblies and associations we join by choice is another new frontier for exploration. Finally, whether these opaque but powerful associations reflect or defy democratic norms of participation and choice is a question whose answers hold significant implications for civil society and democracy.

References

Ausloos, Jeff, Rene Mahieu, and Michael Veale. "Getting Data Subject Rights Right." *Journal of Intellectual Property, Information Technology and E-Commerce Law* 10 (3): 283–309.

Brunton, Finn, and Helen Nissenbaum. 2016. *Obfuscation: A User's Guide for Privacy and Protest.* Cambridge, MA: MIT Press.

Calacci, Dan. Author Interview, February 10, 2022.

Costanza-Chock, Sasha, Inioluwa Deborah Raji, and Joy Buolamwini. 2022. "Who Audits the Auditors? Recommendations From a Field Scan of the Algorithmic Auditing Ecosystem." In *FAccT '22: ACM Conference on Fairness, Accountability, and Transparency.* New York: Association for Computing Machinery.

DeNardis, Laura. 2020. *The Internet in Everything: Freedom and Security in a World with No Off Switch.* New Haven, CT: Yale University Press.

Eijkman, Quirine. 2017. "Indiscriminate Bulk Data Interception and Group Privacy: Do Human Rights Organizations Retaliate through Strategic Litigation?" In *Group Privacy: New Challenges of Data Technologies,* edited by Linnet Taylor, Luciano Floridi, and Bar van der Sloot, 123–138. London: Springer.

Eubanks, Virginia. 2018. *Automating Inequality: How High-Tech Tools Profile, Police and Punish the Poor.* New York: McMillan.

Griffin, Venita E. 2022. "Community-Organized Data Collection." In *Blueprint 2023: Philanthropy and Digital Civil Society,* edited by Lucy Bernholz, 31–36. Stanford, CA: Stanford University.

Hamilton, Michael. 2020. "The Meaning and Scope of 'Assembly' in International Human Rights Law." *International and Comparative Law Quarterly* 69 (3): 521–556.

Hoid. "Flood Your ISP with Random, Noisy Data to Protect your Privacy on the Internet." *Null Byte,* September 5, 2018. https://null-byte.wonderhowto.com/how-to/flood-your-isp-with-random-noisy-data-protect-your-privacy-internet-0186193/.

Lardinois, Frederic. 2022. "Google Kills Off FloC, replaces it with Topics." *TechCrunch,* January 25, 2022. https://techcrunch.com/2022/01/25/google-kills-off-floc-replaces-it-with-topics/.

Mahieu, Rene, Hadi Asghari, and Michel van Eeten. 2018. "Collectively Exercising the Right of Access: Individual Effort, Societal Effect." *Internet Policy Review*, January 30, 2018. http://dx.doi.org/10.2139/ssrn.3107292 .

O'Neil, Cathy. 2016. *Weapons of Math Destruction: How Big Data Increases Inequality and Threatens Democracy*. New York: PenguinRandomHouse.

Privacy International and Others v. UK, European Court of Human Rights. https://privacyinternational.org/legal-action/privacy-international-and-others-v-united-kingdom.

Rutzen, Doug, and Jacob Zenn .2014. "Association and Assembly in the Digital Age." *International Journal of Not-for-Profit Law*. 13 (4). Accessed online July 20, 2022. https://www.icnl.org/resources/research/ijnl/association-and-assembly-in-the-digital-age-2#_ftnref20.

Schneier, Bruce. 2018. *Click Here to Kill Everybody: Security and Survival in a Hyper-Connected World*. New York: W. W. Norton.

Taylor, Linnet, Luciano Floridi, and Bar van der Sloot. eds. 2017. *Group Privacy: New Challenges of Data Technologies*. London: Springer.

Taylor, Linnet, Luciano Floridi, and Bar van der Sloot. eds. 2017. "Introduction." In *Group Privacy: New Challenges of Data Technologies*, 10–24. London: Springer.

Turner, Fred. 2023. "A Brief History of (over) Time." *The New York Times Magazine*, April 16, 2023. https://nytimes.pressreader.com/article/281492165602129.

UN General Assembly. 1948. *Universal Declaration of Human Rights*, art. 20 (Paris 1948). https://www.un.org/en/about-us/universal-declaration-of-human-rights.

Xu, Dongkuan and Yingjie Tian. 2015. "A Comprehensive Survey of Clustering Algorithms." *Annals of Data Science* 2 (2): 165–193.

Six

A Tale of Two Audits

Danaë Metaxa
Deborah Raji

Introduction

It was the best of times, it was the worst of times.

Charles Dickens (1859)

Given the near ubiquity of algorithmic deployments, it comes as no surprise that even the most helpful products can, at times, become the cause of undeniable harm. Many of these harms have arisen due to functional failures—algorithmic deployments that do not live up to articulated expectations of performance, especially in unforeseen circumstances or while deployed on under-considered populations (Raji et al. 2022). These broken promises, often disproportionately impacting the most vulnerable populations, are costly. Historically, faulty algorithmic deployments have led some to lose access to health care (Lecher 2018), housing (Kirchner and Goldstein, 2020), and unemployment benefits (Charette 2018), or have had dire consequences such as the loss of a job or a false arrest (Hill 2022).

But what does it mean for an algorithmic system to "work" in the first place? The reality is that the determination of model performance is not just a technical question but also a political one. In actuality, there exists a multitude of answers to the question of what it means for algorithmic systems to perform, and those answers depend strongly on the priorities and influence of those conducting the assessments.

In this chapter, we explore the politics of evaluation in algorithm auditing. By analyzing how various stakeholders come into play to define what it means for these deployed systems to operate "correctly," we map out the messy sociopolitical process that determines whose narrative will triumph and decide the fate of the analyzed system. At its core, this is a game played by many actors, all jostling for leverage on an uneven playing field. Each involved actor enters the game with their own proposals on how best to assess these systems, and offers counter-narratives to the vendor's initial story of how well these systems function. However, the winner of the game is determined by those with the institutional power to assert their narrative of performance, or the collective power to demand the attention required for accountability.

We examine algorithm auditing through two case studies from two types of algorithmic system: the first, from a system used directly by end users; the second, an automated decision-making system (ADS) in which those most impacted are not direct users of the system. As the case studies demonstrate, the issues that arise when auditing these different systems—and the avenues for recourse—share some commonalities, but can also be distinct in important ways. In the remainder of this chapter, we explore these case studies, using them as examples to discuss the political project of persuasion that follows an algorithm audit. In each case, we outline a high-profile, high-stakes tension that arose due to the potential harms of the platform, how it resolved, and what lessons it offers for the future.

A Primer on Audits

Before going into the case studies, we provide some background on the questions audits ask in the context of both end-user and automated decision-making systems (in which endpoint-impacted individuals are generally not themselves the system's users).

What Does It Mean for an AI System to Work (and for Whom)?

As with any technology, a major question that arises for producers and users of an AI system is whether or not it "works." More specifically, we question whether it satisfies the expectations of those making use of it or being impacted by it. And while AI systems certainly undergo testing during their development, different stakeholder groups may unfortunately have different criteria against which they might evaluate them. As a result, the testing done during the production of such a system can overlook important issues for the system's eventual users and other stakeholders.

One of the most popular examples of the limitations of industry testing standards is the 2018 Gender Shades work, in which researchers Joy Buolamwini and Timnit Gebru showed that already deployed facial analysis technologies performed especially poorly on darker-skinned and female faces.

As this example demonstrates, in many cases performance failures occur most when the system relates to marginalized populations, whose perspectives and data system designers may have failed to consider or did not prioritize. Such groups function as "edge cases" of sorts, with their needs either unanticipated or ignored early in the development process.

To identify such issues, an ecosystem of external testing has sprung up around AI systems, critically scrutinizing claims of what it means for such systems to work—and whether their performance holds for the full range of impacted stake holders. That ecosystem is algorithm auditing.

What Do Algorithm Audits Do?

Most audits have twin goals: evaluation and accountability. The first component, evaluating the system, is in the context of the claims or guarantees (explicit or implicit) that the system makes about its functioning and limitations. In addition to the explicit claims that can be made about a system, these evaluations can include an assessment of implicit expectations, such as legal requirements (such as discrimination-relevant performance disparities) or anticipated system outcomes tied to basic social norms.

Audits, however, are not a mere exercise in knowledge production. Instead, they have the additional goal of accountability. This accountability objective means that there is an intention on the auditor's part to see that the judgment provided by the evaluation is consequential— in other words, that it catalyzes improvements to the system; informs legal sanctions, reparations, or retribution; or raises public awareness of certain issues.

What Kinds of AI Systems Are Audited?

When considering the risks posed by algorithmic systems and the mechanisms available for recourse when things go awry, there are a few key questions. A first central question is who its relevant stakeholders are. That is, who is interacting with the system? Who is impacted by it? A second question is what the goals of the AI system are. Not necessarily the technical goals but the broader socio-technical motivations of the stakeholders developing and operating the system. To investigate this question, we ask: Who pays for the system? What are they paying for?

Algorithms manifest in a variety of deployed products. In this chapter, we see a key distinction between two types of system: online platforms and automated decision-making systems. These differ in important ways that affect the audit process.

For most online platforms, which include search engines and social media sites, the end users of the algorithmic system (private individuals) are a stakeholder group. They are able to sign up and use a service (often free), and make up the majority of external individuals interacting with the algorithmic system, which often ranks, sorts, or filters the content they consume.

There are likely also corporate users of the platform—for example, advertisers connecting with end users through an ad exchange. Corporate actors generally pay for access to the end user population or end user data, and they are often the primary source of capital flowing into the platform. Despite not directly contributing financially in many cases, typical end users have some agency since they provide the data upon which the system depends and can opt out if they so choose. Specific examples of online platforms include social media companies like Meta (owner of Facebook), search engines like Google, e-commerce platforms like Amazon, gig economy services like Uber, and so on. In each of these cases, the individuals impacted by the algorithmic outcomes of the platform overlap completely with the direct users of the platform.

In contrast, other algorithmic deployments manifest as *automated decision-making system* (ADS) tools. These tools tend to be standalone model products integrated into preexisting decision-making processes. As a result, the main users are institutional actors already involved in defining and executing the processes rather than individual consumers. Institutional actors will often leverage the ADS to make decisions about some downstream population of affected nonusers, often without their knowledge or participation. Thus, in such cases the individuals whose fates are enmeshed in the system's machinery do not directly interact with the product. Often, they may be completely unaware of its existence despite its use in decision-making processes that ultimately impact them. Examples of ADS tools are machine learning health-care products (Kim et al. 2023), policing technologies (Zilka et al. 2022), risk assessment tools [for things like child welfare (Chouldechova et al. 2018), credit, health, criminal recidivism risk (Liu et al. 2022), etc.], and application screening [screening potential renters (Kirchner and Goldstein 2020), job applicants (Raghavan et al. 2020), etc.)].

As AI tools are deployed across an inconceivable scope of domains and contexts, this dichotomy is likely not a complete taxonomy of the algorithmic systems that exist today. It does, however, describe a significant proportion of the systems that have been a focus of algorithm audits over the last decade.

CASE STUDY 1: DISCRIMINATORY ADS ON FACEBOOK

Facebook is a prominent example of an online platform, a system whose end users are often private individuals directly impacted by the algorithmic systems integrated into the product. While end users use

Facebook for free, companies seeking to sendads to a consumer base pay Facebook to distribute them, placing the ad content in the web browser or mobile app of relevant users. The advertisers specify a budget and (through various means at issue in the coming case study) a desired target audience, and in exchange the platform distributes their ads to users. This ad exchange accounts for a majority of Meta's revenue. In the remainder of this case study, Meta will generally be referred to as Facebook, its company name at the time of these events and still the name of its platform.

This case study is a representative and high-profile example of such a system gone wrong. For context, discrimination in the housing market (in terms of selecting tenants, advertising for housing, and so on) is illegal in many countries, including the United States. The Fair Housing Act of 1968 made it illegal to advertise housing in any manner that showed preference for (or, equally, bias against) any group along the lines of protected characteristics like race, religion, sex, and national origin. The Civil Rights Act of 1964 banned discrimination in employment, including job advertisements.

In October of 2016, a bombshell article was dropped by a team of reporters led by journalist Julia Angwin at *ProPublica*. In the article, the team provided evidence that, acting as advertisers, they could racially target ads for housing on Facebook using a feature that the platform provided to all advertisers (Angwin and Parris 2016). In the menu used for selecting a desired audience, in the category "demographics" there was a subset of options for advertisers to choose from labeled "ethnic affinity" that was equally available to advertisers posting about housing or jobs as for any other type of advertisement. Contacted for that story, Facebook claimed that such discrimination was prohibited on the platform, and quickly removed the violating ads. They further claimed that the "ethnic affinity" options were offered as part of a "multicultural advertising" effort and technically did not necessarily constitute user race.

Despite this swift action, the article led to the filing of a class action lawsuit less than a week later on November 3, 2016, in a Northern California district court. The allegation in *Onuoha v. Facebook* was that users were harmed by advertisers' ability to exclude certain demographic groups from targeting using this feature. In other words, users may not have seen ads they legally should not have been excluded from seeing (see Mobley v. Facebook 2016). A week later, after their initial insistence that this was normal industry practice, on November 11 Facebook released a statement that they would implement a system to automatically scan ads for housing, employment, and credit that were discriminatory and flag them for human review (Angwin 2016).

After a period of silence on the matter, nearly a year later, in November 2017, *ProPublica* repeated its original tests. Again it found that housing ads could be targeted to exclude user groups on the basis of race, disability, religion, nationality, familial status, and so on—all categories protected by the Fair Housing Act. All ads (set to exclude groups like "Jews" and "people interested in wheelchair ramps") were approved within minutes, most of them fast enough that it was clear they were not triggering any extra layers of automated or human review. The same month, *ProPublica* published another article describing how Facebook enabled advertisers to target users interested in topics like "Jew hater" and "How to burn jews" (Angwin, Varner, and Tobin 2017). Such categories had been automatically and algorithmically created by Facebook's advertising system based on terms frequently added by users to their profiles. These were relatively small ad audiences (a couple of thousand users), but when ProPublica tried to target ads to them, those ads were still approved within minutes. The same day, another outlet, *Slate*, reported on a number of other offensive ad targeting categories (Oremus and Carey 2017). Such ads were all very clearly against Facebook's stated policies. The experiments showed that those policies were not being enforced. This continued into December, with *ProPublica* running stories showing specific instances of discrimination in addition to demonstrating the potential for advertisers to discriminate—for instance, dozens of companies were running real job ads that excluded older adults.

A few months later, in March of the following year, the National Fair Housing Alliance filed a lawsuit in New York's southern district court, alleging discrimination against protected groups like mothers, disabled people, and Spanish speakers (Angwin and Tobin 2018). The US Department of Housing and Urban Development (HUD) filed a statement of interest in the case a few months later. At the same time, Facebook was being investigated by the state of Washington for its discrimination. That investigation was settled in July of 2018, with Facebook announcing "legally binding" changes to its ad platform, including removing the features that allowed advertisers to discriminate in housing, employment, insurance, and credit (Tobin 2018). Citing Section 230 of the Communications Decency Act, which releases platforms from liability for third-party content (like ads), Facebook denied any violation of antidiscrimination law, but still paid fees to the state of Washington and agreed to make permanent fixes that had been ongoing for nearly two years.

Astoundingly, the story was still far from over. In September of 2018, while the ability to target ads by race, religion, and national origin had been removed by the platform, *ProPublica* found and reported that companies, including Uber, were running employment ads on Facebook targeted only to men (Tobin and Merrill 2018). These ads, collected using crowdsourcing by *ProPublica*'s Political Ad Collector project, showed that advertisers could—and were—still targeting by age and sex, again in violation of US law. Notably, the use of crowdsourcing was critical to discovery of the issue; such audits relied on the scale of data collected from many users. In January of 2019, following these discoveries, Facebook responded not by changing their system to prevent illegal advertising but instead by making changes to their platform that blocked ad-tracking tools like the one used by *ProPublica* to make the discovery (Merrill and Tobin 2019).

It took until March of 2019, nearly two and a half years after the original October 2016 story, for Facebook to address gender, age, and zip code discrimination, finally agreeing to stop enabling advertisers' illegal ad targeting for all protected categories (Gillum and Tobin 2019). The company did this as part of another legal settlement in the state of Washington, with civil rights organizations like the American

Civil Liberties Union (ACLU) involved. That settlement required the changes to be made by September 2019.

A week later, and after years of repeated demonstrations that Facebook was engaging in discrimination, HUD finally sued it for violating the Fair Housing Act (Tobin 2019b). The lawsuit alleged that, in addition to allowing advertisers to discriminate on the basis of protected categories, Facebook's own algorithms exacerbated the problem by targeting ads automatically in ways that led to discrimination. Supporting the allegation was an academic article from a few months earlier, in April 2019, by prominent auditing researchers at Northeastern University, which showed that skewed ad delivery occurred because of the optimization effects of the platform as well as the algorithm's estimates of the "relevance" of ads to different groups (Ali et al. 2019). In other words, not only did Facebook enable advertisers to illegally target ads but its own algorithms were allegedly doing the same.

A few months later, in a batch of rulings in July 2019, the US Equal Employment Commission (EEOC), a federal agency tasked with enforcing workplace nondiscrimination law, found that a group of employers violated employment law by excluding groups like women and older adults from seeing their job ads on Facebook (Tobin 2019a). These rulings occurred only after the ACLU and other organizations filed complaints, which were themselves enabled by *ProPublica* and other media organizations' reporting.

Despite the several settlements and rulings, in December 2019, months after the legal settlement with Washington State in March, ProPublica continued to find evidence of discrimination by the algorithm when targeting ads (Kofman and Tobin 2020). Reporters found that anyone could easily circumvent the new portal Facebook had built after having removed discriminatory targeting categories, and that the old one (allowing all the types of discrimination that had been demonstrated over several years) was still active and usable. The same month, the team at Northeastern, which had previously shown discriminatory effects from Facebook's own targeting algorithms, submitted another paper showing that "lookalike audiences" and "special ad audiences" (two features provided by Facebook to advertisers) could also result in biased ad targeting even in the absence of explicit demographic targeting (Sapiezynski et al. 2022).

After a two-year lull (due to ongoing lawsuits, the COVID pandemic, or other factors), in November 2021 Facebook announced that detailed ad targeting options relating to sensitive topics (race, religion, health, politics, sexual orientation) would be removed (Mudd 2021). And yet again, a few months later in May 2022, *The Markup* found that "such ad targeting is very much still available" using other terms that are obvious proxies: "The Tea Party" had been removed as a target category, for example, but "Tea Party" had not. The reporting showed that major advertisers like Starbucks were targeting ads using keywords like "telenovelas" and "Spanish language" despite the illegality of racially targeted ads (Waller and Lecher 2022).

Wrapping up the lawsuits, in June 2022 the Department of Justice settled with Facebook over allegedly discriminatory housing advertising (United States of America v. Meta Platforms 2022). The settlement was the outcome of the 2019 HUD case and required the company to pay the maximum penalty under the Fair Housing Act—$115,054, an unbelievably small drop in the bucket for a company valued at more than $430 billion. Aside from the meager fine, however, the settlement did include some regulatory teeth: Facebook agreed to disband the "special ad audience" functionality that led to the discriminatory ads and to change its algorithm to proactively ensure that disparate targeting was not occurring. This was a technical change that would be approved and overseen by the Department of Justice and an independent review (Tobin and Kofman 2022).

Notably, it is a gray area (both legally and morally) whether some forms of ad targeting should be allowed. Aside from specifically protected categories like housing, employment, and credit, most targeting is legal. And while some forms of advertising might feel uncomfortable or predatory to the people interacting with them, others might be perceived as a legitimate and welcome way for advertisers to interact with specific communities. Given the complexity of these issues and the subjective human judgments entailed, why are companies like Facebook left to make these decisions unilaterally?

Moreover, whether the settlement was a win for civil rights is murky. While an optimistic reader might appreciate its requirement that the company proactively develop and deploy a new system to correct racial, ethnic, and sex-based disparities in the users receiving housing ads, the agreement was narrow in scope, focusing only on a specific subset of ads and characteristics, as the laws themselves are limited in the protections they offer, and it notably encouraged—or rather *required*—that Facebook use its data to infer protected characteristics of its users without their knowledge or consent.

This case has been ongoing for over *seven years*. The same pattern repeats annually: a cat-and-mouse game of journalists making claims of discriminatory or unethical practices and Facebook responding with some change, or some proposed change, and often not delivering on it or delivering only after years of repeated prompting. Now it culminates in a financial slap on the wrist and the requirement that Facebook do even more automated inference and categorization of its users, albeit with some external oversight.

The cost to play this audit-response cyclical game is notably uneven; while journalists and researchers must pour resources and time into meticulously documenting abuses, until the legal system intervenes the company need only respond with a defensive explanation or a half-hearted commitment to change. And most of these scenes play out in the court of public opinion, since even the maximum penalty resulting from years-long lawsuits at the federal level cost Facebook a laughable $115,054 at best. In contrast, the European Union, a jurisdiction known for its more stringent legal stance against online platforms, recently fined Meta $1.3 billion for user data privacy violations (Ziady 2023).

But most important, barred from input in this cat-and-mouse game are everyday users, individuals who cannot afford the cost to play—neither to identify whether and how such discrimination has impacted them individually nor to take legal steps to address it—and whose privacy and personal information continues to be used and abused without their knowledge or consent.

CASE STUDY 2: ADS TOOLS

In October 2018, the American Civil Liberties Union (ACLU) shared an alarming report: Amazon, the technology giant, was pitching its facial recognition product to law enforcement and immigration authorities. Specifically, Amazon was conducting sale conversations with ICE officials (Guliani 2018) and law enforcement agencies in the city of Orlando, Florida, and with the Washington County Sheriff's Office in the state of Oregon (Cagle and Ozer 2018).

Throughout the summer of 2018, this news caused a public uproar. Letters to Amazon leadership from industry leaders, Congress members (Congressional Black Caucus 2018), civil rights groups (ACLU 2018a), shareholders (ACLU 2018b), employees (Conger 2018), academics (*ICRAC* 2018), and the public outlined the many dangers of deploying the technology in such high-stakes settings. The ACLU, joined by other advocacy groups such as Fight for the Future and EFF flagged the major privacy and accuracy risks in deploying the unproven technology on a large scale. The general manager of artificial intelligence at Amazon Web Services at the time, Dr. Matt Wood, remained stubborn in his support for it. In a blog post on June 1, 2018, he claimed, "There have always been and will always be risks with new technology capabilities . . . we believe it is the wrong approach to impose a ban on promising new technologies because they might be used by bad actors for nefarious purposes in the future. . . . Through responsible use, the benefits have far outweighed the risks."

In particular, on June 25, 2018, Joy Buolamwini of the Algorithmic Justice League at the MIT Media Lab sent her own letter to Amazon. Following up on past work exposing the biased performance of commercial facial recognition systems sold by competitors IBM, Microsoft, and the Chinese company Megvii (Buolamwini and Gebru 2018), Buolamwini wrote to Amazon's founder and CEO, Jeff Bezos: "On the easy Pilot Parliaments Benchmark for gender classification, Amazon

Rekognition performs better on lighter-skinned faces than darker-skinned faces with an accuracy difference of 11.45%. It also performs better on male faces than female faces with an accuracy difference of 16.47%. The performance metrics on darker-skinned individuals are especially concerning given the long history of racial bias in policing practices" (Buolamwini 2018). She received no response from Bezos or the company (Buolamwini 2019).

On July 26, 2018, Jacob Snow at the ACLU followed the methodology in Buolamwini's initial Gender Shades study to demonstrate that Amazon's facial recognition model falsely face-matched twenty-eight members of Congress, with 19% more false matches on members of color (Snow 2018). This finding led to yet another wave of public disapproval, with the renewed attention escalating to another letter of Congress—this time from the Congressional Black Caucus (Barrett 2018).

Months later, Buolamwini, along with co-author Inioluwa Deborah Raji (who is also co-author of the chapter you are reading), published a peer-reviewed academic paper (Raji and Buolamwini 2019) reinforcing the findings referenced in the June 2018 letter. In this paper, they reported that the version of Amazon's Rekognition facial analysis product being pitched to ICE the year prior was performing at 68.6% for darker-skinned female–presenting subjects while operating at 100% for lighter-skinned male faces. This represented a performance disparity between the two groups of more than 30 percent.

This new result garnered visibility, and Amazon responded swiftly. In a blog post, Dr. Wood of AWS directly challenged the findings, claiming that in an internal attempt to replicate the study, "across all ethnicities, we found no significant difference in accuracy with respect to gender classification" (Wood 2019). However, he obscured important details—his audit was done with a supposedly upgraded version of Rekognition from November 2018, not the version Amazon had been pitching the summer before to law enforcement and ICE. The internal tests he referenced were also done at a model performance threshold of 99% percent confidence—not the default product threshold of 80% confidence, which Amazon's police client was eventually reported to be using (Menegus 2019) (and which Buolamwini and Raji's study used).

Finally, describing Amazon's overall attitude, Wood claimed, "We are very interested in working with academics in establishing a series of standardized tests for facial analysis and facial recognition and in working with policy makers on guidance and/or legislation of its use. One existing standardized test is from the National Institute of Standards and Technology (NIST)." Less than a year later, however, Amazon opted out of NIST's annual Facial Recognition Vendor's Test—which now included an assessment of demographic disparities following Buolamwini and Raji's study (Harwell 2019).

Despite Amazon's assertions, many reproductions in the following year validated Buolamwini and Raji's finding that the technology habitually performed worse for subjects of marginalized and underrepresented identities (Krishnapriya et al. 2019; Cook, et al. 2019; Raji, et al. 2020; Scheuerman, et al. 2019). Several key researchers came out in defense of Raji and Buolamwini, defending their original results as reproductions increased (Metz and Singer 2019).

By the spring of that year, some Amazon shareholders were frustrated enough to push for a vote to stop the company from continuing to sell its technology. In response to Amazon's attempts to shut it down, in April of 2019 the SEC stepped in to force a shareholder vote (Dastin and Kerber 2019). Unfortunately, despite the support of groups like the ACLU (Rubin and Hautala 2019), Amazon was ultimately successful, with the majority of shareholders voting to continue the sale of the harmful and unproven technology (Whittaker 2019).

In February 2019, the company came out in support of legislative efforts for facial recognition (Punke 2019). By March, there were already signs of this happening. At the municipal level, a flurry of facial recognition bans and moratoriums began to show up, starting in Berkeley, California, and then expanding. By the summer of 2019, critical state and federal bills began to be introduced, in Washington state, California,

Illinois, Idaho, Arkansas, and New York and for applications in housing, education and, of course, policing.[1]

Real-life stories of those impacted began to proliferate as well, including the March 2019 testimonies of tenants at the rent- controlled
Atlantic Towers building, who challenged the facial recognition system
installed by their landlord (Bellafante 2019; Durkin 2019), the January
2020 release of the "Coded Bias" documentary[2] on Netflix, and the
June 2020 reporting on Robert Williams (Hill 2022), in the first case of
several involving the false arrest of an individual due to a faulty facial
recognition match (Johnson 2023).

By June 2020, in the midst of the global struggle to address the death
of George Floyd, Amazon was facing major reputational costs for its
continued sale of Rekognition to police. So, on June 10 2020, following the lead of IBM, it committed to a minimum one-year moratorium
on the sale of facial recognition products to law enforcement, sunset-
ting the pilots in Oregon (Allyn 2020) and Orlando (Roulette 2019).

However, by the following autumn it was clear that the company
had not quite given up, pivoting instead to focus on shaping the up-
coming legislation. Amazon lobbyists were named in several of the
federal and state facial recognition bills, with at least one documented
case of Amazon actively paying (Ongweso Jr 2020) or pestering (Del
Rey 2019) policy makers to adopt its preferred legislative stance on the
technology—that is, omitting clauses for any kind of restriction on
use or denouncing mandated external scrutiny in favor of voluntary
corporate-led reporting on biased performance.

Furthermore, the voluntary nature of Amazon's moratorium allowed for easy loopholes. Although the moratorium was extended from
one year to an indefinite period, proliferation of Amazon's "smart door-
bell", Ring, included facial recognition features for identifying people
caught in the footage, and Amazon routinely released such footage and
features to the hundreds of police they partner with (Biddle 2019; Molla
2020; Bridges 2021; Ng 2022). Ring had become the largest civilian surveillance network in the US by 2021, and was sharing videos to police

partners even without an owner's permission by 2022. From the initial outcry to the first moratorium, there were over two years of advocacy (Hao 2020), but the fight was clearly far from over.

Discussion

Following the high-profile political battles that followed the algorithm audits of Facebook's advertising platform and Amazon's facial recognition tool, there are clear implications both hold for the future of algorithm auditing and AI technology development.

Case Study Reflections

In this chapter, we focus primarily on two types of AI system: online platforms and automated decision-making systems. As the case studies illustrate, this distinction is quite meaningful, since the stakeholders, political battles, and possibilities for recourse vary accordingly.

In both worlds, auditors and vendors engage in the same style of gameplay, a back-and-forth process with each responding to the other's claims with empirical counternarratives of model performance and biases. The role of public attention and outcry—powered by journalism, civil society advocacy, and word of mouth—is equally integral, whether the audit target is an online platform or an ADS vendor. And in both cases, the power differential between auditors and vendors remains significant. ADS vendors may include smaller startups that are less publicly recognizable, especially when compared with large multinational social media platforms, but in comparison auditors are typically the smaller team (at times, as small as one individual), composed of independent actors without the capital, personnel, and other resources to compete on an even playing field. Also, the degree of public and legal scrutiny faced by auditors, in addition to expectations of research reproducibility, increases the risk and consequences associated with exaggerating or misrepresenting the audit's results. On the other hand, corporate audit targets typically possess a highly coordinated and well-compensated machinery for responding to complaints, often through a public relations or marketing lens that is not so wedded to scientific truth.

There are, however, several ways in which these contexts differ meaningfully, with implications for how accountability actors should approach algorithm audits in the separate contexts. These differences include the empirical methodologies available for conducting the audit, the population impacted by the tool, and potential processes for effecting change.

Empirical Methodologies. The first difference, and one of immediate concern to an auditor, is the range of applicable methods. Online platforms and ADS are implemented and accessed differently and as a result require different data collection approaches. Online platforms are designed to sandbox users, showing them a personalized, individualized experience, and therefore auditors must go to great lengths to understand what other users of the system see before beginning to reason why. Thus a range of specific methods have been developed, including crowdsourced audits (collecting data from a large sample of different users) and sock puppet audits (collecting data from fabricated accounts created to trick the system into treating them as a large sample of users). ADS tools, meanwhile, are largely deterministic or reproducible, and auditors using them can be confident that other users are having the same (or a very similar) experience with the product. In addition, ADS tools are generally more stable, being updated less frequently, with changes that are logged or published. Users know what version they use, and can compare it with a version others are using, in order to track changes in product outcomes. Meanwhile, online platform algorithms are understood to change constantly, updated much more frequently, often without any publicly available documentation or logging. It is a huge challenge to understand how much these systems have changed over time or even to identify at what time points change should be meaningfully evaluated. While not exhaustive, these two dimensions (the consistency of user experiences and product stability over time) demonstrate the need for methodological variation required in auditing.

Impacted Population. A second major difference between ADS and online platforms is the impacted population. For online platforms, the impacted population is largely synonymous with the user base of the platform. There may be some exceptions: for instance, downstream social effects of certain algorithms might eventually impact nonusers, as when Facebook researchers found that nudges prompting users to vote led to significant changes in individuals actually turning up at the polls. But in most cases, the affected population comprises platform users. Meanwhile, ADS tools are generally used *on* a separate third-party population by their direct users. In addition to the facial recognition systems that we have discussed, consider bail-setting and sentencing algorithms produced by private companies, paid for by various legal jurisdictions, and used on defendants and incarcerated people—the impacted third parties to those transactions. The obvious result is that anyone taking issue with the algorithm used by an online platform can consider at least partially resolving the issue by ceasing to use it. Of course, this is easier said than done; online platforms like Facebook and Twitter gained massive user bases because of the significant and meaningful benefits they provide. But in comparison with ADS tools, platform users have much more choice. On top of this difference at the level of the individual, group dynamics also change. Online platform users can band together in large-scale data donation efforts to uncover problems, or they can boycott the system en masse. Meanwhile, those affected in the ADS context may struggle to even become aware that they are impacted, and are generally unable to leverage their position to support research or to resist.

Relevant Authorities. A final difference we have alluded to throughout this chapter is the available routes toward changing problematic algorithmic systems. Accountability is, after all, the end goal of an audit. But because of some of the differences explained previously, auditors and other interested parties have different avenues available when seeking to change these systems. Aside from ad hoc or grassroots mechanisms, which we have touched on, regulation stands out as one of the most compelling options for achieving algorithmic accountability.

Laws and regulations, however, require appeals to authority, which must happen at different levels for ADS tools compared with online platforms. ADS tools are used in scoped and specific settings, allowing regulatory action to be taken at the level of a smaller jurisdiction: a specific city can ban the use of these technologies within its limits and often for specific applications. For example, a health care, finance, or housing regulator can restrict tools used in their specified domain. Online platforms, in contrast, are used far and wide, with the very technology predicated on the interconnection of massive swaths of international populations. In this context, even an entity as large as the European Union has struggled to sanction platforms like Facebook. Taking action to force companies to stop or change their algorithmic systems' behaviors requires intervention at the level of one or more countries to have any hope of making a difference. We discuss this point, and the possible forms algorithmic regulation might take, in the next section.

Looking Ahead: A Call for Algorithm Regulation

In too many cases, the auditors lose and the vendors win—it is fundamentally easier to promote a baseless narrative than to dispute that narrative and prove its falsity. This is why, overall, we see a major role for regulation. The ability of anyone to dispute the narratives that these companies promulgate—when building ADS tools and online platforms alike—relies on difficult-to-obtain privileges, such as access to data. As our case studies have demonstrated, audits are a metaphorical boxing match, a dialogue over time that currently rests in the court of public opinion (and occasionally formal court as well) to decide whose narrative holds more water. Regulatory intervention could possibly increase access in a way that provides a more independent, third-party arbiter of truth.

Effective regulation in the context of algorithm audits should establish auditing standards (i.e., a formalization of audit practice and auditor conduct) as well as a regulatory body to execute audits. Whether that body conducts its own audits or hires reputable third parties to do so and makes judgements by interpreting their findings is up for debate.

Regardless, the core function of such a regulatory actor remains: we need a legitimate regulatory entity to be given the resources and authority to sift through the multiple narratives of what it means for a system to work. This mediating agency can then seriously consider the perspectives of those with a public interest motive, who are otherwise easily outmatched by corporate interests and resources, while also pushing for material consequences for identified harms. The act of formalizing audit requirements, standards and protections goes a long way in shielding vulnerable parties in the relentless political exchange of the audit process. It tips the scales in favor of public interest, to give those raising concerns and evaluating them directly a fair shot at achieving accountability.

A Few Notes of Caution

As algorithm auditors ourselves, we are proponents of this tool as a powerful option for identifying harmful technologies and prompting vendors to make changes in favor of public benefit. We want to caution, however, that auditing is not a panacea; there are limitations to the method that bear keeping in mind.

Auditing Standards and the Risk of Audit-Washing

Holding audits to a high standard in terms of empirical methodology but also perceived legitimacy is of the utmost importance. Audits *and auditors* must be prepared to face scrutiny, both by the general public (as they are often currently circulated) and, in the future, by regulators handing down verdicts. This means that audits must be conducted by independent third parties who have minimal conflicts of interest (ideally none, with any conflicts clearly disclosed if that is the case), and they must be held to a rigorous scientific standard in their execution and analysis. Absent such measures, the entire audit enterprise runs the risk of devolving into what other scholars have named "audit washing" (Goodman and Trehu 2022)—the possibility that subpar audits will be strategically deployed (and perhaps even paid for by the entity being audited) to give an undeserved impression of innocence. If we want audits to be believed as reliable assessments of a product's real-world performance and impact, we must vehemently guard against their corruption.

Proving Phenomena with Small Effect Sizes

Some intervention effects are very small and hard to prove using statistical inference (the backbone of many audit analyses). This is a clear limitation of the method; auditing is not the right tool for demonstrating every type of problem. Regulation might help if accused entities are required to share enough data to conduct a rigorous audit of small-effect-size phenomena. But absent this reality, audits are often most useful in contexts where the disparities or performance failures are quite significant.

Beyond Strict Illegality

Finally, many audits today focus on demonstrating evidence for bias or discrimination perpetuated by AI systems. This is illegal in most legal jurisdictions (usually according by US or EU law). While such audits are critical, there are many types of problematic algorithmic behavior that are not strictly illegal—for instance, the promotion of misinformation is not illegal (Keller, 2022). Rather than shutting down the execution of such studies altogether, we may be entering an era in which entirely new legal standards for algorithmic systems are needed, and such audits can provide the basis for making a case for future legislative developments. We thus encourage those interested in this space to focus not only on auditing currently illegal actions but also on efforts acknowledged to be harmful but currently outside the scope of existing law.

Conclusion

Algorithm audits can play a significant role in adequately informing the public and decision-makers about the reality of technology's limitations in deployment. There are important distinctions to keep in mind between online platform–based systems and automated decision-making systems.

The two vary in their impacted audience, appropriate methodologies, and avenues for recourse. Both, however, point in the same direction on how best to move forward: a regulatory system that allows a healthy back and forth between the large, overpowered corporate players in this industry and the persistent public interest entities that meaningfully push back on those players' misleading narratives of product performance. If we—technologists, lawmakers, auditors, and the general public—desire an AI development ecosystem where those creating and deploying new technologies are held accountable for their actions, then we need to contribute to the development of an ecosystem—either through policymaking or otherwise—where algorithm auditors can thrive.

Notes

1. Examples include the No Biometric Barriers to Housing Act of 2019 introduced by Rep. Yvette D. Clarke; New York Senate Bill S7944, Banning The Use of Biometric Identifying Technology in Schools; and Washington Senate Bill 6280, Curbing Unaccountable Use of Facial Recognition, Especially in Policing. An overview of nationwide and State moratorium proposals can be found at https://www.banfacialrecognition.com/map/.

2. Further details on the documentary can be found at https://www.codedbias.com/.

References

ACLU et al. 2018. "Letter from Nationwide Coalition to Amazon CEO Jeff Bezos regarding Rekognition." June 18, 2018. https://www.aclu.org/documents/letter-nationwide-coalition-amazon-ceo-jeff-bezos-regarding-rekognition

Ali, Muhammad, Piotr Sapiezynski, Miranda Bogen, Aleksandra Korolova, Alan Mislove, and Aaron Rieke. 2019. "Discrimination Through Optimization: How Facebook's Ad Delivery Can Lead to Biased Outcomes." *Proceedings of the ACM on Human-Computer Interaction* 3 (CSCW): 1–30.

Allyn, Bobby. 2020. "Amazon Halts Police Use of Its Facial Recognition Technology." *NPR*, June 10, 2020. https://search.yahoo.com/search?fr=mcafee&type=E210US1144G0&p=Allyn%2C+Bobby.+2020.+%E2%80%9CAmazon+Halts+Police+Use+of+Its+Facial+Recognition+Technology.

Angwin, Julia, and Terry Parris, Jr. 2016. "Facebook Lets Advertisers Exclude Users by Race." *ProPublica*, October 28, 2016. https://www.propublica.org/article/facebook-lets-advertisers-exclude-users-by-race.

Angwin, Julia, and Ariana Tobin. 2018. "Fair Housing Groups Sue Facebook for Allowing Discrimination in Housing Ads." *ProPublica*, March 28, 2018. https://www.propublica.org/article/facebook-fair-housing-lawsuit-ad-discrimination.

Angwin, Julia, Madeleine Varner, and Ariana Tobin. 2017. "Facebook Enabled Advertisers To Reach 'Jew Haters.'" *ProPublica*, September 14, 2017.

Angwin, Julia. 2016. "Facebook Says It Will Stop Allowing Some Advertisers to Exclude Users by Race." *ProPublica*, November 11, 2016. https://www.propublica.org/article/facebook-to-stop-allowing-some-advertisers-to-exclude-users-by-race.

Barrett, Brian. 2019. "Lawmakers Can't Ignore Facial Recognition's Bias Anymore." *Wired*, July 26, 2018. https://www.wired.com/story/amazon-facial-recognition-congress-bias-law-enforcement/.

Bellafante, Ginia. 2019. "The landlord wants facial recognition in its rent-stabilized buildings. Why?" *The New York Times*, March 29, 2019. https://www.nytimes.com/2019/03/28/nyregion/rent-stabilized-buildings-facial-recognition.html.

Biddle, Sam. 2019. "Amazon's Ring Planned Neighborhood "Watch Lists" Built on Facial Recognition." *The Intercept*, November 26, 2019. https://theintercept.com/2019/11/26/amazon-ring-home-security-facial-recognition/.

Bridges, Lauren. 2021. "Amazon's Ring Is the Largest Civilian Surveillance Network the US Has Ever Seen." *The Guardian*, May 18, 2021. https://www.theguardian.com/commentisfree/2021/may/18/amazon-ring-largest-civilian-surveillance-network-us.

Buolamwini, Joy, and Timnit Gebru. 2018. "Gender Shades: Intersectional Accuracy Disparities In Commercial Gender Classification." *Proceedings of the 1st Conference on Fairness, Accountability and Transparency*, PMLR 81:77–91.

Buolamwini, Joy. 2019. "Response: Racial and Gender Bias in Amazon Rekognition—Commercial AI System for Analyzing Faces." *Medium*, January 25, 2019. https://medium.com/@Joy.Buolamwini/response-racial-and-gender-bias-in-amazon-rekognition-commercial-ai-system-for-analyzing-faces-a289222eeced.

Buolamwini, Joy. 2018. Letter to Jeffrey Bezos, "Re: Audit of Amazon Rekognition Uncovers Gender and Skin-Type Disparities" June 25, 2018. https://uploads.strikinglycdn.com/files/e286dfe0-763b-4433-9a4b-7ae610e2dba1/RekognitionGenderandSkinTypeDisparities-June25-Mr.%20Bezos.pdf?id=125030.

Cagle, Matt, and Nicole Ozer. 2018. "Amazon Teams Up With Government To Deploy Dangerous New Facial Recognition Technology." *American Civil Liberties Union*, May 22, 2018. https://www.aclu.org/news/privacy-technology/amazon-teams-government-deploy-dangerous-new-facial-recognition-technology.

Charette, Robert N. 2018. "Michigan's MiDAS Unemployment System: Algorithm Alchemy Created Lead, Not Gold." *IEEE Spectrum*, January 24, 2018. https://spectrum.ieee.org/michigans-midas-unemployment-system-algorithm-alchemy-that-created-lead-not-gold.

Chouldechova, Alexandra, Diana Benavides-Prado, Oleksandr Fialko, and Rhema Vaithianathan. 2018. "A Case Study Of Algorithm-Assisted Decision Making In Child Maltreatment Hotline Screening Decisions." In Conference on Fairness, Accountability and Transparency. *PMLR* 81: 134–148.

Conger, Kate. 2018. "Amazon Workers Demand Jeff Bezos Cancel Face Recognition Contracts With Law Enforcement." *Gizmodo*, June 21, 2018. https://gizmodo.com/amazon-workers-demand-jeff-bezos-cancel-face-recognitio-1827037509.

Congressional Black Caucus. 2018. "Letter to Amazon about Facial Recognition Technology," May 24, 2018. https://cbc.house.gov/news/documentsingle.aspx?DocumentID=896.

Cook, Cynthia M. et al. 2019. "Demographic Effects in Facial Recognition and Their Dependence on Image Acquisition: An Evaluation of Eleven Commercial Systems." *IEEE Transactions on Biometrics, Behavior, and Identity Science* 1(1). https://ieeexplore.ieee.org/document/8636231.

Dastin, Jeffrey, and Ross Kerber. 2019. "U.S. Blocks Amazon Efforts to Stop Shareholder Votes on Facial Recognition." *Reuters*, April 5, 2019. https://www.reuters.com/article/technology/us-blocks-amazon-efforts-to-stop-shareholder-votes-on-facial-recognition-idUSKCN1RG32N/

Del Rey, Jason. 2019. "Jeff Bezos Says Amazon Is Writing Its Own Facial Recognition Laws To Pitch To Lawmakers." *Vox*, September 25, 2019. https://www.vox.com/recode/2019/9/25/20884427/jeff-bezos-amazon-facial-recognition-draft-legislation-regulation-rekognition

Durkin, Erin. 2019. "New York Tenants Fight As Landlords Embrace Facial Recognition Cameras." *Slashdot*, May 31, 2019. https://yro.slashdot.org/story/19/05/31/1759225/new-york-tenants-fight-as-landlords-embrace-facial-recognition-cameras.

Gillum, Jack, and Ariana Tobin. 2019. "Facebook Won't Let Employers, Landlords or Lenders Discriminate in Ads Anymore." *ProPublica*, March 19, 2019. https://www.propublica.org/article/facebook-ads-discrimination-settlement-housing-employment-credit.

Goodman, Ellen P., and Julia Trehu. 2022. "AI audit washing and accountability." *SSRN 4227350*, September 22, 2022. https://ssrn.com/abstract=4227350 or http://dx.doi.org/10.2139/ssrn.4227350

Guliani, N. S. 2018. "Amazon Met with ICE Officials to Market Its Facial Recognition Product." *ACLU*, October 24, 2018. https://www.aclu.org/news/privacy-technology/amazon-met-ice-officials-market-its-facial.

Hao, Karen. 2020. "The Two-Year Fight to Stop Amazon from Selling Face Recognition to the Police." *MIT Technology Review*, June 12, 2020. https://www.technologyreview.com/2020/06/12/1003482/amazon-stopped-selling-police-face-recognition-fight/.

Harwell, Drew. 2019. "Federal Study Confirms Racial Bias of Many Facial-Recognition Systems, Casts Doubt on Their Expanding Use." *The Washington Post*, September 19, 2019. https://www.washingtonpost.com/technology/2019/12/19/federal-study-confirms-racial-bias-many-facial-recognition-systems-casts-doubt-their-expanding-use/.

Hill, Kashmir. 2022. "Wrongfully Accused by an Algorithm." In *Ethics of Data and Analytics*, 138–142. Abington, UK: Auerbach Publications.

ICRAC. 2018. "Open Letter to Amazon against Police and Government use of Rekognition." n.d. https://www.icrac.net/open-letter-to-amazon-against-police-and-government-use-of-rekognition/.

Raji, Inioluwa Deborah, Timnit Gebru, Margaret Mitchell, Joy Buolamwini, Joonseok Lee, and Emily Denton. 2020. "Saving Face: Investigating the Ethical Concerns of Facial Recognition Auditing." *IAES '20: Proceedings of the AAAI/ACM Conference on AI, Ethics, and Society*. New York: Association for Computing Machinery.

Johnson, Khari. 2023. "Face Recognition Software Led to His Arrest. It Was Dead Wrong." *Wired*, June 26, 2023. https://www.wired.com/story/face-recognition-software-led-to-his-arrest-it-was-dead-wrong/.

Keller, Daphne. 2022. "Lawful but Awful? Control over Legal Speech by Platforms, Governments, and Internet Users." *University of Chicago Law Review Online*. https://lawreview.uchicago.edu/online-archive/lawful-awful-control-over-legal-speech-platforms-governments-and-internet-users.

Kim, Jee Young, William Boag, Freya Gulamali, Alifia Hasan, Henry David Jeffry Hogg, Mark Lifson, Deirdre Mulligan et al. "Organizational Governance of Emerging Technologies: AI Adoption in Healthcare." In *FAcct '23: Proceedings of the 2023 ACM Conference On Fairness, Accountability, And Transparency*, 1396–1417. New York: American Association for Computing Machinery.

Kirchner, L., and Matthew Goldstein. 2020. "Access Denied: Faulty Automated Background Checks Freeze Out Renters." *The Markup*, May 28, 2020. https://themarkup.org/locked-out/2020/05/28/access-denied-faulty-automated-background-checks-freeze-out-renters.

Kleinberg, Jon, Himabindu Lakkaraju, Jure Leskovec, Jens Ludwig, and Sendhil Mullainathan. 2018. "Human Decisions And Machine Predictions." *The Quarterly Journal Of Economics* 133 (1): 237–293.

Kofman, Ava, and Ariana Tobin. 2020. "Facebook Ads Can Still Discriminate Against Women and Older Workers, Despite a Civil Rights Settlement." *ProPublica*, December 13, 2020. https://www.propublica.org/article/facebook-ads-can-still-discriminate-against-women-and-older-workers-despite-a-civil-rights-settlement.

Krishnapriya, KS, Kushal Vangara, Michael C. King, Vitor Albiero, and Kevin Bowyer. 2019. "Characterizing the Variability in Face Recognition Accuracy Relative to Race." *Proceedings of the IEEE Conference on Computer Vision and Pattern Recognition Workshops*, May 8, 2019. arXiv: 1904.07325 [cs.CV].

Lecher, Colin. 2018. "What Happens When An Algorithm Cuts Your Health Care." *The Verge*, March 21, 2018. https://www.theverge.com/2018/3/21/17144260/healthcare-medicaid-algorithm-arkansas-cerebral-palsy.

Liu, Jiachang, Chudi Zhong, Boxuan Li, Margo Seltzer, and Cynthia Rudin. 2022. "FasterRisk: Fast and Accurate Interpretable Risk Scores." *Advances in Neural Information Processing Systems* 35: 17760–17773.

Menegus, Brian. 2019. "Defense of Amazon's Face Recognition Tool Undermined by Its Only Known Police Client." *MIT Media Lab*, January 31, 2019. https://www.media.mit.edu/articles/defense-of-amazon-s-face-recognition-tool-undermined-by-its-only-known-police-client/.

Merrill, Jeremy B., and Ariana Tobin. 2019. "Facebook Moves to Block Ad Transparency Tools—Including Ours." *ProPublica*, January 28, 2019. https://www.propublica.org/article/facebook-blocks-ad-transparency-tools.

Metz, Cade, and Natasha Singer. 2019. "AI Experts Question Amazon's Facial-Recognition Technology." *The New York Times*, April 3, 2019. https://www.nytimes.com/2019/04/03/technology/amazon-facial-recognition-technology.html

Mobley v. Facebook (Onuoha v. Facebook, 2016. 5:16-cv-06440 | U.S. District Court for the Northern District of California. November 3, 2016).

Molla, Rani. 2020. "How Amazon's Ring Is Creating a Surveillance Network with Video Doorbells." *RSN*, September 5, 2020. https://readersupportednews.org/news-section2/318-66/58542-how-amazons-ring-is-creating-a-surveillance-network-with-video-doorbells.

Morgan Klaus Scheuerman, Jacob M Paul, and Jed R. Brubaker. 2019. "How Computers See Gender: An Evaluation of Gender Classification in Commercial Facial Analysis Services." *Proceedings of the ACM on Human-Computer Interaction* 3 (CSCW): 1–33

Mudd, G. 2021. "Removing Certain Ad Targeting Options and Expanding Our Ad Controls." *Facebook*, September 9, 2021. https://www .facebook.com/business/news/removing-certain-ad-targeting -options-and-expanding-our-ad-controls.

Ng, Alfred. 2022. "Amazon Gave Ring Videos To Police Without Owners' Permission." *Politico*, July 13, 2022. https://www.politico.com/news/2022/07/13/ amazon-gave-ring-videos-to-police-without-owners-permission-00045513.

Ongweso, Edward Jr. 2020. "Amazon Spent $24,000 to Kill Portland's Facial Recognition Ban." *Vice*, September 9, 2020. https://www.vice.com/en/ article/g5p9z3/amazon-spent-dollar24000-to-kill-portlands-facial -recognition-ban.

Oremus, Will, and Bill Carey. 2017. "Facebook's Offensive Ad Targeting Options Go Far beyond 'Jew Haters.'" *Slate*, September 14, 2017. https://slate.com/ technology/2017/09/facebook-let-advertisers-target-jew-haters-it-doesnt -end-there.html.

Punke, Michael. 2019. "Some Thoughts On Facial Recognition Legislation." *AWS Machine Learning* (blog), February 7, 2019. https://aws.amazon.com/ blogs/machine-learning/some-thoughts-on-facial-recognition-legislation/.

Raghavan, Manish, Solon Barocas, Jon Kleinberg, and Karen Levy. 2020. "Mitigating Bias in Algorithmic Hiring: Evaluating Claims and Practices." In *Proceedings of the 2020 ACM Conference on Fairness, Accountability, and Transparency*, 469–481. New York: Association for Computing Machinery.

Raji, Inioluwa Deborah, and Joy Buolamwini. 2019. "Actionable Auditing: Investigating the Impact of Publicly Naming Biased Performance Results of Commercial AI Products." In *Proceedings of the 2019 AAAI/ACM Conference on AI, Ethics, and Society*. New York: Association for Computing Machinery.

Raji, Inioluwa Deborah, I. Elizabeth Kumar, Aaron Horowitz, and Andrew Selbst. 2022. "The Fallacy of AI Functionality." In *Proceedings of the 2022 ACM Conference on Fairness, Accountability, and Transparency*, 959–972. New York: Association for Computing Machinery.

Roulette, Joey. 2019. "Orlando Cancels Amazon Rekognition Program, Capping 15 Months of Glitches and Controversy" *Orlando Weekly*, July 18, 2019. https:// www.orlandoweekly.com/news/orlando-cancels-amazon-rekognition- capping-15-months-of-glitches-and-controversy-25669272

Rubin, Ben Fox, and Laura Hautala. 2019. "ACLU Pushes Amazon Shareholders To Vote For Facial-Recognition Ban" *CNET*, May 20, 2019. https://search.yahoo .com/search?fr=mcafee&type=E210US1144G0&p=Rubin%2C+Ben+Fox %2C+and+Laura+Hautala.+2019.+%E2%80%9CACLU+Pushes+Amazon+ Shareholders+To+Vote+For+Facial-Recognition+Ban.

Sapiezynski, Piotr, Avijit Ghosh, Levi Kaplan, Aaron Rieke, and Alan Mislove. 2022. "Algorithms That 'Don't See Color' Measuring Biases in Lookalike and Special Ad Audiences." In *Proceedings of the 2022 AAAI/ACM Conference on AI, Ethics, and Society*, 609–616. New York: Association for Computing Machinery.

Scheuerman, Morgan Klaus, Jacob M. Paul, and Jed R. Brubaker. 2019. "How Computers See Gender: An Evaluation of Gender Classification in Commercial Facial Analysis Services." In *Proceedings of the ACM on Human-Computer Interaction*, 1–33. New York: Association for Computing Machinery.

Snow, Jacob. 2018. "Amazon's Face Recognition Falsely Matched 28 Members of Congress with Mugshots." *ACLU*, July 26, 2018. https://www.aclu.org/news/privacy-technology/amazons-face-recognition-falsely-matched-28.

Tobin, A., and J. B. Merrill. 2018. "Facebook Is Letting Job Advertisers Target Only Men." *ProPublica*, September 18, 2018. https://www.propublica.org/article/facebook-is-letting-job-advertisers-target-only-men.

Tobin, Ariana. 2019a. "Employers Used Facebook to Keep Women and Older Workers from Seeing Job Ads. The Federal Government Thinks That's Illegal." *ProPublica*, September 24, 2019. https://www.propublica.org/article/employers-used-facebook-to-keep-women-and-older-workers-from-seeing-job-ads-the-federal-government-thinks-thats-illegal

——. 2019b. "HUD Sues Facebook over Housing Discrimination and Says the Company's Algorithms Have Made the Problem Worse." *ProPublica*, March 28, 2019. https://www.propublica.org/article/hud-sues-facebook-housing-discrimination-advertising-algorithms.

Tobin, Ariana, and Ava Kofman. 2022. "Facebook Finally Agrees to Eliminate Tool That Enabled Discriminatory Advertising." *ProPublica*, July 27, 2022. https://mediastreet.ie/facebook-finally-agrees-to-eliminate-tool-that-enabled-discriminatory-advertising/.

Tobin, Ariana. 2018. "Facebook Promises to Bar Advertisers from Targeting Ads by Race or Ethnicity. Again." ProPublica, July 25, 2018. https://www.propublica.org/article/facebook-promises-to-bar-advertisers-from-targeting-ads-by-race-or-ethnicity-again.

United States of America v. Meta Platforms, Inc. f/k/a Facebook, Inc., 22 Civ. 5187 (2022).

Waller, Angie, and Colin Lecher. 2022. "Facebook Promised to Remove "Sensitive" Ads. Here's What It Left Behind." *The Markup*, May 12, 2022. https://themarkup.org/citizen-browser/2022/05/12/facebook-promised-to-remove-sensitive-ads-heres-what-it-left-behind.

Whittaker, Zack. 2019. "Amazon Defeated Shareholder's Vote on Facial Recognition by a Wide Margin." *TechCrunch*, May 28, 2019. https://techcrunch.com/2019/05/28/amazon-facial-recognition-vote/.

Wood, Matt. 2019. "Thoughts on Recent Research Paper and Associated Article on Amazon Rekognition." *Amazon Web Services* (blog), January 26, 2019. https://aws.amazon.com/blogs/machine-learning/thoughts-on-recent-research-paper-and-associated-article-on-amazon-rekognition/.

Ziady, Hanna. 2023. *"Meta Slapped with Record $1.3 Billion EU Fine over Data Privacy."* *CNN*, May 22, 2023. https://www.cnn.com/2023/05/22/tech/meta-facebook-data-privacy-eu-fine/index.html.

Zilka, Miri, Holli Sargeant, and Adrian Weller. "Transparency, Governance and Regulation of Algorithmic Tools Deployed in the Criminal Justice System: A UK Case Study." In *Proceedings of the 2022 AAAI/ACM Conference on AI, Ethics, and Society*, 880–889. New York: Association for Computing Machinery.

Seven

Thinking Alternately, from Elsewhere

Noopur Raval

Introduction: Against AI Communities

Critical theorist Miranda Joseph, in her phenomenal book *Against the Romance of Community* (2002), pondered the complicity and power of communities in capitalism, particularly through her ethnographic work with Theatre Rhinoceros, a historic queer performance space in San Francisco. Among the many brilliant arguments that Joseph put forward, a particularly relevant proposition is for us not to consider constituency and collective existence as benign and radical in and of themselves but to seriously consider the limits and terms upon which a community comes together. Drawing on a range of postcolonial neo-Marxist theorists, Joseph cautions us against falling back on premodern, ethno-nationalistic, nostalgic notions of community.

All this is to say that there is something to be considered about so-called good and desirable concepts—the visions of a good (communal) life that we put forth as we mount critiques and stage a refusal of a variety of techno-logics under global capitalism. This subtle point is at the heart of this chapter, which arrives in the midst of critiques of corporate and extractive AI systems. We stand at a juncture where there is *a* community of critical AI scholars (albeit not all in agreement), calling for different socially minded regulatory, pedagogical, and activist responses to the onslaught of the "AI disruption" and dog whistles of "existential threats"(Roose, 2023) to workers, creatives, and others.

Within this splintered AI community there is a rhetoric of standing up for community and communities and protecting communities, especially marginalized communities in the face of commercial and extractive AI. This chapter contends that, even as we begin to make claims in the name of various communities globally, there is a need to simultaneously think about the "terms of assembly"—the shared understandings of interests, desired futures, risks, harms, and ongoing struggles of these same communities—on whose behalf we make the claims for community-centered technology or responsible AI. Heeding Joseph's advice, we need to think about the terms of AI assembly for at least two important reasons.

The first, of course, is the automatic sanctifying of various humanistic and social science concepts including the term "community" and by extension "community-washing," a variety of "inclusive AI" project, without really thinking through the terms of inclusion. This is certainly an ongoing trend, especially as we urge a humanistic turn in computer science and associated technical disciplines. What is missing, of course, is deeper and longer-term critical engagement between computational and humanistic scholars that could allow computer scientists to confidently interrogate and meaningfully contribute to, for instance, developing notions such as community or assembly as sociotechnical and political. This is not to ignore the rich scholarship in interdisciplinary fields such as science and technology studies (STS), human-computer interaction (HCI), media studies, and digital humanities, but it is to say that within "core" and mainstream disciplines, the two-way traffic of concepts, methods, and approaches is still largely informed by the epistemic standpoints of those major disciplines as well as their own imperatives for training computer scientists, engineers, or historians as certain kinds of interventionists in the world. All of this is also largely based on how we conduct the business of AI ethics education in US academia.

Which leads us to the second reason that we must urgently and critically examine the social and political assumptions even as we constitute

AI publics and imagine "good futures" in their names. *Who gets to shape AI assemblies and the assembling of AI systems?* Many at the forefront of US AI and policy debates have long remarked, rather soberingly, that shaping AI futures—through technical innovation or design or regulation—, has very much remained the domain of elite actors and experts in elite institutions, mostly in North America and to some extent the European Union and China. Very simply, the infrastructure and resources required to develop large language models (LLMs) for instance, still rest with those working on AI in big technology companies or smaller companies funded through such corporations and government-backed contractors globally. Simultaneously, we are witnessing the erosion of humanities departments and a general depletion in research support for social sciences as well. This makes it harder to import social ideas and make interventions from nontechnical scholars into technical AI development. Importantly, even as non-Western, nonwhite, women, queer scholars, activists, and others get a seat at the table, the power dynamics and the sociotechnical imaginaries of AI continue to be shaped by techno-capitalists and top-down technical experts without any community engagement—all mostly located in the US and some in western Europe and China.

Imaginaries: Why They Matter

The *work* of imagination and imagining different futurities is often key to shaping how technologies make a landing and are interpreted as objects relevant to social life. This work is done by a range of actors—in the form of speeches and op-eds by heads of big and small technology companies to speculative reports on the "future of X" (for example the future of work) by think tanks and government departments to public pedagogy programs in order to develop a collective orientation and stance toward emergent technologies, even and especially as they remain in experimentation mode. STS scholars, particularly building on the work of Jasanoff and Kim (2009, 2015) have championed the analytic of "sociotechnical imaginaries" to attend to technological development as *always* intertwined with and being informed by projects of nation-building, modernity, sovereignty, and other collective visions for macro and micro futures. Extending Jasanoff and Kim's argument, Mager and Katzenbach (2021), in their introduction to a *Media & Society* special issue on imaginaries in making and governing digital technologies, talk about sociotechnical imaginaries (SIs) of corporate origin as well as "alternate" imaginaries, emphasizing the role of talk, imagination, affective circulations around technological developments (public anxiety), and attempts at reclaiming and reinscribing technological futures with communal and emancipatory meanings.

Briefly, then, the purpose of *A New AI Lexicon* project as well as this reflection chapter is to extend that work of alternate imaginaries in response to the behemoth of Big AI (Qumer 2023). The project is an intervention and hence is prescriptive rather than normative. As the curated essays in it demonstrate, the purpose is to generate and collect sociotechnical imaginaries of what could and should be the collective futures of AI. But additionally, as the essays discussed in the later parts of this chapter show, the *Lexicon* project pays special attention to Jasanoff and Kim's call to attend to the geopolitical, colonial, and hence ontological specificities of sociotechnical imaginaries in the "majority world" (or Global South). By calling for contributions especially from those other than the dominant perspectives in North America and Western Europe, the project attempts to unpack the given-ness of categories like "development" and "social good" that are often reified as deficits and challenges experienced in regions of the Global South where legal protections and recourse to regulatory enforcement are seen as not strong enough or where economic impoverishment is seen as the dominant feature of social and political life (through the eyes of Global North interlocutors).

A New AI Lexicon: Imagining AI Centered on Difference

The project that this chapter draws on, *A New AI Lexicon*, is a set of forty-five essays curated by the author with her former colleagues at the AI Now Institute at New York University(*A New AI Lexicon (Archives)* 2021). The project started with an open call to activists, journalists, scholars, and others situated in global contexts, especially those out-side of North America and Europe. Inspired by Maya Ganesh's project *A is for Another: A Dictionary of AI* (2021), our attempt at curating these essays was to produce concrete and imaginative responses to a pervasive desire for inclusive and global AI futures—*What would such futures entail and who would they serve? How do we materialize the good fantasies of inserting marginalized voices from the world over into AI for good? How do these attempts at building inclusive AI run into existing tensions and struggles of grassroots communities?* These are some of the guiding questions that led to the call for the *Lexicon* with the intention to form community without necessarily foreclosing consensus or pro-posing solutions. A small note to add here is that, especially in global contexts, as the chapter demonstrates through select writings later, it is not easy or possible to shuttle only between reforming or abolishing carceral technologies. However, I suspect that the binary does not hold true for the proverbial West either, especially when confronted with some of the contexts from which our contributors are making demands of technology, the need to be included and counted, as well as the ur-gency to shape the terms on which one is "seen" by techno-political systems (Singh 2021). Further, the aspirations and individual projects of progress and modernity and attempts to create a "good life" for one-self, especially for those in the majority world, *need* engagement, par-ticipation, and reliance on existing technological infrastructures, even as these infrastructures compute, extract, discipline, and fail the same subjects. As readers might see, many thematic essays in the *Lexicon* il-luminate this bind effectively, emphasizing the need for a range of tac-tical positions and responses vis-à-vis AI imaginaries and development.

Structurally, as we curated the *Lexicon*, inspired by the work of friends and collaborators Nishant Shah and Maya Ganesh and conver-sations with them, we also attempted to experiment with the format of curation by arranging multiple essays along a single keyword (for ex-ample, "care," "dissent," "language"). Often, as one might see in the in-dividual essays, each thematic keyword holds together overlapping but also divergent meanings and demands of care, dissent, sustainability, rights, and more, as articulated vis-à-vis AI from diverse vantage points (someone writing from Palestine, an essay framing care in AI from an indigenous Mexican cosmology, another making sense of descriptions of AI in India, and yet another writing about the language of scams in China). While not always neat and uniform, the experiment of communing around what we all recognize as familiar or shared language, while also realizing how differently we interpret AI and finally dwelling on the incommensurability of the different articulations by putting AI imaginaries all in one compendium felt like a great formal exercise in maintaining and working through difference and aiming for pluriversality (Escobar 2018; Mignolo 2010) within AI imaginaries.

The project started with the intention to respond to the plethora of writing coming out of various academic and adjacent spaces as well as the FAccT conferences that continue to shape thinking around fairness, transparency, social justice, and inclusion in AI- and ML-powered systems. Legal scholar Frank Pasquale wrote on the *Law and Political Economy* blog (Pasquale 2019), describing the evolution of critical AI discourse as waves (drawing on the history of feminism), that we were past the first big wave of AI and algorithmic accountability. The "first wave" for Pasquale "focused on improving existing systems" where the emphasis was often on finding technical solutions to computational problems. But, as Pasquale noted, drawing on Julia Powles and Helen Nissenbaum (2018), and as many others have started asking, it is not enough to engage in fighting fires and fixing bugs, hoping to make AI systems less discriminatory. Instead, the time had come to ask what systems even deserve to be built, what problems need to be solved through the intervention of AI, and who is involved in every step of the crucial decision-making that shapes the final form and eventual outcomes of AI systems.

In this chapter, I draw on a select set of contributions to highlight the thematic interventions that illustrate what the "work of imagination" can do for a pluriversal AI agenda. The two themes discussed in the chapter are the role of language and, relatedly, the exercises of translation, meaning making, and interpretation in order to *realize* AI on the ground. As the following discussion shows, the thing called AI is not self-evident and easily recognized across contexts of deployment. In fact, in the contemporary moment many older media technology forms as well as more recent deployments once called "big data" or data science innovation are now in the AI fold. Further, as one moves away from the Western centers of AI innovation, across global contexts where the underlying infrastructure to support AI deployment (such as updated and comprehensive digital databases, forms of digital literacies, reliable internet connectivity and electricity, existing regulation to inform deployment) is yet to be worked out, talking about AI, identifying and marketing something as AI, and building a discourse of specific promises of progress and development around those technologies already provides us important clues as to whose progress, prosperity, safety, and well-being is privileged and who is being called upon to comply and make sacrifices in order to realize these imminent AI futures.

Although neat distinctions do not hold, the essays I describe here are divided into writings that attend to the literal work of language (describing, coining new terms, translating) and then others that demonstrate the politics of AI imaginaries (the political role of descriptions, silences, and omissions in collectively imagining AI futures around the world).

In the first group are essays that explore the alternate meanings, definitions, and historical contexts through which universal concepts are imbued with different emphases and actionability. For instance, Lujain Ibrahim's essay, "(In)Justice" (2021), explores the notion of justice as it comes to be defined and aspired to in Arabic as well as among Arabic-speaking communities and Islamic cosmologies. Ibrahim offers the "negative definition of justice" in Arabic where, unlike in English, the presence and achievement of *adalah*/justice not only is the removal of *thulm*/injustice (its opposite) but also crucially hinges upon the removing of *jawr*/oppression. In a simple sense, the imagination of justice rests upon remedying instances of injustice as well as a longer-term commitment to fighting various forms of oppression. Worlding "justice" with such commitments inadvertently expands and imbues the imagination of just and equitable AI with an inherent duty to resisting existing forms of systemic oppression. Ibrahim states: "The inclusion of oppression dictates a much-needed emphasis on the uneven distribution of power when we conceptualize AI fairness and justice" (Ibrahim, 2021). Thought of another way, this expanded definition of justice routed through the Arabic meanings of the word aligns with what many AI critics have also been asking for in Western regulatory discourse—to fight a flattening of "fairness" as only narrowly conceptualized and achieved by making technical systems more accurate, efficient, and unbiased.

In a slightly different direction, three entries in the *Lexicon* playfully cleave the role that literal acts of translation play in materializing the ethereal and spectral thing that are AI in local non-Western contexts. For instance, Asvatha Babu's essay describes the making of "Muga adaiyaalam thozhilnutpam" (2021), which literally translates to "face identity technology" as well as "face knowing technology" or "technology to identify through face." As Babu explains in detail, the lack of an English equivalent for facial recognition technology (FRT) inspired a proliferation of application-oriented descriptions as well as terms that easily port to journalistic and publicly accessible writing on the deployment of FRT in the South Indian state of Tamil Nadu. But, additionally, existing sociotechnical systems and the accrued knowledge in translation systems like Google Translate have curiously added to the project of defining something as a "face knowing technology." Google Translate and, relatedly, the Tamil *Wikipedia* page on FRT describe the term as "muga angeegaaram," where "angeegaaram" literally means recognition. However, in this context, to be recognized or to have recognition, as Babu explains, in fact means that something is officially recognized and credible, vesting the systems thus described with some authority and endorsement from the powers that be. The bulk of Babu's essay describes how important these incidental and somewhat utilitarian translations become so critical to the eventual deployment, sale, and acceptance of an FRT-powered school surveillance system as well as the acceptance of FRT as a necessary tool to update policing and public safety projects in the state.

In yet another essay, Yung Au (2021) discusses how AI is being translated and made sense of in Cantonese speaking and writing contexts. In Cantonese, as Au shows, "telephone" literally translates to "electric speech"; television, to "electric sight"; and computer, to "electric brain." Before moving to names for AI, the larger point that Au makes is worth reflecting on and similar to Babu's point: that technological objects gain meanings, recognition, and identification as they are folded into global processes of circulation, production, and distribution, as well as their historical contexts of industrial, military, educational, and other uses. In Cantonese, as Au explains, while AI translates to "intelligence that is artificial/man-made," when further broken down, the combination of the four characters used includes terms such as salary, work/labor, wisdom, and ability/degree. In short, the aspect of manual labor that is otherwise obfuscated in laudatory discourses on AI innovation, is foregrounded when AI is spoken of in Cantonese. Something that Au mentions briefly but also something that media theorist Nishant Shah has written about in his work on Chinese language and protest tactics across Sinophone regions (Shah 2013), is that historically protestors have frequently leveraged wordplay and the polysemy of homophones to produce and disseminate subversive speech and political messaging. Whether and how playful and subversive practices extend to specific AI/ML-powered technologies remains to be studied, but the lesson here is that, as we look across global cultural, political, and economic contexts, many of the binaries that currently inform US-Euro tech and policy-centric agendas do not necessarily appear as urgent or dominant across global contexts. Even more important, as Au states and as all three essays discussed above illustrate as well, far from aspiring to complete and wholly fixed meanings in our demands regarding how AI is described, relayed, and imagined, paying attention to the use of active and passive voice and synonyms—as well as interrogating the plasticity and possibilities of "good concepts" such as fairness and justice as articulated globally—can truly help us de-link from corporate-driven imaginaries of good and bad

AI. Looking at wordplay, changing vendor descriptions of commercial technologies, poetry, journalistic explanations, and more can help us arrive at popular democratic imaginaries of AI."

The second thematic set in the *Lexicon*, also relevant to this chapter's discussion on expanding AI imaginaries, covers AI descriptions, including naming and labels as well as more structural priorities of so-called linguistic, cultural, and geopolitical inclusion. Two essays (among others) make this argument quite effectively. Palestinian feminist scholar and activist, Islam al Khatib, in "Dissent" (al Khatib 2021), recounts multiple instances of "dangerous" and "indecent" speech, including a variety of dissenting social media posts on different platforms, that have resulted in the incarceration of many activists across the Middle East and North Africa (MENA) region. She poignantly juxtaposes state-sponsored narratives about economic development and "progress" through AI across MENA countries against the same countries' "computational propaganda" and punishment of citizens for unsanctioned digital expression. Her essay opens up the important tension that lies in the whitewashed efforts toward "AI inclusion." Even as global entities such as UNESCO, as well as nonprofits, governments, and others, claim to be working toward "inclusive AI," the centralization of political power and sources of corporate and government-funded innovation ensures that the imagination of development and "AI for good" remains aligned to state-sanctioned behavior and expression, including forms of digital expression. To circle back to Ibrahim's essay defining (technological) justice earlier in this chapter, while it may seem straightforward to imagine how the definition of justice could expand to include not only the lack of injustice but also the removal of systemic oppression, it becomes clear, when considering al Khatib's argument about the parallel trajectory of oppression and development as enacted by multiple countries across the world, that developmental efforts can well exist and thrive while dissenting individuals and communities in the same country are silenced and denied existing human rights and constitutional liberties. Not only this, to add to al Khatib's argument, the apparent alignment of what we consider national welfare, security, and development with technological innovation can result in perverse and oppressive outcomes. Consider the example of engineering students from the Indian Institute of Technology (IIT) Madras in South India (HT Correspondent 2019), who enthusiastically prototyped a facial recognition system that would help the police identify and catch dissenting stone pelters in the Kashmir Valley, an occupied territory of India and one of the most militarized zones in the world. Importantly, such slippages are not just about mass indoctrination in the name of chauvinistic nationhood; they are also ideological extensions enabled by the fact that we are not allowed to question inclusion, development, and terms like "AI for good" *for whom*. What are the implied limits of AI for national and economic development, and what do they inhibit when we port over democratic principles and the exercise of dissent across global contexts?

Aside from national governments, another key actor in the tech innovation ecosystem is multinational technology corporations. Companies such as Alphabet, Meta, and others are primary introducers of new technologies globally and by extension also responsible for introducing terms and policies surrounding technology use that provide the initial normative frameworks for our relationships with various platforms and other users on them. Historically, digital activists have fought against Facebook's Real ID policy, enumerating how the demand to prove one's official name and have it match one's identity on the platform has excluded hundreds of users of Natives American, South Asian, Vietnamese, Chamoru, and other ethnicities, as well as trans users who often use social media platforms to represent their authentic identities. In the struggles that ensued to push the platform to relax and modify Real ID, it also became apparent how minority communities in the physical world are recast into new forms of digital minoritization through such policies (Haimson and Hoffmann 2016). In terms of understanding the malleability of platform power, it also became evident that the political, social, and economic power of communities directly impacts their collective power as user groups as well. The same could be said for why, despite being directly implicated in the spread of rumors and incitement of violence against Rohingya Muslims in Myanmar, not much has changed materially in WhatsApp or Facebook content moderation, security, or antibias measures, since the impacted community constitutes a very small number of platform users for Meta.

Mashinka Firunts Hakopian makes a similar point in "Algolinguicism"(2021) in the *Lexicon*, where she describes how "language justice unsettles the dynamics of linguicism, a term coined by Tove Skutnabb-Kangas and collaborators (Skutnabb-Kangas and Cummins 1988; Skutnabb-Kangas and Phillipson 1996) referring to ideological structures that advantage dominant language-users by inequitably distributing power and resources between discrete linguistic communities (Skutnabb-Kangas 1988)." Hakopian engages with the ongoing ethnic cleansing of Armenian minorities by the Azerbaijan government, specifically where so-called Azerbaijani "cyber militia" have launched a network of "coordinated inauthentic behavior," including progovernment propaganda on social media platforms as well as sophisticated cyberattacks on those dissenting through the platforms.

Algolinguicism has come into play when dissenting activists and minoritized Armenian users have complained about the platforms not being vigilant enough or hiring enough content moderators fluent in Azeri who could work on removing hateful speech and propaganda. Platforms like Meta have simply stated that they do not have enough moderators and that Facebook's own tools and features are not yet fully translated into Azeri, leading to harmful content inadvertently slipping through. Harking back to the politics of linguicism, Hakopian demonstrates how sociolinguistic injustice carries over not only in the form of user participation but also, importantly, as the language infrastructures underlying the training of various machine learning models and tools inside commercial platforms are simply absent for the majority of the world. In this "algolinguicist map" of the world, non-Western countries, but also countries that do not offer either the potential of user growth markets or pose significant security threats to global governments, do not make it onto the priority list for developing language expertise or tools. Unsurprisingly, if we simply focus on "linguistic inclusion" by demographics that *do* include proverbial Global South countries, we would still leave out the concerns of countries and communities that do not neatly fit into the North-South divisions. Not in the same way but Hakopian's argument powerfully extends Ibrahim's expansion of the concept of "justice" as it offers us more considerations for linguistic justice qua technical justice in the age of AI. This articulation also brings into critical examination the buzzword "Global South" that has entirely been co-opted by corporations, academics, governments, and other entities. To frame a truly international and pluriversal agenda for care-*ful* inclusion in AI systems, we would have to reimagine the maps of inclusion in our minds to account for countries and communities as well as stateless people that are most vulnerable to digital harm as well as negligence from platforms.

In the process of writing up the call for contributions for the Lexicon and receiving contributions, editing them for clarity, and now engaging with their arguments, it became clear that we need to keep collecting and foregrounding the plurality of "good futures" as envisioned from different standpoints as well as by multiple communities. To recapitulate, one may ask a very instrumental question: *Global AI imaginaries to what end?* I offer two tactical directions for action that emerge from communing around pluralistic AI futures. Just before I do that, I want to briefly consider Ranjit Singh's argument from "Resolution" in the *Lexicon*. In this essay as well as in another essay on data justice, Singh emphasizes infrastructural contingencies and zooms in how large-scale technological infrastructures produce data portraits that vary in what he calls "resolution" or fidelity—not just in how authentically they represent us but in how these slow, often circuitous processes of inscription, technological representation, and forms of collective awareness and advocacy that insist on careful and empowering modes of alignment with one's data portraits—are key to producing high-resolution portraits in technical systems. Such resolution (pun intended) not only results in high visibility but also reorients the terms of becoming visible through big data and AI systems.

Knowing that people across the world are engaged in complex and tactical movements in order to precisely attain such "resolution" makes the work of collecting and populating pluralistic AI imaginaries urgent. The introductory chapter of this book offers a schema of tripartite relationships between AI and assembly wherein (the shapes of) AI matter for assembly in physical and online spaces, and the specific shapes of assembly for AI—how individuals and groups come together to shape the development and deployment of AI. This chapter, along with the experimental project it reports on, has attempted to populate the specifics and politics of those "shapes" of assembly/community and the (good) troubles that accompany humanitarian and egalitarian fantasies of democratic participation in technology building. Now more than ever, there is a need to recover AI assemblies from Euro-centric humanitarian programs (Madianou 2021) and to ask tougher, messier questions about decolonization and majority-world participation *in practice.*

Populating the specific, sometimes converging but at other times diverging, stakes that are vested in vast nebulous terms like "fairness" and "justice," prevents them from being hijacked by various conciliatory agendas such as AI for good. They offer evidence and material to think with, to question whether abstract principles for AI fairness or accountability are fulfilling already existing demands made by communities. Harking back to Miranda Joseph's critique of community, the *Lexicon*'s (always unfinished) work is to bring the interests of communities to bear upon universal articulations of communal good. Most important, as the essays highlight, there is obviously not a neat consensus across communal imaginaries of dissent, climate justice, and more. Holding space for difference is key to informing a truly pluriversal global agenda for progressive AI futures. Also, as this chapter demonstrates, there is utility in thinking about the "work" that imaginaries perform and how integral they are to the meanings and social relationships that we establish with emergent technologies. As the sample essays from the *Lexicon* discuss, AI futures are being assembled, contested, commodified, and challenged globally. The fact that these futures are not yet foreclosed and, importantly, that AI futures are inadvertently being shaped through quotidian transactions should hopefully alert us to avenues where such "future talk" is happening. As each *Lexicon* essay demonstrates, there is also opportunity to articulate alternate, grounded, and emancipatory sociotechnical imaginaries surrounding AI.

References

Al Khatib, I. 2021. "Dissent." *A New AI Lexicon*, July 6, 2021. https://ainowinstitute .org/publication/a-new-ai-lexicon-dissent.

Au, Y. 2021. "Electric Brain." *A New AI Lexicon*, June 29, 2021. https://ainowinstitute .org/publication/a-new-ai-lexicon-an-electric-brain.

Babu, A. 2021. "Muga adaiyaalam thozhilnutpam [face identity technology]." *A New AI Lexicon*, September 1, 2021. https://ainowinstitute.org/ publication/a-new-ai-lexicon-muga-adaiyaalam-thozhilnutpam-face-identity-technology.

HT Correspondent. 2019. "IIT-Madras Offers AI-Based Tech to Help Army Predict Stone Pelting In Jammu And Kashmir." *Hindustan Times*, January 23, 2019. https://www.hindustantimes.com/india-news/iit-madras-offers-ai-based -tech-to-help-army-predict-stone-pelting-in-jammu-and-kashmir/story -nFpvW68m42WNLXmu2AnIBN.html.

Escobar, A. 2018. *Designs for the Pluriverse: Radical Interdependence, Autonomy, And the Making of Worlds*. Raleigh-Durham, NC: Duke University Press.

Ganesh, M. 2021. *A is for Another: A Dictionary of AI*, April 2021. https:// aisforanother.net/.

Haimson, O. L., and A. L. Hoffmann 2016. "Constructing and Enforcing 'Authentic' Identity Online: Facebook, Real Names, and Non-Normative Identities." *First Monday*, June 6, 2016. https://firstmonday.org/ojs/index.php/ fm/article/view/6791/5521.

Hakopian, M. F. 2021. "Algolinguicism." *A New AI Lexicon*, October 21, 2021. https://ainowinstitute.org/publication/a-new-ai-lexicon-algolinguicism-2.

Ibrahim, L. 2021. "(In)Justice." *A New AI Lexicon*, September 16, 2021. https:// ainowinstitute.org/publication/a-new-ai-lexicon-injustice.

Jasanoff, S., and S.-H. Kim. 2009. "Containing the Atom: Sociotechnical Imaginaries and Nuclear Power in the United States and South Korea." *Minerva* 47: 119–146.

———. 2015. *Dreamscapes of Modernity: Sociotechnical Imaginaries and the Fabrication of Power*. Chicago: University of Chicago Press.

Joseph, M. 2002. *Against the Romance of Community*. Minneapolis: University of Minnesota Press.

Madianou, M. 2021. "Nonhuman Humanitarianism: When 'AI For Good' Can Be Harmful." *Information, Communication & Society*, 24(6): 850–868.

Mager, A., and C. Katzenbach. 2021. "Future Imaginaries in the Making and Governing of Digital Technology: Multiple, Contested, Commodified." *Media & Society* 23 (2): 223–236.

Mignolo, W. 2010. "The Communal and the Decolonial." In *Rethinking Intellectuals in Latin America*," edited by Mabel Moraña and Bret Gustafson, 245–261. Frankfurt a. M, Germany: Vervuert Verlagsgesellschaft.

AI Now Institute. 2021. *A New AI Lexicon* (Archives). 2021. https://ainowinstitute .org/series/new-ai-lexicon.

Pasquale, F. 2019. "The Second Wave of Algorithmic Accountability." *Law and Political Economy Project* (blog), November 25, 2019. https://lpeproject.org/ blog/the-second-wave-of-algorithmic-accountability/

Powles, J., and H. Nissenbaum, 2018. "The Seductive Diversion of 'Solving' Bias in Artificial Intelligence." *One Zero*, December 7, 2018. https:// onezero.medium.com/the-seductive-diversion-of-solving-bias-in-artificial -intelligence-890df5e5ef53.

Qumer, S. M. 2023. "Timnit Gebru: Seeking to Promote Diversity and Ethics in AI." *The Case For Women*, September 12, 2023. https://www.researchgate .net/publication/373886701_Timnit_Gebru_seeking_to_promote _diversity_and_ethics_in_AI.

Roose, K. 2023. "AI Poses 'Risk of Extinction,' Industry Leaders Warn." *The New York Times*, May 30, 2023. https://search.yahoo.com/search?fr=mcafee &type=E210US1144G0&p=AI+Poses+%E2%80%9CRisk+of+Extinction %2C%E2%80%9D+Industry+Leaders+Warn.

Shah, Nishant. 2013. "Citizen Action in the Time of the Network." *Development and Change* 44 (3): 665–681.

Singh, R. (2021). "Resolution." *A New AI Lexicon*, August 18, 2021. https://ainow institute.org/publication/a-new-ai-lexicon-resolution.

Skutnabb-Kangas, T., and J. Cummins, eds. 1988. *Minority Education: From Shame to Struggle*. Bristol, UK: Multilingual Matters, 1988.

Skutnabb-Kangas, T., and R Phillipson. 1996. "Linguicide and Linguicism." In *Kontaktlinguistik. Contact Linguistics. Linguistique de contact. Ein Internationales Handbuch zeitgenössiger Forschung. [An International Handbook of Contemporary Research; Manuel international des recherches contemporaines]*, edited by Hans Goebl, Peter H. Nelde, Zdenek Stary, and Wolfgang Wölck, vol. 1, 667–675. Berlin: Walter de Gruyter.

Acknowledgments

Lucy Bernholz

The COVID-19 pandemic has not ended. The virus continues to circulate and people continue to suffer. In addition, the acute form of the disease has a chronic and devastating sibling known colloquially as long COVID, which affects tens of millions around the globe, including me. I am grateful to the Stanford faculty, staff, fellows, and students affiliated with the Digital Civil Society Lab. They, along with my family and friends, demonstrate daily the importance of community, our human need for connection, and the power of gathering.

Toussaint Nothias

I am grateful to all the contributors for their willingness to embark on such a collaborative and demanding project during a time of global upheaval.

This book originates from exploratory research done at the Digital Civil Society Lab (DCSL), before the pandemic, on digital technologies and associational life, and in the early months of the pandemic when we launched the Digital Assembly Research Network (DARN)—many thanks to Wren Elhai, Amélie-Sophie Vavrovsky, and Estelle Ciesla for their work on these projects. The community of DCSL postdoctoral and practitioner fellows provided constant inspiration and reminders of the relevance of the issues discussed here. We are particularly honored that Tawana Petty offered some words to open the volume. I cannot imagine a better way to foreground the purpose and context of the book than with her poetry.

Our editor at Stanford University Press, Marcela Maxfeld, has been a fantastic ally since the early days of this book: thank you for your professionalism and decisive input at various stages. To the reviewers of both the proposal and the full manuscript: I am grateful for your work, supportive words, and, most of all, your piercing comments, which made the manuscript more robust and cohesive.

The Stanford Institute for Human-Centered Artificial Intelligence (HAI) supported the project through a seed research grant, which made it possible to publish the book as open access. The project and this grant would not have been possible without the enduring support of DCSL's faculty director, Rob Reich: thank you for your enthusiasm, leadership, and trust. Many thanks to our colleague Rebecca Abela, program manager of the DCSL, for her work and consistent positive energy throughout the project life cycle.

Finally, endless love and gratitude to my wife and our kids for their incredible kindness, enthusiasm, and appetite for new adventures, always.

About the Contributors

Lucy Bernholz is a senior research scholar at Stanford University's Center on Philanthropy and Civil Society and was the founding director of the Digital Civil Society Lab. She has been a visiting scholar at the David and Lucile Packard Foundation and a fellow at the Rockefeller Foundation's Bellagio Center, the Hybrid Reality Institute, and the New America Foundation. Lucy is the author and editor of numerous books about philanthropy, policy, and technology, including *Philanthropy in Democratic Societies* (University of Chicago Press, 2016), *Digital Technology and Democratic Theory* (University of Chicago Press, 2021), and *How We Give Now. A Philanthropic Guide for the Rest of Us* (MIT Press, 2021). She writes extensively on philanthropy, technology, and policy on her award-winning blog www.philanthropy2173.com. She studied history and has a B.A. from Yale University, where she played field hockey and captained the lacrosse team, and an M.A. and Ph.D. from Stanford University.

Lisa Garbe is a research fellow in Institutions and Political Inequality at the WZB Berlin Social Science Center. She earned a Ph.D. in political science from the University of St. Gallen in Switzerland and was a visiting researcher at the Oxford Internet Institute (2019–2020) and the Centre for Digital Governance at the Hertie School (2020–2021). Her research analyzes the ownership of internet service providers in Africa and the consequences for the availability of internet access and censorship. Currently, she investigates the determinants and effects of internet censorship, notably in authoritarian developing contexts.

Michael Hamilton is a visiting associate professor at the University of East Anglia (UEA) Law School, having been associate professor of public protest law at UEA from 2012 to 2022. He is a legal advisor on the right to protest in the International Secretariat of Amnesty International, and chair of the OSCE-ODIHR Panel of Experts on Freedom of Assembly. Previously, he was acting chair of the Human Rights Program in the Legal Studies Department of Central European University in Budapest and before that co-director of the Transitional Justice Institute at the University of Ulster in Belfast. His research on protection of the right of peaceful assembly includes articles in the *Oxford Journal of Legal Studies* and the *International & Comparative Law Quarterly*. He is a co-editor of the *Oxford Handbook of Peaceful Assembly*.

Ashley Lee is an assistant professor in the School of Information at the Pratt Institute in New York City. As a computer scientist and empirical social scientist, Dr. Lee examines the implications of technology design and use for democracy, social equality, and civil society, focusing on youth and marginalized communities. Prior to joining Pratt, Dr. Lee was a postdoctoral scholar with the Digital Civil Society Lab at Stanford University's Center on Philanthropy and Civil Society. Outside of academia, she has worked on issues at the intersection of computer science, design, and tech policy at Microsoft Research, the Stanford Research Institute, and the United Nations.

Danaë Metaxa is the Raj and Neera Singh Term assistant professor of Computer and Information Sciences at the University of Pennsylvania, with a secondary appointment in the Annenberg School for

Communication. In their research, Dr. Metaxa studies bias and representation in algorithmic systems and content across high-stakes social settings like politics, employment, and education, especially as these pertain to marginalized populations. Prior to joining Penn, Dr. Metaxa was a postdoctoral scholar with the Stanford Center of Philanthropy and Civil Society's Program on Democracy and the Internet and, prior to that, completed a Ph.D. in computer science at Stanford University.

Daniel Mwesigwa is a Ph.D. candidate in the information science department at Cornell University and an affiliate at the Berkman Klein Center for Internet & Society at Harvard University. Daniel has a decade of experience in tech policy, having worked as an ICT policy analyst and researcher at the Collaboration on International ICT Policy for East and Southern Africa in Kampala, Uganda. His research interests lie at the intersection of artificial intelligence and its effects on social, economic, and political experiences in the Global South.

Toussaint Nothias is a communication scholar researching journalism, digital technologies, and civil society. He is a clinical associate professor at NYU, where he is also the associate director and director of graduate studies at XE: Experimental Humanities and Social Engagement and an affiliate faculty member in Media, Culture and Communication. Broadly, he is interested in how inequalities inherited from colonialism play out in contemporary media systems and how they can be challenged. He has written on a range of topics, from stereotyping in the news to tech projects to provide "free" connectivity across the Global South. Prior to joining NYU, he spent eight years at Stanford University, where he was a senior research scholar in the Center on Philanthropy and Civil Society and research director at the Digital Civil Society Lab. He holds a Ph.D. in Media and Communication from the University of Leeds, and an MA and BA in Philosophy from Paris Nanterre University.

Deborah Raji is a Mozilla fellow and computer science Ph.D. candidate at the University of California, Berkeley. Her research explores a range of questions related to algorithmic auditing and evaluation. In the past, she worked closely with the Algorithmic Justice League initiative to highlight bias in deployed AI products. She also worked with Google's Ethical AI team and was a research fellow at the Partnership on AI and the AI Now Institute at New York University, focusing on various projects to operationalize ethical considerations in machine learning engineering practice. Recently, she was named to *Forbes*'s 30 Under 30, *MIT Technology Review*'s 35 Innovators Under 35, and was among *Time* magazine's 100 most influential people in AI.

Noopur Raval is assistant professor of information studies at UCLA. Raval holds a Ph.D. in informatics from UC Irvine and a M.Phil. in Cinema Studies from JNU, New Delhi. Raval is an interdisciplinary interpretivist scholar trained in humanistic social sciences and critical technology studies. Raval is interested in historically examining contemporary technologies with a special focus on majority world phenomena and the enduring legacies of colonialism in information and communication technologies. Raval is an alumna of the Berkman Klein Center for Internet and Society at Harvard University and the CTSP at UC Berkeley and has worked with the Wikimedia Foundation, Microsoft Research labs, and NYU.

Index

The authorized representative in the EU for product safety and compliance is:
Mare Nostrum Group
B.V Doelen 72
4831 GR Breda
The Netherlands

www.ingramcontent.com/pod-product-compliance
Lightning Source LLC
Chambersburg PA
CBHW031131270326
41929CB00011B/1583